Media, Gender and Identity

An introduction

SECOND EDITION

David Gauntlett

Routledge
Taylor & Francis Group

LONDON AND NEW YORK

This edition published 2008
by Routledge
2 Park Square, Milton Park, Abingdon, Oxon OX14 4RN

Simultaneously published in the USA and Canada
by Routledge
711 Third Avenue, New York, NY 10017

First edition published 2002

Routledge is an imprint of the Taylor & Francis Group, an informa business

© 2002, 2008 David Gauntlett

Typeset in Galliard by Wearset Ltd, Boldon, Tyne and Wear

British Library Cataloguing in Publication Data
A catalogue record for this book is available from the British Library

Library of Congress Cataloging in Publication Data
Gauntlett, David.
Media, gender and identity: an introduction / David Gauntlett. – 2nd ed.
p. cm.
1. Mass media and sex. 2. Sex differences in mass media. 3. Sex role in mass media.
4. Mass media and culture. I. Title.
P96.S45G28 2008
305.3–dc22
2007036666

ISBN10: 0-415-39660-3 (hbk)
ISBN10: 0-415-39661-1 (pbk)
ISBN10: 0-203-93001-0 (ebk)

ISBN13: 978-0-415-39660-8 (hbk)
ISBN13: 978-0-415-39661-5 (pbk)
ISBN13: 978-0-203-93001-4 (ebk)

For Jenny (1977–)
and Finn (15 January 2008–),
always

CONTENTS

ILLUSTRATIONS

FIGURES

TABLES

ACKNOWLEDGEMENTS

At the start of this second edition, I would like to thank all the readers of the first one (2002), especially those who took the time to e-mail me with their comments. The book was meant to be readable, and to connect the sometimes-complex theories with everyday examples from the media and social experience, and I am glad that people seemed to think that I achieved that. This time around, I've tried to do a *proper* second edition, revising and updating the material, tweaking some of the wonky opinions, and adding new stuff. I hope you like it.

The first edition was helped considerably by those people who were kind enough to read parts of the text and provide their perceptive comments: Ross Horsley, Susan Giblin, Clare O'Farrell, Nick Stevenson and Kirsten Pullen. I am also very grateful to the people who generously gave their time to be interviewed by e-mail about lifestyle magazines, pop stars and other matters.

For the second edition, I am grateful to Per Kristiansen and Jesper Just Jensen of Lego Serious Play, Sara Bragg, Nick Couldry, Anja Hirdman, Peter Holzwarth, Ross Horsley, Knut Lundby, Stuart Nolan, Jon Prosser, Jon Shore and Paul Sweetman, for their help and ideas. I had useful discussions with Fatimah Awan, who also helped to find some new material on role models. At the University of Westminster I have enjoyed the support of Annette Hill, Peter Goodwin, Colin Sparks, Sally Feldman, Jeanette Steemers, David Hendy, Edmund de Waal, Rachel Groom and many others.

At Routledge, Natalie Foster and Charlie Wood have been extremely helpful and supportive.

Visitors to the Theory.org.uk website regularly send me thought-provoking responses, so I am grateful to them; and my ideas about media, gender and identity have been most thoroughly challenged by several cohorts of ruthlessly intelligent students at the Universities of Leeds, Bournemouth and Westminster, so a big and broad thanks to all of them too.

Finally, all my love and thanks to Jenny and Finn, who supported me so much doing this second edition, even though one of them wasn't even born yet.

PICTURE CREDITS

All photographs and images are by David Gauntlett, except:

- page 80, photograph of Silver Surfer advertising promotion on the London Eye by Judith Duddle, reproduced by kind permission.
- page 92, 'The chart' from *The L Word*, reproduced under GNU Free Documentation License, from http://en.wikipedia.org/wiki/The_L_Word.
- page 105, photograph of Anthony Giddens, courtesy of LSE Press Office.
- page 127, photograph of Square Michel Foucault in Paris by Cameo M. Kaisler, reproduced by kind permission.
- page 146, photograph of Judith Butler by Richard Moran, reproduced by kind permission of University of Leeds Press Office.

Chapter 1

INTRODUCTION

W HY EXPLORE THE relationship between media, gender and identity? Media and communications are a central element of modern life, whilst gender and sexuality remain at the core of how we think about our identities. With the media containing so many images of women and men, and messages about men, women and sexuality today, it is highly unlikely that these ideas would have no impact on our own sense of identity. At the same time, though, it's just as unlikely that the media has a direct and straightforward effect on its audiences. It's unsatisfactory to just assume that people somehow copy or borrow their identities from the media. To complicate things further, we live in changing times. What we learned in the 1960s, 1970s or 1980s about media and gender might not be so relevant today, because the media has changed, and people's attitudes have changed. The 'role models' of times gone by might be rather laughable and embarrassing now.

Even the idea of media 'audiences' has become more complex in recent years. Since the first edition of this book was published in 2002, we have seen the launch of MySpace (in 2003), YouTube (in 2005), and numerous other social networking sites where people can be creative media producers, sharing their work with thousands and sometimes millions, or just communicating with friends. This was all possible previously, of course – in particular, the World Wide Web had become a popular place for people to share their life stories and creative products during the 1990s (see Gauntlett, 2000; Gauntlett and Horsley, 2004). The promise of the Web, to connect people and enable them to create, share and collaborate, was there from the start, but has only really taken off since around 2003, with the growth of 'Web 2.0' tools which make this especially easy for people. Today, YouTube and MySpace are the fourth and sixth most popular websites globally (see Alexa.com for latest rankings). Apart from search services, these are *the most popular websites in the world*.

We know from various studies that individuals – especially young people – are spending less time with traditional media, such as television, and more time online, interacting with others through these popular websites (see, for example, BBC, 2006a, 2006b). So people's relationship with media today is more often characterised by the role of 'user' or 'participant' than 'audience member'. Nevertheless, each of us is still 'audience' of a lot of electronic and print messages every day – and 'audience' seems to be the best word we have for it at the moment. Perhaps we can accept that the idea of 'audience' itself has now changed, and incorporates a level of interactivity.

This book, then, sets out to establish what messages the media suggests to contemporary audiences about gender, and what the impact of those messages might be. We will consider some of the previous writings on media and identity, but rather than dwell on the same set of works that textbooks have covered in the past – a set of concepts and ideas which I will suggest are not always so helpful today – this book seeks to introduce the reader to particular social theorists (such as Anthony Giddens, Michel Foucault and Judith Butler), whose ideas about identity give us more to work with when considering the role of the media in the formation and negotiation of gender and sexual identities. This second edition also gives you a taste of new 'creative methods' which have been used to explore identities in unconventional ways.

WHY MEDIA INFLUENCES ARE IMPORTANT

In modern societies, people typically consume many hours of television each week, look at magazines and other publications, surf the internet, pass billboards, go to the movies, and are generally unable to avoid popular culture and advertising. In the most obvious example, people in Europe and the USA typically spend three or four hours per day watching TV. That's a lot of information going into people's heads – even if they don't see it as 'information', and even if they say they're not really paying much attention to it. (For statistics on leisure activities and media consumption, see www.worldopinion.com, www.statistics.gov.uk.)

It seems obvious and inevitable, then, that we will be affected by these experiences somehow. The media shows us situations and relationships from other people's points of view – indeed, it is part of the eternal fascination of drama that we can see 'how the world works' in lives other than our own. This could hardly fail to affect our own way of conducting ourselves, and our expectations of other people's behaviour. For example:

- Domestic or romantic dramas (including soap operas) show us how neighbours, friends and lovers interact. When a person has a lover for the first time in their lives, how do they know how to behave? And where do we learn the typical shape and content of friendships? Our main reference points are surely films and TV.
- Magazines aimed at women, and increasingly those for men, contain all kinds of advice on how to live, look and interact. Even if we only read these items in an ironic state of mind, it must all sink in somewhere.
- Movie heroes, female or male, are almost uniformly assertive and single-minded. The attractive toughness of these stars, whilst not necessarily a problem, is 'advertised' to us continuously, and therefore should have *some* impact on our own style and preferences.
- Images of 'attractive people' abound. This may have absolutely no influence on how we rate our own appearance, and that of others – but that's improbable.

So it is imperative that, as students of contemporary culture, we try to investigate the ways in which everyday popular media material affects people's lives. Researchers have tried to do this before, of course – not always with great success, as we will see in the next chapter.

MEN AND WOMEN TODAY

Before we consider the media's role further, it is worth establishing the relative positions of women and men in modern Western democracies. If there is a 'battle of the sexes', who is winning nowadays? Women and men generally have equal rights – with a few exceptions within various laws, which we see being campaigned against and changed. The sexes today are generally thought to be 'equal', to the extent that the cover of *Time* magazine wondered if feminism was 'dead' in June 1998. There is even a noisy minority who argue that feminism has 'gone too far' and that it is now men who have the worst deal in society (Farrell, 2001; Nathanson and Young, 2001, 2006; Hise, 2004; Ellis, 2005).

Equality and inequality

The modern Western world is an odd mix of equal and unequal. Women and men may 'feel' equal, but at the same time are aware that this is kind-of inaccurate. Women have the formal *right* to do most things that a man can do, and vice versa; situations where this is not the case become well-publicised courtroom battles. More informally, women and men generally believe themselves to be equals within the sphere of personal relationships. The sociologist Anthony Giddens (of whom more in Chapter 5) asserts that intimate relationships have become 'democratised', so that the bond between partners – even within a marriage – has little to do with external laws, regulations or social expectations, but is based on the internal understanding between two people – a trusting bond based on emotional communication. Where such a bond ceases to exist, modern society is generally happy for the relationship to be dissolved. Thus we have 'a democracy of the emotions in everyday life' (Giddens, 1999).

A 1999 study based on longitudinal data from the US General Social Survey, run by the National Opinion Research Center at the University of Chicago, concluded that over the previous 27 years:

> Marriage has declined as the central institution under which households are organized and children are raised. People marry later and divorce and cohabitate more. A growing proportion of children have been born outside of marriage. Even within marriage the changes have been profound as more and more women have entered the labor force and gender roles have become more homogenous between husbands and wives.
>
> (Smith, 1999)

Compared to the findings of similar studies in 24 other advanced industrial countries, Americans were found to be 'on the middle range of many of the attitude scales' and could be expected to further 'evolve in their attitudes towards acceptance of more non-traditional attitudes', the study found (ibid.). In other words, the new 'democracy of the emotions' which is beginning to take hold means that adults are less willing to stay in unhappy relationships or dysfunctional households, and are increasingly likely to 'vote with their feet' and go in search of happiness elsewhere.

Women increasingly reject dated ideas regarding their gender role, and men are changing too. The UK's National Centre for Social Research (2000) reported that their annual survey of social attitudes had found that:

> The traditional view of women as dedicated 'housewives' seems to be all but extinct. Only around one in six women, and one in five men [mostly older people], think women should remain at home while men go out to work.

This sounds like a huge break with tradition, then. But note that this is a change in *attitudes*. The reality of actual *behaviour* is somewhat different. The government's Time Use Survey for 2005 found that:

> Women in Great Britain spent more time on shopping and other domestic work in 2005 than on paid work, 228 minutes and 146 minutes respectively. In comparison, men spent more time on paid work (225 minutes) than on domestic work (129 minutes). If paid work and domestic work are combined, women still spent 20 minutes more on average per day on work than men.
>
> Overall, women carried out about two thirds of the time spent on housework (178 minutes a day compared with 100 minutes for men). Women spent more time than men cooking and washing up, cleaning and tidying, washing clothes and shopping (159 minutes per day compared with 71 minutes per day for men). Men spent more time performing DIY repairs and gardening (23 minutes per day compared with 11 minutes per day for women).
>
> (National Statistics, 2006a)

It is worth remembering, of course, that paid work can be difficult and tedious. But housework is almost *always* tedious, and exhausting. Men, we note from this study, only really pull the stops out for the satisfaction of putting up some shelves and growing potatoes. Young fathers seem to be doing a bit better: *New Scientist* (2005) reported that British fathers of under-fives spend an average of two hours per day on child-related activity; in the 1970s it was just 15 minutes.

Meanwhile, there are obvious inequalities on the 'macro' level of Western states. Most visibly, those people we see on TV running governments and businesses are more often men than women. For example, the proportion of female politicians in Western European parliaments was 19 per cent on average in 2007. In the USA, this was just 16 per cent. In Sweden and Finland, by contrast, it was 47 and 42 per cent respectively (all data from Inter-Parliamentary Union, 2007).

In the UK, just 15 per cent of businesses are owned by women (ESRC, 2006), whilst in the United States, women own 26 percent of all non-farm businesses (US Department of Labor, 2002). According to the research organisation Catalyst, women held just 15.6 per cent of the top corporate officer positions in *Fortune* 500 companies in 2006, and occupied only 14.6 per cent of all board seats in those companies. The number of women in top-paying positions was 6.7 per cent (Catalyst, 2007). A United Nations report on women's impact in business, academia, civil society, the media and the judiciary, in 2006, was surprisingly stark: Rachel Mayanja, the Special Adviser to the Secretary-General on Gender Issues, officially summarised it by saying, 'Women remain largely invisible, their voices unheard' (United Nations, 2006).

The principal jobs in businesses and organisations are no doubt protected by a 'culture of men' at the top. For example, when Cambridge University – a supposedly 'enlightened' institution – commissioned a report from external consultants to find out why women were not well represented in its top jobs, the researchers identified 'an insular and secretive "macho" culture, dominated by white males' (BBC Online, 2001a) – revealing how everyday attitudes at the 'micro' level can have an impact upon the 'macro' level employment statistics.

Macho work cultures are detrimental to women's chances of progression – and may not be so great for men either. The pressure of work in the City, London's financial centre, was highlighted in 2007 by a spate of male breakdowns, suicides and a murder. 'It is a very macho culture, a very competitive culture', commented Andrew Kinder of the British Association of Counselling and Psychotherapy. 'It is surely no coincidence that there are more Alcoholics Anonymous, Narcotics Anonymous and Gamblers Anonymous meetings in the City than anywhere else', noted the *Independent* (Mesure, 2007).

Traditional attitudes can have an impact on other people's lives at all levels. Although girls in the UK tend to do better than boys at school, for instance, studies by the Equal Opportunities Commission (EOC) have shown that they still tend to be pushed by their teachers and careers advisors towards 'the five "C"s – cleaning, catering, caring, cashiering and clerical' (EOC, 2006). Masculine stereotypes meanwhile mean that young men still tend to avoid precisely these careers, even though they say that they might enjoy them (EOC, 2005). Furthermore, a study in 2007 found that Black and Asian women were 'missing' from almost a third of workplaces in areas with significant ethnic minority populations: 'Those who want to work are finding it more difficult to get jobs, progress within them and are more likely to be segregated into certain types of work, despite leaving school with the same career aspirations as white girls and similar or better qualifications than white boys', the study found (EOC, 2007). All of these stories – which are mirrored around the world – are about *other people's expectations* getting in the way of individual choices and achievements.

All bad news?

In spite of the depressing facts and figures above, there is still a lot of on-going transformation for us to be reasonably pleased about. Society clearly changed a great deal in the second half of the twentieth century, and sexual equality is something that almost everybody in power at least *says* they are in favour of. On the everyday level, as noted above, women and men expect to be treated equally, and are frustrated if this does not happen. As we will see in later chapters, magazines for women encourage their readers to be assertive and independent. Pop stars like Beyoncé, and other media icons such as Oprah Winfrey, convey the same message. Magazines for men, whilst sometimes going overboard with macho excess, encourage men to understand women, and face up to modern realities. Women and men are usually equals in today's movies and TV shows; we raise an eyebrow when this isn't so. Things have changed quite quickly, and there is still some way to go, but equality within everyday life is now quite well established. This needs to be carried forward into the formal world of work and government where a disproportionate number of men are running the show. Other changes are needed in the world of work too – amazingly in the 'modern' world, working fathers are allowed few concessions to spend time with their children, and paternity leave, which is typically minimal or non-existent, is viewed as a luxury. (Tony Blair set a poor example by refusing to take paternity leave upon the birth of his son in 2000; instead he said he would work less for a short period so that he would be able to 'help out', but insisted 'I have to run the country', as if no Prime Minister had ever taken a break (BBC Online, 2000a).) Mothers are still seen as the natural carers of children. But attitudes and regulations are changing, albeit very slowly, in this area too.

Masculinity

Every so often there is a wave of media coverage about contemporary 'masculinity' and the idea that it is 'in crisis'. In Australia in 2006, for example, former political leader Mark Latham prompted such a debate when he complained, in print, about the decline of 'Australian male culture':

> This has been squeezed out of society by a number of powerful influences: the crisis in male identity brought about by changes in the workplace and family unit; the rise of left-feminism in the 1970s and 1980s, with its sanitising impact on public culture;

and, more recently, the prominence of neo-conservatism and its timid approach to social behaviour and language.

(Latham, 2006)

This observation led to his forthright conclusion: 'Australian mates and good blokes have been replaced by nervous wrecks, metrosexual knobs and toss-bags' (ibid.). Unsurprisingly, Australian columnists took this prompt to spend a few weeks discussing the state of Australia's men in general, and toss-bags in particular.

In Britain, a somewhat more temperate debate was prompted by the publication of Anthony Clare's book *On Men: Masculinity in Crisis* in 2000 – which gained publicity since Clare was a well-known broadcaster – and, separately, London's Royal Festival Hall ran a series of public discussions on 'Masculinity in Crisis' in spring 2001. Similar discussions were prompted in the USA by the publication of Susan Faludi's *Stiffed: The Betrayal of the Modern Man* (1999), in which Faludi, well-known as the bestselling feminist author of *Backlash: The Undeclared War Against Women* (1991), appeared to come out in sympathy for the modern man.

Anthony Clare sets out the 'masculinity in crisis' idea at the start of his book:

> Now, the whole issue of men – the point of them, their purpose, their value, their justification – is a matter for public debate. Serious commentators declare that men are redundant, that women do not need them and children would be better off without them. At the beginning of the twenty-first century it is difficult to avoid the conclusion that men are in serious trouble. Throughout the world, developed and developing, antisocial behaviour is essentially male. [...] And yet, for all their behaving badly, they do not seem any the happier. Throughout North America, Europe and Australia, male suicides outnumber female by a factor of between 3 and 4 to 1. [...] Men renowned for their ability and inclination to be stoned, drunk or sexually daring, appear terrified by the prospect of revealing that they can be – and often are – depressed, dependent, in need of help.
>
> (2001: 3)

Men used to know their place, as provider for their family, says Clare, and this was a role to be proud of. But today, as women show that they can do everything that men can, this provider role becomes diminished. Women are also finding that they can bring up families perfectly well without the father being present at all, and scientific advances seem to be making men unnecessary to reproduction itself (Clare 2001: 7).

All this adds up to the modern men's 'crisis' although, of course, it's a bit over-excitable to call it a crisis. It's a set of changing circumstances, and men, most certainly, need to renegotiate their place within this new culture. But – without wanting to sound too masculine and rational about it – it's surely nothing to have a crisis about. Men may not be able to fit into their *traditional* role, but that's no reason to conclude that life is over for men. Men just have to find a new, modern, useful place for themselves in the world – just as women have to. And this is where the mass media and popular culture come in, because they offer important tools to help men – and women – adjust to contemporary life. Many of the academic books on 'masculinity' are disappointing, as they dwell on archetypes from the past, and have little to say about the real lives of modern men; whereas top-selling magazines and popular self-help books – and, to a lesser but significant extent, TV shows and movies – are full of information about being a man in the here-and-now. So these are discussed later in this book.

To be fair, Anthony Clare doesn't think that men need to have a crisis, either, but they do need to change. Emotional communication, and the expression of love and vulnerability, are important. Men don't need to become 'like women' but can develop a new form of masculinity which places 'a greater value on love, family and personal relationships and less on power, possessions and achievement', he suggests (2001: 221). He carefully sifts through scientific evidence in order to reject the idea that men cannot help themselves for biological reasons. As one reviewer noted,

> Clare does a thorough job of demolishing the 'unreconstructable caveman' that pop science peddles to the media. It's easy (but false) to say that testosterone causes aggression; the truth – that [testosterone]-levels and aggressive behaviour are linked in a circular relationship dependent on a multitude of environmental factors – is hard to fit into a tabloid headline.
>
> (Kane, 2000)

Clare is particularly good on the masculine drive to 'prove' oneself through work – perhaps because, as he admits in the book, he has suffered from this himself. He marshals evidence from major studies, though, to support his point that the quality of personal relationships has a much greater impact on a person's levels of life satisfaction than their success in work. Indeed, 'once a person moves beyond the poverty level, a larger income contributes almost nothing to happiness' (2001: 100; see also Layard, 2006). Therefore he recommends social changes to allow men and women to spend less time in work, and more time experiencing their relationships with each other, with children, and with the world in general – which, the evidence shows, makes for happier people and – lest employers be worried by all this talk of leisure – better workers.

In Susan Faludi's *Stiffed* (1999), as mentioned above, the well-known feminist surprised readers by arguing that contemporary culture damages men just as much as women, albeit in different ways. (This, of course, is not actually inconsistent with the basic idea of feminism, which originally sought to free both women and men from constricting gender stereotypes.) Explaining the book's title in a 1999 interview, Faludi said:

> To me it has three meanings: working stiff; the way guys have been cheated by this society; and the fact that men are supposed to be stiff – that they have to show their armoured self to the world all the time. Having to do that hurts them as much as it hurts everyone else.

> (Halpern, 1999)

Like Clare, Faludi notes that men who spend their lives in work miss out on a proper engagement with their partners, children and friends, and don't get anything for it except an early death. Faludi finds that the traditional male 'provider' role also bitterly hurts men who cannot find employment. In this sense, Faludi feels that men have been 'betrayed' by a society which had seemed to promise them that the traditional masculine role would deliver some ultimate happiness. She also implies that feminism was mistaken to see men's traditional role as being one of 'power', and wrong to think that men had kept the best lifestyle for themselves and only given women the boring responsibilities. A role which turns men into breadwinning robots, subject to the whims of the employment market and disconnected from quality relationships and parenthood, is not particularly powerful or desirable, she observes. It is important to note that Faludi does not renounce feminism, or suggest that women now have a better deal in society than men; her point is more that contemporary society is just as depressing and constricting for the average man as it is for the average woman, and that men deserve to be heard.

Faludi further argues that both sexes have now become victims of the culture of consumerism, appearances and glamour:

Truly, men and women have arrived at their ornamental impris-
onment by different routes. Women were relegated there as a
sop for their exclusion from the realm of power-striving men.
Men arrived there as a result of their power-striving, which led
to a society drained of context, saturated with a competitive
individualism that has been robbed of craft and utility, and ruled
by commercial values that revolve around who has the most, the
best, the biggest, the fastest. The destination of both roads was
an enslavement to glamour.

(1999: 599)

It is our media-saturated consumer culture which now has men as well as
women 'by the throat' (1999: 602), she suggests, and she urges men to
overthrow the overly competitive, uncommunicative and ultimately unre-
warding world they have created for themselves.

There is general agreement, then, that this is not a particularly stable
time for the 'male identity', if such a singular thing exists. Some parts of
popular culture are said to be 'reasserting' the traditional forms of masculinity, whilst others are challenging them – and as we will see later in the book,
it's even debatable which media products are conveying which messages.
More of that later; now we'll turn to masculinity's opposite – or counterpart
– femininity.

Femininity

The ideas of 'masculinity' and 'femininity' have been pulled through the
social changes of the past few decades in quite different ways. Masculinity is
seen as the state of 'being a man', which is currently somewhat in flux.
Femininity, on the other hand, is not necessarily seen as the state of 'being a
woman'; instead, it's perceived more as a stereotype of a woman's role from
the past. Men like their identities to fit within 'masculinity', even if we have
to revise that term as attitudes change. Modern women are not generally
very bothered about fitting their identity within the idea of 'femininity',
though, perhaps because feminists never really sought to *revise* femininity,
preferring to dispose of the fluffy, passive concept altogether. Femininity is
not typically a core value for women today. Instead, being 'feminine' is just
one of the performances that women can choose to employ in everyday life
– perhaps for pleasure, or to achieve a particular goal.

There's plenty of evidence that traditional femininity is no longer
popular. Virtually everybody wants young women to be successful, so the
characteristics of femininity – passivity, reticence, assuming that men and

authority figures are probably right and that you are probably wrong – are therefore redundant. Schoolgirls today have shaken off 'feminine' docility and are out-performing boys at all levels of school education in both the UK and the USA (www.statistics.gov.uk; www.nces.ed.gov). Sales of the Barbie doll are reported to be falling because only the youngest girls will accept such a 'girly' toy nowadays, and the pretty-but-passive Barbie doll is easily beaten at Christmas time by toys and games related to Dora the Explorer, the inquisitive and multi-lingual adventurer whose animated TV series is hugely popular around the world (Gogoi, 2006). Meanwhile, young women have a wide range of other assertive 'girl power' role models to choose from in magazines, movies and pop music – all of which will be discussed in the following chapters.

Traditional ways of thinking are still present in modern society, of course, so we can think of occasions when a woman may be criticised for her 'lack of femininity'. And elements of fashion, say, might be commended for adding 'a dash of femininity' to a woman's appearance. Even these examples of the term in use, however, incorporate a recognition of the broadly 'optional' role which femininity has today. Whole books have been written about how Madonna showed that femininity is a 'masquerade' or a 'performance' in her videos from the early 1990s such as *Express Yourself* and *Justify My Love* (Schwichtenberg, 1993; Lloyd, 1993; Frank and Smith, 1993). For example, E. Ann Kaplan wrote that '[Madonna's] image usefully adopts one mask after another to expose the fact that there is no "essential" self and therefore no essential feminine but only cultural constructions' (1993: 160). Madonna was seen to be playing with 'the given gender sign system' where 'femininity' was just one of the available guises. And indeed, the idea of a woman being seductively 'feminine' in order to get her own way is a dramatic cliché appearing in various movies from throughout the last century, so the idea of femininity as a mere performance, to be used by wily women, is not new.

Today, magazines such as *Cosmopolitan* suggest ways in which cunning women might use 'feminine' tricks to get certain things from gullible men, but traditional femininity is far from being essential to the modern female reader – instead, it is just one technique amongst many, and an amusing, lightweight one at that. In a fascinating in-depth study of a group of British working-class women, Beverley Skeggs (1997) finds that her subjects had a complex relationship with 'femininity', since they sought the 'respectability' which was associated with the 'feminine' role, but had no interest in being associated with its connotations of passivity or weakness. The women rejected the historical idea of women's 'divine composure' in favour of their modern 'having a laugh'. As Skeggs explains, 'They had knowledge and competencies to construct feminine performances, but this was far removed from *being* feminine. They usually "did" femininity when they thought it was necessary' (1997: 116). The women found that they were compelled to invest in femininity in order to succeed economically – such as when applying for a job – and that femininity was also a kind of 'cultural capital' which brought both pleasures and problems.

> Their forays into femininity were immensely contradictory. Femininity offered a space for hedonism, autonomy, camaraderie, pleasure and fun whilst simultaneously regulating and generating insecurities. The women simulated and dissimulated but did not regard themselves as feminine. [...] Aspects of femininity are, however, something which they have learnt to perform and from which they can sometimes take pleasure.
>
> (Ibid.)

Femininity, then, whilst seen as a 'nice' thing for women traditionally, is increasingly irrelevant today. Whilst 'masculinity' always included a number of positive attributes which men are keen to hang on to – assertiveness and independence, for example, are clearly good things when not taken to extremes – 'femininity' was traditionally lumbered, by the unsubtle patriarchs of yesteryear, with feeble qualities like subservience and timidity. The sensible woman of today has little enthusiasm for these traits, and so the meaning of 'femininity' now is just a swishy kind of glamour – and ideally is just a masquerade, utilised by a confident woman who knows *exactly* what she's doing.

SEXUAL IDENTITIES TODAY

Although lesbians, gays and bisexuals continue to face prejudice and discrimination, there is a growing amount of evidence that Western societies – especially younger generations – are becoming more accepting of sexual diversity. When the first edition of this book was published, we were able to report that British attitudes had largely broken with tradition: a 2001 study by Britain's largest market research group, Mintel, suggested that gay and straight lifestyles were increasingly convergent, and that an atmosphere of tolerance and social mixing dominated in cities (Arlidge, 2001). A MORI poll in the same year found that just 17 per cent of people in England said that they felt 'less positive' towards lesbians and gays, and three-quarters of people with children in their household said that they would be comfortable if the child had a gay or lesbian teacher (MORI, 2001). In the USA, however, surveys suggested some less open-minded views: surveys conducted by Gallup had found acceptance of homosexuality as 'an acceptable alternative lifestyle' rising from 38 per cent in 1992 to 52 per cent in 2001 (Newport, 2001), but almost half the population (42 per cent) felt that 'homosexual relations between consenting adults' should *not be legal*. So – have things changed since then?

In 2004, the large-scale Pew Global Attitudes Project found that the question 'Should homosexuality be accepted by society?' gained an affirmative response from 69 per cent of Canadians and 77 per cent of Western Europeans, but only 51 per cent of Americans. Fewer than half of American men (46 per cent) felt that homosexuality was acceptable (Pew Research Center, 2004a). It is worth noting that elsewhere in the world, there are more trenchant views: in Kenya, for instance, 99 per cent of people said that the answer to the question 'Should homosexuality be accepted by society?' was 'No' (ibid.).

Recent polls on legal issues in this area give us a little more information on attitudes in the United States. A CNN/Opinion Research Corporation poll in 2007 found that around half of Americans would support the legal recognition of same-sex marriages or civil unions for gay or lesbian couples (24 per cent accepting the idea of same-sex marriages, and a further 27 per cent approving of civil unions but not same-sex marriages). However, almost as many respondents (43 per cent) said that they would approve of neither. Asked whether 'people who are openly gay or homosexual' should be allowed to serve in the US military, 79 per cent said yes, 18 per cent said no. On the question of whether gay or lesbian couples should have the legal right to adopt a child, however, only 57 per cent were in favour, with 40 per cent opposed (*Polling Report*, 2007). As mentioned above, these attitudes can differ by age: for instance, the Pew Research Center in 2006 found that among the over-65s, three-in-four (73 per cent) opposed the legalisation of gay marriage, whereas more than half (53 per cent) of the under-30s were in favour (Pew Research Center, 2006).

As these polls indicate, the legal status of gay and lesbian partnerships has become a hot issue in various parts of the world. Same-sex marriages have been legally recognised in the Netherlands (since 2001), Belgium (2003), Spain (2005), Canada (2005) and South Africa (2006). The US state of Massachusetts recognised same-sex marriages in 2004, a decision which to date has withstood various attempts to overturn it (see the Wikipedia article 'Same-sex marriage in Massachusetts' for up-to-date coverage). Same-sex civil unions, similar to but legally not the same as marriage, have been introduced in Nordic countries and Western Europe since Denmark led the way in 1989. In the UK, civil partnerships came into effect in 2005. (The helpful Wikipedia article 'Civil union' provides much detail.) Again, the picture is less positive elsewhere in the world: homosexual acts can result in the death penalty in countries including – at the time of writing – Iran, Mauritania, Pakistan, Saudi Arabia, Sudan, United Arab Emirates and Yemen.

It is not possible to measure the relative influence of the mass media upon changing attitudes to sexuality, of course (although when questioned, MORI respondents said that the media was an important source of information about minorities (MORI, 2001)). In his book *Striptease Culture*, Brian McNair (2002) shows how sex and sexuality have come to be represented in a diverse range of ways in popular culture, and makes a strong case for the central role of popular culture in the rejection of tradition and the transformation of society. It seems likely that as the media introduces the general audience to more everyday gay and lesbian (and bisexual and transgendered) characters, tolerance should grow. Discussions of the representations of sexual minorities in television and film appear in Chapter 4.

OTHER AXES OF IDENTITY

Identities, of course, are complex constructions, and gender is only one part of an individual's sense of self. Ethnicity is obviously an important aspect of identity, and like gender may be felt to be more or less central to self-identity by each individual, or might be *made* significant by external social circumstances (such as a racist regime or community). Other much-discussed axes of identity include class, age, disability and sexuality. In addition, a range of other factors may contribute to a sense of identity, such as education, urban or rural residency, cultural background, access to transportation and communications, criminal record, persecution or refugee status. Furthermore, whilst usually less significant in terms of overall 'life chances', any aspects of the physical body can be relevant to self-identity: for example, whether one is seen as overweight or underweight, tall or short, hairy or shaven or bald, or wearing spectacles, unusual clothes, or piercings. Researchers have studied all of these aspects of identity. This book generally confines itself to discussing gender, though, as one particular *part* of identity which all individuals, in whatever way, have to integrate and express within their personalities.

MEDIA, *ETHNICITY* AND IDENTITY

See also the valuable books that have been written on representations of 'race' and their implications. See, for example, *Representing 'Race': Racisms, Ethnicity and the Media* by John Downing and Charles Husband (2005), *Watching Race: Television and the Struggle for 'Blackness'* by Herman Gray (2004), *Race/Gender/Media: Considering Diversity Across Audience, Content, and Producers* by Rebecca Ann Lind (2003), *Say It Loud!: African-American Audiences, Media, and Identity* edited by Robin Means Coleman (2002), *Representing Black Britain: Black and Asian Images on Television* by Sarita Malik (2002), and *Ethnic Minorities and the Media: Changing Cultural Boundaries* edited by Simon Cottle (2001). For a thought-provoking black feminist perspective, see the work of bell hooks, in particular *Black Looks: Race and Representation* (1992) and *Reel to Real: Race, Sex, and Class at the Movies* (1996).

OUTLINE OF THIS BOOK

In Chapter 2, we catch up on previous debates about the power of the media within cultural theory and psychological research. Then we consider representations of gender in the media, both in the past (Chapter 3) and today (Chapter 4). In Chapters 5 to 7, we look at some theoretical approaches which we can employ to help us understand how people form their sense of self and identity in relation to the media: Chapter 5 takes up the work of Anthony Giddens, Chapter 6 employs Michel Foucault and Chapter 7 makes use of queer theory. (No previous knowledge of these approaches is assumed.) In Chapters 8 to 10, we turn back to actual contemporary media, and seek to relate some of these theoretical ideas to popular culture. In Chapter 8 we consider popular lifestyle magazines aimed at men, such as *FHM* and *Maxim*, and Chapter 9 looks at those for women, such as *Cosmopolitan* and *Glamour*: do these glossy publications play a role in shaping gender identities, or are they pure entertainment? Chapter 10 looks at some aspects of popular culture which provide ideas about 'ways of living', from the notion of 'role models', to self-help books and their more explicit advice about self-fulfilment. Chapter 11, which is all-new for this edition of the book, discusses ways of exploring identities in which particip-ants are asked to engage in creative visual tasks – including my own recent study in which participants were asked to build metaphorical models of their

Figure 1.1   Identities can be explored in a number of ways: Lego identity study
        discussed in Chapter 11

identities in Lego. Finally, the conclusion brings together a number of key themes which emerge through the course of the book.

A note on methodology

The book mixes an analysis of previous theories and research with some new material. Quotations from e-mail interviews are included in the chapters on men's magazines, women's magazines and role models, providing qualitative information about how people relate to media texts. E-mail interviews are very similar to any other kind of interview, except that the researcher is able to contact people from different parts of the world quite easily. As a means of surveying the general population, this is a bad method (the most obvious problem is that only people with internet access are even *potentially* reachable). For interviewing *fans* or users of a particular media artist or artefact, though, the internet is extremely valuable – fans can be found via websites and message boards dedicated to the performer or thing in question, and are often happy to share their thoughts about the object of their affection. It's also not too hard to find people willing to be interviewed about their other media habits and interests.

Some people say 'You don't know who you're talking to on the internet – they might be lying to you', but this is often a weak reservation; people are no more likely to waste their time lying in an e-mail interview, than in a face-to-face interview. Where in-depth interviews about magazine reading or pop music idols are concerned, in particular, it seems unlikely that anyone would bother making fictional submissions. Of course, respondents may leave out or 'modify' parts of their account, but that is the case in any interview situation.

Elsewhere, I have sometimes taken the responses of consumers (of a movie, or a self-help book, say) from websites where everyday people are requested to post their views – such as The Internet Movie Database (www.imdb.com) for movies, and Amazon (www.amazon.com) for books and music. Whilst comments from these sites could not be used as the basis for a whole thesis – because their authors are a self-selected bunch of people interested in reviewing things on websites (who may not, therefore, represent the 'general audience') – quotes from these sites are useful for fleshing out an idea or illustrating a point, and they do represent the spontaneously-offered views of people who are actually interested in the media product in question.

Funny way of talking

This book is not intended to be written in pointlessly complex language, but a few specific terms from the worlds of sociology and cultural studies will spring up here and there. Most students will probably be familiar with them already, but for clarification, here's what I mean by the following terms:

Text – In media studies, 'text' can refer to any kind of media material, such as a television programme, a film, a magazine, or a website, as well as a more conventional written text such as a book or newspaper.

Discourse – Broadly means 'a way of talking about things' within a particular group, culture or society; or a set of ideas within a culture which shapes how we perceive the world. So when I talk about 'the discourse of women's magazines', for example, I am referring to the ways in which women's magazines typically talk about women and men and social life, and the assumptions that they commonly deploy.

Biological determinism – The view that people's behaviour patterns are the result of their genes and their biological inheritance. Biological determinists typically argue that women and men are fundamentally different, and that they cannot help it – they were born that way.

Social constructionism – The view that people's personality and behaviour are *not* pre-determined by biology, but are shaped by society and culture. People are not fixed from birth, and can adapt and change.

Modern life and *modernity* – The present time in developed Western countries. Although postmodernists have correctly observed a range of cultural features of developed societies (such as scepticism towards science, religion and other 'macro' explanations; consumerism; superficiality, and the importance of appearance and media image), I agree with Anthony Giddens that it's not really worth calling these features 'post'-modern, because we do not really live in a wholly new era. The term 'post-traditional' is certainly useful, however. More on these terms appears in Chapter 5.

Other terminology will be explained as it appears.

WHAT'S WRONG WITH THIS BOOK

Like all books, this one spends time discussing things that the author considers to be relevant and interesting, at the expense of other matters which are judged to be less pertinent, or which there simply wasn't room for. This section offers brief explanations for some of its limitations:

The emphasis tends to be more on the choices of individuals, and less on the social constraints which they may face

There is a growing social perception, which is certainly encouraged by popular media, that people can make what they want of their own lives. This book explores this idea of personal autonomy – and therefore might occasionally appear to be assuming that we all live in a 'middle class' world where people are free to do what they like and not be inhibited by lack of money, or fear of social rejection or violence. Needless to say, however, most people do face social, cultural and financial constraints, which have been well documented by social scientists for many decades. These constraints can be very powerful. At the same time, though, individuals do have *choices*, and we are surrounded by media which celebrates a range of possible lifestyles (whilst also, perhaps, selecting and channelling what seems to be available). Rather than simply rehash the sociological pessimism which assumes that any sense of individual autonomy is more-or-less irrelevant because of the poverty and sexism imposed by capitalism and patriarchy, this book takes individual identities – and their relationship with popular media – more seriously, because changes in people's consciousness will ultimately lead to changes in the wider society (an idea developed further in Chapter 5). We should also note that the notion that you can choose a way of living, as suggested by some of the theorists and media which are discussed in this book, is not actually limited to the middle classes, even if it sounds, to some people, like a 'middle class' discourse.

The book doesn't spend much time criticising media texts themselves

A number of previous books on media and gender have consisted of detailed criticism of particular representations of women (e.g. MacDonald, 1995; Tasker, 1998; Gateward and Pomerance, 2002), or representations of men (e.g. Cohan and Hark, 1993; Lehman, 2001; Spicer, 2001). Even Liesbet van Zoonen's excellent introduction to *Feminist Media Studies* (1994) spends more time on critical approaches to texts than on the more significant question of how audiences relate to them. Although these text-based approaches may reveal 'hidden' (i.e. not-so-obvious) aspects of media messages, they often do not help us to understand why such texts are appealing or popular, or how they are consumed by actual audiences. (They may also suggest interpretations of texts which are not apparent to most viewers, and it is difficult to assert that a particular academic reading of a text is superior to that made by any other person.) In this book I will discuss the changing representations of gender in Chapters 3 and 4, and elsewhere, but rather than describing worrying aspects of texts *in themselves*, I will be considering – in later chapters in particular – how we can understand the ways in which popular media are connected to the gendered identities of real people. In other words, how do mass-produced items (from the 'outside' world) become significant in how we think of ourselves (in our 'inner' world)?

The book only focuses on popular, mainstream media

Although many delightful challenges to the status quo are made by small-scale or minority media producers and artists, this book is concerned with the messages about identity, gender and lifestyle *which people most commonly encounter*, which means that there is a deliberate focus on the popular and mainstream.

The book doesn't simply spell out the process by which we acquire gender

This book argues that there is not a single, straightforward psychological process through which gender identities are formed; instead, there is a complex interaction of thoughts, evaluations, negotiations, emotions and reactions. We are therefore never going to be able to produce a simple flow chart showing how identities are 'formed'; other, more subtle, approaches are needed. Chapter 11 discusses some recent attempts to explore identities and media influences in a more sophisticated way.

The book is focused on Western media and culture

Indeed, this book's remit is the discussion of media and gender identities in developed Western countries, with examples from the USA and the UK in particular. Of course, the question of media influences on gender and identities in non-Western countries around the world is very important too (Thussu, 2006; Machin and Van Leeuwen, 2006; Altman, 2002; Stald and Tufte, 2001), but is beyond the scope of the present volume.

THE BOOK'S WEBSITE

A website for this book can be found at www.theoryhead.com. The site contains additional resources, including some extended analyses, extra articles, discussions between the author and other people, and links to related websites. You can also send suggestions and comments via the site.

Chapter 2

SOME BACKGROUND DEBATES

IN THIS CHAPTER we will consider some existing theoretical and empirical approaches to the impact of the mass media. Is the media a powerful force, shaping the consciousness of the modern public? What do we know about the 'effects' of the media? What have psychologists had to say about the development of gender and identity? And what has the academic sphere of 'film studies' claimed about media, gender and identity? This chapter considers some of the previous theories – ones which are often, for different reasons, unsatisfactory, and which we might hope to go 'beyond' later in the book.

MEDIA POWER VERSUS PEOPLE POWER

One of the biggest debates about the social impact of the media – perhaps *the* debate – can be boiled down to one question: does the mass media have a significant amount of power over its audience, or does the audience ultimately have more power than the media? It is, perhaps, not very sensible to consider the matter in such extreme, polarised terms, but we shall put that thought to one side temporarily, because it is at least *instructive* to consider both sides of the debate in their most clear-cut form.

In one corner, then, we have Theodor Adorno, who felt that the power of mass media over the population was enormous and very damaging, and in the opposite corner we have John Fiske, who argues that it is the audience, not the media, which has the most power. We could have picked other theorists to represent these views, perhaps, but Adorno and Fiske are probably the most celebrated exponents of each position.

Adorno: media power

Theodor Adorno (1903–69) was a member of the Frankfurt School for Social Research (established in 1923), a group of mostly German, Jewish intellectuals, who fled from Frankfurt to New York and Los Angeles when the Nazis rose to power in the 1930s. Many of them returned to Germany at the end of the 1940s. Their antipathy towards the mass media will likely have been increased by the observation that Hitler had apparently been able to use the media organisations as a tool for widespread propaganda, and also by their sudden encounter with American popular culture, which was clearly not to their 'high art'-centred, bourgeois tastes. Even more crucially, the revolution predicted by Karl Marx in the middle of the nineteenth century – in which the workers were meant to recognise their exploitation, and overthrow the rulers and factory owners – had not come to pass. Instead, the workers of the world seemed to be reasonably happy; the work itself may not have been rewarding, but they had some decent films to watch, and the radio played nice songs to cheer them up.

And so Adorno and his colleague Max Horkheimer (1895–1973) wrote the book *Dialectic of Enlightenment* (1979), first published in 1947, which contains the essay 'The Culture Industry: Enlightenment as Mass Deception', encapsulating their views on the mass media and its impact upon society. The essay alternates between sharp, lucid points about media power, and rather more rambling prose about the nature of mass culture – as if Adorno and Horkheimer were fighting for control of the typewriter, and one of them was drunk. It's well worth reading. Adorno also helpfully revisited these ideas in a shorter essay, 'Culture Industry Reconsidered', published in English after his death (see Adorno, 1991).

The mass media was referred to as the 'culture industry' by Adorno and Horkheimer to indicate its nature: a well-oiled machine producing entertainment products in order to make profit. Whilst this comes as no surprise to us today – we are happy to recognise the 'music industry' or the 'movie business' as such – the German intellectuals were clearly disturbed by the reduction of culture to a set of manufactured products. They explain that they deliberately avoided referring to this business as 'mass culture', because they wanted to make it clear that this is not a culture produced by the people. Instead, the culture consumed by the masses is imposed from above – churned out by the culture industry. Because of this commercial context, media products (whether films, music, TV dramas or whatever) can never be 'art' which just happens to be a commodity: instead 'they are commodities through and through' (Adorno, 1991: 86).

All products of the culture industry are 'exactly the same' (Adorno and Horkheimer, 1979: 122) – not literally, of course, but in the sense that they all reflect the values of the established system. 'Each product affects an individual air', explains Adorno, but this is an 'illusion' (1991: 87). Unusual talents who come along are quickly 'absorbed' into the system (1979: 122): think of the 'challenging' rock acts who almost always end up signing big-money deals with the major record labels – themselves part of even bigger media and business conglomerates – and generating fat profits for their masters. Marilyn Manson and 50 cent may be scary to middle America, but in Wall Street terms they are embodiments of the American capitalist dream. The teen 'rebels' who are fans of such acts, Adorno would suggest, are just consumers: buying a CD is not rebellion, it's buying a CD. The tough guy who has just bought the latest angry rap CD, takes it home and plays it loud, may be thinking 'Yeah! Fuck you, consumer society!', but as far as Adorno is concerned, he might as well say 'Thank you, consumer society, for giving me a new product to buy. This is a good product. I would like to make further purchases of similar products in the near future.'

We might think that the media offer a range of different forms of entertainment, giving different groups what they want, but Adorno and Horkheimer fit this into their account too: 'Something is provided for all so that none may escape' (1979: 123). They remind us that the person seeking entertainment 'has to accept what the culture manufacturers offer him' (p. 124), so choice is an illusion too. We can choose what we like, certainly, but from a limited *range* presented by the culture industry. And our consumption merely fosters 'the circle of manipulation and retroactive need in which the unity of the system grows ever stronger' (p. 121). Because we've never really had anything different, we want more and more of the same. 'The customer is not king, as the culture industry would have us believe, not its subject but its object,' states Adorno (1991: 85).

Adorno and Horkheimer's points can seem worryingly relevant in relation to the Hollywood blockbusters of today. Even back in the 1940s, they observed that new films were usually a set of 'interchangeable' elements borrowed from previous successes, with slight modifications or upgrades in terms of expense, style or technology (1979: 123–125). The authors say: 'As soon as the film begins, it is quite clear how it will end, and who will be rewarded, punished, or forgotten' (p. 125). Some more recent ironic, knowing movies have tried to get around the formula by admitting it – the Hollywood blockbuster *Swordfish* (2001), for example, opens with John Travolta saying 'You know what the problem with Hollywood is? They make shit. Unbelievable, unremarkable shit'; *Transformers* (2007) is both deadly serious and knowingly ludicrous; and disaster movie *The Core* (2003) features a super-strong vehicle made of a metal called 'Unobtainium'. But whilst we may pat ourselves on the back for selecting a movie with such clever, 'postmodern' concepts, the formula remains pretty much intact.

So far we've considered Adorno and Horkheimer's criticisms of the *quality* of popular culture – they think it's all very similar, formulaic and manufactured. Now we'll turn to their view of its *impact* on society. Their concern is, in part, unrelated to the content of any particular TV show, film, or magazine, but is more generally focused on the fact that this 'rubbish' (1979: 121) takes up so much time in people's everyday consciousness – 'occupying [their] senses from the time they leave the factory in the evening to the time they clock in again the next morning' (p. 131), leaving no opportunity for resistance to develop. If your response to this is, 'But I enjoy watching TV – I choose to watch it and I enjoy it!', then you are merely confirming Adorno and Horkheimer's view: they do not deny that people have a 'misplaced love' for popular culture (p. 134). The programmes are well-made and provide enjoyment. We may well watch an educational or political documentary occasionally, but these things make no difference to the main argument: we are still just people consuming TV. We may feel emotions, or have a conversation about an interesting show with friends, but Adorno would say that we are still drones, manipulated by the system to want the pleasures which it offers, and satisfied (in a rather passive, brainless way) with the daily diet of entertainment which it pours forth.

So it is the *passivity* which media consumption brings to people's lives that is Adorno's main concern. In addition there is a belief that the media's content encourages conformity:

> The concepts of order which [the culture industry] hammers into human beings are always those of the status quo ... It pro-claims: you shall conform, with no instruction as to what; conform to that which exists anyway, and to that which every-one thinks anyway as a result of its power and omnipresence. The power of the culture industry's ideology is such that confor-mity has replaced consciousness.
>
> (1991: 90)

He further argues that the culture industry 'impedes the development of autonomous, independent individuals who judge and decide consciously for themselves' (1991: 92). Critical thinking is closed off by mass-produced popular culture.

This all sounded like the kind of argument that a sophisticated media-literate society could shrug off without too much difficulty. But then along came the hit TV series *Pop Idol* (UK, 2001–03), and its successful international franchise which includes *American Idol* (US, 2002–), and successors such as *The X Factor* (2004–). Prior to this, pop stars who were seen as 'manufactured' stooges were often rejected by the public, who did not like the idea that a pop star could be wholly 'invented' by millionaire producers who would tell them what clothes to wear and what songs to sing. *Pop Idol*, however, explicitly *showed* this process of market-driven selection and grooming takes place, over several weeks of mainstream TV; and rather than rejecting the manufactured winners, the public made all of them top pop stars selling millions of records. The first single from UK *Pop Idol* winner Will Young, for instance, became the fastest-selling debut in UK chart history, and US winner Kelly Clarkson's debut single 'A Moment Like This' shot from #52 to #1 in the Billboard chart, breaking a record set by The Beatles. The song had been written specifically *as* the first single for the winner, and had correspondingly been recorded by all four finalists, in case they won, in a clear refutation of the idea that particular songs and stars might go together.

Even after several years, the public do not seem to be tiring of the manufacture-me-a-pop-star format. In December 2006, for instance, the debut single by Leona Lewis, winner of the third series of *The X Factor*, broke a world record by being downloaded 50,000 times within 30 minutes of being available online, and in its first week outsold the rest of the Top 40 combined, making it the fastest selling single in the UK by a female artist. The hit song was not a new one but was, unimaginatively enough, a repeat of Kelly Clarkson's US debut 'A Moment Like This'.

You could say that this all shows that the public will buy any old rubbish if they have been shown it enough times on TV. The *Idol* and *X Factor* stars are produced by a capitalist machine which is happy to reveal its own cynical workings, and which barely pretends to care about the individuality of its 'stars' – and yet still we lap it up. For Adorno, of course, this explains why Marx's revolution didn't happen: pacified by pleasant, shallow entertainments offered by the culture industry, people didn't really feel the need. With communities fragmented into a world of individuals staying in their homes watching TV or listening to pop music, or isolated in the darkness before a cinema screen, resistance was unlikely to find a space to develop, and was further discouraged by the broadly 'conformist' media.

Even if you disagree with Adorno and Horkheimer's snobbish attitude to popular culture and its consumers, their argument about its role in society still seems to stand up. This is partly because it's a 'false consciousness' argument – you might be certain that the mass media hasn't damaged you, but the argument says that you wouldn't notice this anyway, and so your protestations are in vain; only Adorno and Horkheimer know better. Even if you think that they are fantastically arrogant and elitist for taking that position, you still haven't proven them wrong. You need a better argument than that. So let's consider the case for the opposition.

Fiske: audience power

John Fiske is best known for a pair of books, *Understanding Popular Culture* and *Reading the Popular*. At the time of their simultaneous publication in 1989, Fiske was a fiftysomething professor, and a self-confessed fan of pop culture, who had taught in Britain, Australia and the USA. The time-pressed modern consumer may like to note that an article by Fiske called 'Moments of Television' (1989c) offers a decent introduction to the views which he discusses in much more depth in the books.

Fiske's work represents a view diametrically opposed to Adorno's. Near the start of *Understanding Popular Culture* he tells Adorno fans bluntly:

> Popular culture is made by the people, not produced by the culture industry. All the culture industries can do is produce a repertoire of texts or cultural resources for the various formations of the people to use or reject in the ongoing process of producing their popular culture.
>
> (1989a: 24)

In other words, the power of the audience to interpret media texts, and determine their popularity, far outweighs the ability of media institutions to send a particular message or ideology to audiences within their texts. This position did not, of course, appear out of the blue. Stuart Hall's 'encoding/ decoding' model (1973) had already suggested, in more modest terms, that a media message could be 'decoded' by the audience in different and unpredictable ways (see box, pp. 30–31) – a point which, you might think, was pretty obvious anyway. Fiske, however, offers a radically exaggerated version of this view, which – no doubt as a reaction to the pessimism of Adorno and his followers – often appears to be a gleeful celebration of the audience's power of interpretation and choice.

We should note that although Fiske was opposed to the cynical stance of left-wing critics like Adorno, Fiske's arguments are not (intended to be) a 'right-wing' response. Instead, Fiske comes across as an upbeat leftie and a 'man of the people' who wants to show that 'the people' are not foolish dupes. He says, indeed, that we can't even talk about 'the people' or 'the audience' because a singular mass of consumers does not exist: there is only a range of different individuals with their own changing tastes and a 'shifting set of social allegiances' which may or may not relate to their social background, and which are complex and contradictory (Fiske, 1989a). Fiske does not deny that we live in a capitalist and patriarchal society, but suggests that it is silly to think of popular culture as a manufactured thing imposed by capitalists upon the unsuspecting masses. 'Culture is a living, active process: it can be developed only from within, it cannot be imposed from without or above' (p. 23). Therefore the pop charts are not a set of recordings that people have been somehow duped into liking and purchasing, in a uniform way; instead they reflect what is genuinely popular. Fiske supports this by pointing out that record companies and movie studios put out many products which fail: flops outnumber the hits, showing that the public choose which items they actually want and like. Furthermore, people relate to their current favourite single or film, as they relate to all media texts, in a complex, shifting way, based in their own identity, which is unique to themselves. And rather than the people accepting a stream of similar products, as Adorno would suggest, Fiske says that there is a 'drive for innovation and change [which] comes from the audience activity in the cultural economy' (1989c: 62).

Our media choices are limited, to an extent. Fiske says that 'My argument in favour of difference and a relatively empowered, relatively loosely subjected, subject must not blind us to the determining framework of power relations within which all of this takes place' (1989c: 58). Nevertheless, Fiske says there is an 'overspill' of meanings (p. 70), so that most texts contain the 'preferred' meaning – the one intended by its producers – but also offer possibilities for consumers to create their own alternative or resistant readings. Indeed, Fiske says that people are not merely consumers of texts – the audience rejects this role 'and becomes a producer, a producer of meanings and pleasures' (1989c: 59). Following the French theorist Michel de Certeau (1984), Fiske talks about the 'guerrilla tactics' by which everyday media users snatch aspects of the mass-produced media but then (re-)interpret them to suit their own preferred readings. The text is the source from which the viewer *activates meanings* to make sense of their material existence (1989c: 58).

Let us take, for example, the case of Madonna, who was discussed by Fiske almost two decades ago, but – incredibly – remains popular today. The 2005 *Confessions on a Dancefloor* album, for instance, sold 8 million copies in a year, and by 2007, Madonna had sold over 200 million albums worldwide. Her *Confessions* world tour in 2006 made US$260 million (Billboard, 2007) and was the highest-grossing tour ever by a female artist. For Adorno, this would well illustrate his thesis that the culture industry can mass-produce one product (or a set of similar products) and successfully flog it to an audience of passive consumers – millions of them – who do not seek out their own preferred entertainments, but settle for the work of a manufactured icon whose image is successfully promoted and marketed around the world. For Fiske, it is quite the reverse. Madonna has sold so many million albums because of her ability to connect with an audience, to be meaningful to individuals. Each album sold may be just another 'unit' to record company executives, but at an individual level, it is a unique item which its purchaser invests with a unique set of meanings. Fiske says that Madonna is 'an exemplary popular text because she is so full of contradic- tions – she contains the patriarchal meanings of feminine sexuality, and the resisting ones that her sexuality is *hers* to use as she wishes in ways that do not require masculine approval.... Far from being an adequate text in herself, she is a provoker of meanings whose cultural effects can be studied only in her multiple and often contradictory circulations' (1989a: 124). By saying that Madonna is not an 'adequate' text, Fiske is not commenting on Madonna *per se*, but is reminding us of his argument that the meaning of any text is not complete until interpreted by an individual within the context of their lives.

Madonna's image, then, becomes 'a site of semiotic struggle between the forces of patriarchal control and feminine resistance, of capitalism and the subordinate, of the adult and the young' (1989b: 97). In short, Madonna is 'a cultural resource of everyday life' who can be used by each individual fan in a different way to add some meanings or pleasures to their existence. This can be carried through to their whole *way of being* in the world, too. 'Madonna offers her fans access to semiotic and social power; at the basic level this works through fantasy, which, in turn, may empower the fan's sense of self and thus affect [their] behaviour in social situations' (p. 113).

This process is not meant to be unique to Madonna and her audience, of course – Fiske would say that this is just an illustration of a mode of media consumption which happens all the time. Fiske therefore answers the *Pop Idol* conundrum: consumers have not simply been duped into conforming to the demands of the culture industry; rather, viewers have taken the con- testants into their hearts, literally and individually. They buy the singles and albums by the winners because they feel that they have developed a personal connection with these people over several weeks of televised trials and tribu- lations. Their struggles are our struggles, as it were. We have supported them through their battles with smug music industry executives such as Simon Cowell, and want to share in their triumph, Fiske might suggest; we

STUART HALL AND HIS PREDECESSORS

Born in Jamaica in 1932, Stuart Hall came to be the best-known figure in the development of British cultural studies. As a leader, facilitator, theorist and editor, he developed key approaches and strands of theory within the field. In some cases he took up the work of influential European theorists and helped to bring them to the attention of English-speaking audiences. A lot of his work was produced in collaboration with colleagues from the Birmingham Centre for Contemporary Cultural Studies and the Open University.

Hall's famous 'encoding/decoding' model (1973) suggested that a media producer may 'encode' a certain meaning into their text, which would be based on a certain social context and understandings, but noted that when another person comes to consume that text, their reading ('decoding') of it – based on their own social context and assumptions – is likely to be somewhat different. This might seem obvious, but one benefit of this model was that it highlighted the importance of understanding the meanings and interpretations of significant actors in both media production (journalists, writers, producers, editors) and media reception (the numerous audiences) – as well as those intermediaries in media distribution (executives, marketers, broadcasters, distributors, regulators).

Hall's writings on ideology were more sophisticated, and sought to understand how particular political positions could become meaningful and popular when articulated in terms which people could identify with. (Such communication would primarily take place, of course, through the mass media.) This approach reflected Hall's interest in the work of Antonio Gramsci (1891–1937), who had noted that leaders could win the assent of the people ('hegemony') if they were able to make their policies appear to be 'common sense'. Hall's studies of Thatcherism were rooted in this idea: Thatcherism became successful because it was able to articulate a right-wing political agenda in terms which addressed the concerns of 'ordinary people' and made the solutions seem sensible and obvious (Hall, 1983, 1988). In studying the media and gender, one could use this kind of approach to see how the media might make certain formations of masculinity, femininity and sexuality seem to be natural, inevitable and sexy.

Hall's work on ideology also drew on a critical reading of the French Marxist thinker Louis Althusser (1918–90), whose concept of 'interpellation' purported to show how an individual's identity or sense of self is absorbed into – and, indeed, produced by – the dominant ideologies within a society (Althusser, 1971). Interpellation is typically explained as a kind of hailing – like when a figure of authority calls out 'hey you!', and the individual turns round to recognise that they are being addressed. In this moment the person is constituted as a subject – which means that they recognise and acquiesce to their position within structures of ideology. Interpellation occurs when a person connects with a media text: when we enjoy a magazine or TV show, for example, this uncritical consumption means that the text has *interpellated* us into a certain set of assumptions, and caused us to tacitly accept a particular approach to the world. This can be a fruitful notion, then: it could be said, for example, that lifestyle magazines use glamour, humour and attractive photography to seduce (interpellate) readers into a particular worldview. However, as Hall and others have noted, the approach is limited by its determinism – it attributes power to grand ideologies, and none to individuals.

Hall's work on the media has focused more on productions and representations than audiences, although he assumes the two are connected: Hall suggests that we can try 'to theorise identity as constituted, not outside but within representation; and hence of cinema [or other media], not as a second-order mirror held up to reflect what already exists, but as that form of representation which is able to constitute us as new kinds of subjects, and thereby enable us to discover places from which to speak' (Hall, 1997: 58). This is a clear rationale for studying media representations – although such work can remain at the level of interesting speculation, unless backed up by some responses from actual audiences.

Further reading: *Stuart Hall: Critical Dialogues in Cultural Studies* (Morley and Chen, 1996); *Stuart Hall* (Procter, 2004); *Althusser: A Critical Reader* (Elliot, 1994); *Louis Althusser* (Ferretter, 2005).

buy their records not because we are idiotic dupes, but because we are empathic people. We identify with their emotional 'journey' of self-fulfilment – even if our own personal goals happen to be different. Similarly, for example, the *TV Living* study found that people used TV science fiction shows as a way of thinking through their sense of 'otherness' – even though they were not, themselves, eccentric Time Lords like the Doctor in *Doctor Who* or alienated androids like Data in *Star Trek: The Next Generation* – and thereby arrived at a comfortable sense of their own identity (Gauntlett and

Hill, 1999). The media is thus an 'enabler' of ideas and meanings, promoting diversity and difference, which might lead to social change (Fiske, 1989c: 73).

The obvious criticism of Fiske's work is that it is far too optimistic about the challenging impact of mainstream texts – or to be precise, the challenging consequences of people's own unique readings of mainstream texts. But it's certainly a thought-provoking response to Adorno's extreme pessimism. At this stage in the book I'll leave it for you to decide who you think is closer to the truth. Now we'll move on to consider the empirical, rather than theoretical, studies of the media's impact.

UNHELPFUL PSYCHOLOGY RESEARCH

In the previous chapter we mentioned several ways in which everyday popular media could be expected to affect people's feelings, responses and actions, both in general terms and in relation to ideas about gender. Those were not wholly new observations. Researchers, in particular psychologists, have been studying these matters for a few decades now. When I tell people that I am studying the relationship between media and gender, I sometimes get a sympathetic, puzzled smile, because people assume (quite reasonably) that psychologists must have 'done that' quite satisfactorily already. But, in fact, whilst many studies have indeed been produced, the level of useful insight remains low.

There are two relevant streams of existing research: the research on 'media effects' in general, and the work within psychology on 'development of gender identity'. In this part of the chapter, then, we will look at the shortcomings of 'media effects' studies, followed by the gender-development studies.

Problems with media 'effects' studies

Media 'effects' studies – by which we mean those studies which seek to identify a particular 'effect' which is the result of exposure to a particular type of media content – have had a most unusual history. The majority of this research has been centred, predictably enough, on the question of whether watching violence on screen will lead individuals to be aggressive in real life. On the one hand these studies have been quite popular, with newspapers and politicians always eager to have more of them, and with several (usually American) academics keen to build entire careers around producing them. On the other hand they have been almost entirely useless, showing nothing except the somewhat interesting fact of their own redundancy.

The central problem for these studies is that isolating one particular thing, such as TV viewing or magazine reading, as the cause of a person's behaviour, is basically impossible. The idea that a bit of media content 'made' somebody do something will always seem silly, for the perfectly good reason that, as we all know, the influences upon any decision to do something are a complex mix of many elements, including previous experiences, opinions, values and suggestions from various sources.

It might seem overhasty to dismiss these studies out of hand. Instead one could consider each piece of research in some detail, as I tried to do once in a whole book dissecting these studies (*Moving Experiences*, 1995, 2005). But to do that is really to take these studies much too seriously. Their individual flaws were often curious, amusing, and a bit depressing, but would not usually be worthy of much attention, were it not for the fact that 'media effects' continues to be a subject of public discussion – and also because some 'experts' like to cheekily claim that the case for negative media effects has been proved. (On a UK television discussion about screen violence back in 1994, for example, American psychologist Leonard Eron confidently told the audience that in the USA this was no longer an issue for debate: 'The search for media effects is *over*', he declared, asserting that 'conclusive proof' had finally persuaded everyone that media content could have a clear and identifiable effect on people's behaviour. This claim was, of course, not true.) For this reason it remains important to be able to look at the studies themselves – to show, for what it's worth, that they don't show anything.

Generally, however, it makes more sense to tackle the 'media effects' studies in a broader way, considering the paradigmatic problems which almost always dog such research. These I have grouped together in the following list of overarching flaws (Gauntlett, 1998, 2001).

TEN THINGS WRONG WITH THE 'MEDIA EFFECTS' MODEL

1 The effects model tackles social problems 'backwards'

If researchers are concerned about the causes of problematic behaviour, such as violence, it seems obvious that they should study people who engage in these activities, and try to ascertain the roots of their behaviour. Media effects researchers, however, have typically started at the wrong end of this question: informed only by speculation (and often, it seems, a grimly unsympathetic attitude to youth culture), they start with the idea that the media is to blame, and then try to make links *back to* the world of actual violence. This approach to a social problem is, in a literal sense, backwards.

To understand violent people, we should study violent people. But in the uncommon cases where researchers have sought to identify links between screen violence and real-life violence by interviewing actual violent individuals (e.g. Hagell and Newburn, 1994), they have found no such connection.

2 The effects model treats children as inadequate

The media effects studies position children exclusively as potential 'victims' of the mass media, and (rather cruelly) allow young people no opportunity to express their critical abilities, intelligence or free will. Hundreds of shallow quantitative studies, usually conducted by 'psychologists', have often been little more than traps for the subjects, and ironically allow no scope for developing psychological insights. More generous research methods, which are willing to listen to children, have shown that children can talk intelligently and indeed cynically about the mass media (Buckingham, 1993, 1996), and that children as young as seven can make thoughtful, critical and 'media literate' video productions themselves (Gauntlett, 1997).

3 Assumptions within the effects model are characterised by barely-concealed conservative ideology

Media effects studies support conservative and right-wing ideologies, even if that is not necessarily the conscious intention of the people producing them. The studies typically suggest that social problems are not rooted in the organisation of society, and inequalities, but are actually the evil magic products of popular culture. Their conception of screen violence as a meaningless but measurable 'thing' also helps those who want to blame modern media instead of considering the serious social causes of violence. The researchers' categorisations of 'antisocial' behaviour often reveal that they are worried about challenges to the status quo. And the tendency to patronise and devalue children and young people, by assuming that they have no competencies worth considering, also fits with these illiberal trends.

4 The effects model inadequately defines its own objects of study

Media effects studies are usually extremely undiscriminating about how they identify worrying bits of media content, or subsequent behaviour by viewers. An act of 'violence', for example, might be smashing cages to free some trapped animals, or using force to disable a nuclear missile. It might be kicking a chair in frustration, or a horrible murder. In many studies, 'verbal aggression' is included within the categories of aggression, which means that studies which are interpreted by most people as being about physical violence may actually be more about the use of swear words. Once processed by effects research, any of these depictions or actions simply emerge as a 'level of aggression', but without a more selective and discriminating way of compiling these numbers, the results can be deceptive and virtually meaningless.

5 The effects model is often based on artificial studies

Careful sociological studies of media influences require large amounts of time and money, and so they are heavily outnumbered by simpler studies which often put their subjects into artificial, contrived situations. Laboratory and field experiments involve compelling participants to watch a particular programme or set of programmes, and – just as artificially – observing them in a particular setting afterwards. Here, behaviour of the children towards an inanimate object is often taken (artificially) to represent how they would behave towards a real person. Furthermore, this all rests on the artificial belief that children's behaviour will not vary even though they know that they are being manipulated, tested and/or observed. (Studies by researchers such as Borden (1975) have shown that this is quite erroneous – children's behaviour in experiments changes in accordance with what they think the adults would like to see.)

6 The effects model is often based on studies with misapplied methodology

The studies which do not use the experimental method, and so may not be guilty of the flaws described in the previous point, nevertheless often fall down by applying a methodological procedure wrongly, or by drawing inappropriate conclusions from particular methods. Meaningless comparisons are made, glaring inconsistencies are overlooked, and sometimes methods which are unable to demonstrate any causal links are treated as if they have found them (details in Gauntlett, 1995, 2001, 2005). This reckless abuse of research procedures seems to be acceptable when people are pinning blame on 'media effects'.

7 The effects model is selective in its criticisms of media depictions of violence

The ideological motive behind effects studies (see point three above) may mean that some media representations are criticised, whilst others are strangely exempt. Violence in news and factual programmes, for example, which is often presented suddenly and without much context, is not seen as a worry, whereas violence in popular drama and movies is of great concern. This again suggests that researchers are more interested in blaming an aspect of popular culture for social problems, than they are in making a coherent and thoughtful argument.

8 The effects model assumes superiority to the masses

Researchers always assume that media effects happen to *other people*. Ironically, surveys show that almost everybody feels this way: whilst varying percentages of the population say they are concerned about media effects, almost nobody ever says that they have been affected *themselves*. Sometimes the researchers excuse their approach by saying that they are mature adults, whereas their concerns lie with *children* (see point two above: 'The effects model treats children as inadequate').

9 The effects model makes no attempt to understand meanings of the media

As hinted above, the media effects model rests on simplistic assumptions about media content. Controversial material, such as a scene containing violence, is not treated as part of a relationship between characters, but is seen as a 'thing' cynically inserted by media producers. The meanings of the action, and understandings of character motivation held by the audience, are of no interest in effects research, because media content is just a set of measurable threats. Regardless of the tone and intentions of any piece of media content, the media effects model will always assume that its sole meaning is 'Hey kids! Here's some stuff that you might like to copy!'. But qualitative studies have unsurprisingly given support to the view that media audiences routinely arrive at their own, often quite varied and unpredictable interpretations of everyday media texts (e.g. Hill, 1997, 2004, 2007; Buckingham, 1993, 1996; Buckingham and Bragg, 2004; Gauntlett and Hill, 1999; Schlesinger *et al.*, 1992; Gray, 1992; Palmer, 1986).

10 The effects model is not grounded in theory

The media effects model would make much more sense if it suggested a coherent theory which could explain *why* people might become motivated to copy actions seen in the media. But no decent explanation is offered. Sometimes the idea that violence is 'glamorised' is mooted and can seem relevant, but effects researchers tend to suggest that children must be protected from the most violent media depictions, which are usually the least 'glamorous' depictions. The violence used by dashing spies in 'family' films, say, usually looks much more attractive, but attracts little criticism. The model just isn't subtle or well-thought-out enough to cope with these things.

This lack of theory has led to the proliferation of half-baked ideas outlined above – that the media (rather than people) should be the unproblematic starting-point for research; that children will be unable to 'cope' with the media; that categories such as 'antisocial behaviour' are clear and self-evident; that a veneer of 'science' is more important than developing methods which might actually show us something; that screen fictions are of concern, whilst news pictures are not; that researchers have the unique capacity to observe and classify social behaviour and its meanings, but that those researchers need not attend to the various possible meanings which media content may have for the audience. Each of these substantial problems has been able to develop because there is no-one with a decent theory to keep them on the straight and narrow.

So much for that, then

The studies which seek to find a simple causal link between seeing something in the media, and subsequent behaviour, are therefore of little use. That's a disappointment at first, but then you realise it's not a great surprise: we all knew the relationship between media and identity was never going to be that simple anyway. So we can move on.

PSYCHOLOGISTS ON GENDER IDENTITY

Within the field of psychology, the 'received wisdom' and general level of insight about the development of gender identities remains rather shallow and disappointing. If we look at the contemporary general understanding of the area, such as that passed on in psychology textbooks, we find explanations which are alarmingly simple and mundane (e.g. Malim and Birch, 1998; Carver and Scheier, 2006; Phares and Chaplin, 1998; Huffman,

2006). This shortcoming is not the fault of the textbook writers, but reflects the lack of valuable theory in the psychology field. There are two main positions on gender role development:

- Some psychologists believe that chromosomal and hormonal differences are the main cause of differences between male and female behaviour. They typically point to evidence from situations where people have grown up with different hormone levels and emerge as more 'masculine' or 'feminine'; but the implications of such findings are rarely clear-cut (see, for example, Malim and Birch, 1998: 516–518).
- Other psychologists argue that socialisation is much more important – gender roles are *learned* during development, and reinforced throughout everyday life. There is a lot of evidence to support this case, and it is often conceded that 'most investigators agree that cultural influences and socialization processes are the main determinants of an individual's gender role identity and roles' (ibid.: 518).

This division of views – the standard 'nature vs. nurture' debate – will be familiar to many people from TV documentaries, magazine articles and even everyday conversations about how one might bring up children. What is more interesting, perhaps, is the way that the arguments and theories don't get *much* more genuinely varied or complicated than this. Those who assign the most importance to biological factors may come up with further bits of 'evidence', but this will always be viewed with suspicion by those who feel that there is something inherently odd about modern-day scientists trying to 'prove' that sex differences are important.

Meanwhile, social learning theory seems to have surprisingly little flesh on its bones. It includes the idea of *modelling* – that we may imitate and take on behaviour which we observe in same-sex role models (such as a parent, peers and others); and *reinforcement* – that behaviour which is socially approved-of will be well-received, and so we learn to continue and develop it, whereas socially inappropriate actions will not get a good reception and so will be cut from our repertoire. This seems to ring true to everyday experience, and several studies can be cited which appear to show the theory in action (e.g. Malim and Birch, 1998: 518–519). There's not much *to* it, though, is there?

There is another approach, 'cognitive-developmental theory', which also regards gender roles as learned, but sees the child as more active in the creation of their own gender identity. In this model, the child's own cognitions (thought processes) are imperative, as they organise and make sense of the messages about gender which they receive. The child's journey through stages of cognitive development is also important. Once a child has acquired 'gender constancy' – the understanding that they are expected to have a continuous gender identity which does not change between different situations – they will then seek to develop their personality within an appropriately 'masculine' or 'feminine' mould (Kohlberg, 1966). This model, then, has the child *actively seeking* information about how to act like a boy or girl, rather than the somewhat more passive modelling described in social learning theory. A development of this approach, called 'gender schematic processing theory' (Martin, 1991), suggests that children initially learn that certain activities and interests are appropriate for one sex or the other – that's the gender schema of the title; and then they learn about and interpret the world in terms of this schema, paying most attention to material which will reinforce their own gendered identity.

Like a lot of social psychology, these theories are blandly descriptive on the one hand, whilst also being rather deterministic (or fatalistic) in tone on the other – as if relating a process which will *always* occur. In other words, they make it sound like a natural and necessary part of child development, that a young boy has to recognise the importance of cultivating a masculine identity, or that a girl has to reach a point where she realises the need to develop feminine traits. To be fair, the theories could also be read as critiques of a society which compels children to see these things as important (but the flatly 'scientific', descriptive tone of most child development writing is unlikely to suggest this).

Furthermore, there is the fear that these theories could be used in ways which would reinforce the traditional status quo. People who did not want to conform to gender conventions could be seen to have 'failed' to have acquired 'gender constancy', whilst children interested in non-stereotypical activities could be said to have an incomplete gender schema. This has certainly been an acceptable part of 'psychology' work to date, where people who don't fit within a traditional cultural norm end up being told that they have a medical disorder. For example, whilst the official diagnostic manual of American psychiatrists ceased to define homosexuality as pathological in 1973, in 1980 it introduced a new illness called 'Gender identity disorder', which explains that girls or boys who are interested in non-stereotypical activities may have fallen prey to this psychological malady. This 'disorder' is still officially recognised today (see Bartlett *et al.*, 2000; O'Keefe and Fox, 2003; Icon, 2004).

We should acknowledge that there is one more complex section of the 'nurture' camp: the theories based on Sigmund Freud's psychoanalytic approach. Gender identity is here seen as an outcome of the Oedipus and Electra complexes; ideally, the developing child will achieve stability by identifying with their same-sex parent at the end of this stage. Like most Freudian theory, however, this is unproven and speculative – indeed, it's not even clear whether we are meant to take it literally. It might be of value as a metaphor which can be used in some psychiatric situations, but otherwise seems to have little authority. Freud made an outstanding contribution to our understanding of the role of the unconscious, and human development generally; but his ideas about gender roles today seem unhelpful, and unlikely to really work in a modern context. Nevertheless, psychoanalytic theory played a key role in some feminist film theories, which we turn to now.

GENDER DIFFERENCES ARE FOR OTHER PEOPLE

In one of the more interesting psychology studies, Williams and Best (1977, 1990) produced a 'sex stereotype index' by showing a long list of adjectives to men and women, and asking them to rate each word according to whether it was most associated with women or men. Subsequent studies could then ask people to pick words which described themselves, or others, from this list.

It was found that when participants were asked to pick words which described themselves, there was considerable overlap in the adjectives picked by men and women. Indeed, over 25 per cent of men had self-descriptions that were more stereotypic of women than the average women's stereotype, and over 25 per cent of women had self-descriptions that were more stereotypic of men than the average men's stereotype.

However, when asked to describe *friends*, participants typically gave them somewhat more stereotypical characteristics, and in describing men and women in general, the assessments were clearly divided along stereotyped lines.

These findings suggest that we don't really expect gender stereotypes to apply to ourselves – complicated beings that we know ourselves to be – but that we still apply them to everyone else!

LAURA MULVEY AND THE 'MALE GAZE'

The publication of Laura Mulvey's article 'Visual pleasure and narrative cinema' in 1975 (reproduced in Hollows *et al.*, 2000, and elsewhere), had a huge impact on feminist film studies in particular, and the study of film, gender and representation more generally. Mulvey's argument rested on a number of psychoanalytic (Freudian) concepts and assumptions, combined with a rather fatalistic form of feminism (and heterosexuality), all of which were clearly popular at the time.

Mulvey argued that one of the pleasures of cinema is 'scopophilia', a voyeuristic gaze directed at other people. This kind of viewing is encouraged in the cinema, Mulvey suggests, because the conventions of mainstream film 'portray a hermetically sealed world which unwinds magically, indifferent to the presence of the audience', and the darkness of the theatre contrasts with the light of the screen, again helping to promote the 'voyeuristic separation' (1975: 9). Mulvey asserts that a second form of pleasure offered by cinema is a *narcissistic* voyeurism – seeing oneself in a primary character and identifying with them (or, in Mulvey's terms, *him*). At this point in the argument, Mulvey's clear-cut sense of imposed sex roles becomes apparent:

> In a world ordered by sexual imbalance, pleasure in looking has been split between active/male and passive/female. The determining male gaze projects its phantasy onto the female figure, which is styled accordingly. In their traditional exhibitionist role women are simultaneously looked at and displayed, with their appearance coded for strong visual and erotic impact so that they can be said to connote *to-be-looked-at-ness*.
>
> (1975: 10)

Male viewers identify with the (male) protagonist, and the female characters are the subject of their desiring gaze. Female viewers, Mulvey says, are also compelled to take the viewpoint of the central (male) character, so that women are denied a viewpoint of their own and instead participate in the pleasure of men looking at women. ('Men look at women; women watch themselves being looked at', as John Berger had put it (1972: 47).) The female character has no importance in a film, Mulvey says, except as a 'spectacle', the erotic object of both the male characters and the cinema spectators; her role is to drive the hero to act the way he does. (This can certainly be seen in many films – think of *Die Hard* (1988) and *Die Hard II* (1990), say, where Bonnie Bedelia is in peril and can do very little, whilst her husband Bruce Willis is thereby motivated to go to extremes to save her – and a lot of other people, of course, to underline his heroism. Some thrillers today, such as *Firewall* (2006) and *Déjà Vu* (2006), still casually use a man's desire to save a woman as his motivation.) Male viewers would not want to view the male hero as a sexual object, Mulvey says, 'according to the principles of the ruling ideology' (1975: 14), but since he drives the story and makes things happen, identification means he can be admired *narcissistically*, as an ideal version of the self.

Mulvey's article is well-written, thoughtful and interesting. She is also able to illustrate her thesis with some examples from classic cinema – Hitchcock's films in particular. However, the argument is based on some premises which make it (arguably?) untenable. Mulvey says that the heroes that drive the story are always male, whilst female characters are passive erotic objects. Although it is not difficult to think of films where this occurs, particularly ones made in the time prior to Mulvey's mid-1970s text, today we can list many films with heroic females, and only note a few recent films where women are passive; Chapter 4 of this book gives many examples. (Of course, there is still a troublesome imbalance, and room for many more female heroes and leaders in mainstream movies.)

Perhaps a bigger problem with Mulvey's argument is that it denies the heterosexual female gaze altogether. Within her model, the audience, both male and female, is positioned so that they admire the male lead for his actions, and adopt his romantic/erotic view of the women. There is value in the idea that women come to learn to view themselves and other women through the 'male gaze', given the dominance of male-produced media; but to deny the 'female gaze' altogether does little service to women (although Mulvey's point is not that women are *inadequate* in this respect; rather, she is making a critique of *the position that patriarchy puts women into*). But since their earliest days, movies have included and often *celebrated* physically attractive men, whose sexual allure has surely drawn women into cinemas. The relaunch of the James Bond franchise with *Casino Royale* (2006), for example, was helped considerably by shots of Daniel Craig emerging from the sea in tight trunks: 'Phwoar!', said *Heat* magazine (14 November 2006), and, in common with several other women's magazines, urged female audiences to see this spectacle.

Mulvey's argument cannot be too strong if mainstream films like *Lara Croft: Tomb Raider* (2001), *Elektra* (2003) and *Aeon Flux* (2005) can bounce it off the rails altogether. Mulvey would be right to note that Angelina Jolie, Jennifer Garner and Charlize Theron in these films are 'coded for strong visual and erotic impact [which] can be said to connote *to-be-looked-at-ness*' (although as we saw above, you could say just the same of the typically attractive male action heroes such as James Bond). But rather than being the object of desire who inspires the hero to action, these women *are* the hero, driving the story forward on their own, and reserving the right to eye certain men with desire – none of which can fit into the Mulvey model at all.

FILM STUDIES BEYOND MULVEY

Ultimately, then, Mulvey's argument may help to illuminate certain films, and some male spectator positions, but simply *does not work* as a comprehensive account of gendered viewings of film today. (The idea that women learn to absorb the 'male gaze' is provocative, though, and will appear again in this book.) Mulvey's article is still discussed and reprinted in film studies textbooks, but feminist film studies have advanced in the meantime. As Liesbet Van Zoonen put it in 1994, 'Mulvey's dark and suffocating analysis of patriarchal cinema has lost ground to a more confident and empowering approach which foregrounds the possibilities of "subversive", that is, non-patriarchal modes of female spectatorship' (1994: 97). Here, the 1970s idea that inevitably-sexist cinema could offer no pleasures to women, was replaced by the 1980s idea that women could find their *own* pleasures in inevitably-sexist cinema (Arbuthnot and Seneca, 1982; Stacey, 1987). Whilst rightfully assigning more agency to women, this approach seems almost as tragically resigned to the patriarchal nature of movies as its predecessor: instead of seeking social change, or even just change in the movies, viewers resign themselves to making 'subversive' readings, or highlighting unusually subversive texts.

By the late 1990s, film studies had begun to change again. Yvonne Tasker's book *Working Girls: Gender and Sexuality in Popular Cinema* (1998) offered a thoughtful, intelligent discussion of newer Hollywood representations of women. Although the roles and images of women in popular movies were generally far from feminist ideals, Tasker does not dwell on the easy-to-find examples of embarrassing sexism in the Hollywood product, but provides a thoughtful analysis of the newer roles played by women: as action heroes, detectives, cowgirls and empowered music stars. She also notes the growing number of equal male/female partnerships (e.g. *Speed*, *Strange Days*, *Broken Arrow*). Some baggage from the history of film studies remains: for example, the clothing of the female heroes in *Aliens*, *Terminator 2* and *The Long Kiss Goodnight* is observed to be 'masculine' (p. 68), which is a silly concern to raise about their sensible apparel (the critic would presumably be no happier to see these women in impractical long dresses ... or short skirts). The discipline of film studies has a long-standing interest in masculine and feminine archetypes, though – even though these terms are beginning to shed meaning. At least Tasker sought to bring back a well-observed engagement with texts. Audience studies are needed too, of course, but these should engage with *actual* viewers. Mulvey's work – which doesn't warrant a single mention in Tasker's book – only considered the viewer as a theoretical psychoanalytic construct in any case.

SUMMARY

At the start of this chapter we considered two rather polarised approaches to the potential power of the media. One view, represented by Theodor Adorno, suggested that the mass media has considerable power over the population. The 'culture industry' churns out products which keep the audience blandly entertained, but passive, helping to maintain the status quo by encouraging conformity and diminishing the scope for resistance. Representing the opposite view, John Fiske argued that popular culture is created by the people. Rather than being turned into submissive zombies, media audiences have an active and creative engagement with popular culture, using 'guerrilla' tactics to reinterpret media texts to suit their own purposes. Meaning is not sent from 'above' by the culture industry, but is generated 'on the ground' by media users. Neither one of these views can be seen as the 'correct' one – although it's partly a matter of opinion and ideology. (We might like to consider whether a more useful account, matching neither extreme in this polarised debate, can be found. Stuart Hall's ideas, for example, suggest just one kind of 'third way' approach, and others are available.)

The chapter then took a more pessimistic turn as we considered previous empirical studies of media power. The 'media effects' research tradition, which had gone to great lengths to identify the effects of exposure to particular instances of popular media, was seen to have failed for a variety of reasons. The attempts of psychologists to account for the development of gender identities were also found to be rather lacking in depth. Furthermore, the whole approach of the psychology discipline was attacked for its tendency to reinforce the status quo, instead of helping to generate more progressive, challenging or optimistic approaches.

Some classic 'cultural studies' approaches to media, gender and identity developed from Mulvey's feminist film studies thesis, but as we saw, this rested on a monolithic view of male and female roles (in both film and reality). These arguments have fallen from grace more recently, but in the absence of other big ideas, they still are discussed in film classes. This, then, is the historical background to the study of media, gender and identity, and it is not short of some rather disappointing, simplistic and/or sexist ideas. Having set out this series of disappointments, we'd better get on with the rest of the book.

Chapter 3

REPRESENTATIONS OF GENDER IN THE PAST

Tнıs снартек AND the next one provide an overview of representations of gender in the media. Attempting to talk about such a broad topic, the images of women and men – that's all people – within such a broad field – 'the media' – is a very tall order. Each week a new set of movies is released. Every day, television broadcasters put out dramas, news, current affairs programmes, documentaries, children's entertainment, game shows, chat shows, lifestyle programmes, films, soap operas, music videos and more. Magazines, newspapers and adverts all contain images of women and men, and even songs on the radio (or played in shops and cafes) might feed into, or challenge, our ideas about gender. The internet and World Wide Web bring even more information and ideas into our lives; the material we see online is more likely to be material we have requested quite specifically, but as online magazines and general entertainment sites become increasingly popular, and these merge with digital television, electronic media becomes yet another source of gender information.

So there are many sources of images and ideas about gender, and each one contains a colossal amount of information. This chapter will, then, be a radically simplified overview of general trends in the representations of genders from around the middle of the previous century up to the start of the 1990s. The subsequent chapter covers representations of gender from the 1990s to the present.

WOMEN AND MEN ON TV

Gunter (1995) and Elasmar *et al.* (1999) provide useful summaries of the findings of various content analysis studies, which have counted the prevalence of women and men in significant speaking roles in TV shows. In the 1950s, 1960s and 1970s, only 20 to 35 per cent of characters were female. By the mid-1980s, there were more women in leading roles, but still there were twice as many men on screen. (These figures are generally based on reliable studies of US television; there is no evidence that in Europe the proportions were much different.)

Gender disparities varied between programme types, of course. In the mid-1970s, Miles (1975) found that there were nearly equal proportions of men and women in situation comedies – although of course the gender roles and the humour could still be traditional and sexist, despite this statistical parity – whereas in action-adventure shows, only 15 per cent of the leading characters were women. A decade later, a 1987 study found female characters to be most common in comedy programmes (43 per cent), but outnumbered two to one in dramas, and in action-adventure shows women had almost doubled their showing to a still-low 29 per cent of characters (Davis, 1990).

Gunter goes on to show how studies in the 1970s consistently found that marriage, parenthood and domesticity were shown on television to be more important for women than men (1995: 13–14). A study by McNeil (1975) concluded that the women's movement had been largely ignored by television, with married housewives being the main female role shown. Women's interactions were very often concerned with romance or family problems (in 74 per cent of cases) whereas men's interactions were not frequently concerned with these matters (only 18 per cent of cases). Female characters were unlikely to work, especially not if they were wives or mothers, and even when they did, this work was typically not seen on screen, McNeil found. Furthermore, various other studies in the 1970s found men to be the dominant characters and the decision-makers on TV; for example, men were twice as likely to make decisions or to give orders, whilst women who were successful at work – where they were to be found – did not get on well with men, or have happy relationships (ibid.: 16–17).

Overall, men were more likely to be assertive (or aggressive), whilst women were more likely to be passive. Men were much more likely to be adventurous, active and victorious, whereas women were more frequently shown as weak, ineffectual, victimised, supportive, laughable or 'merely token females' (Gunter, 1995).

The potential consequences of this were highlighted by Gaye Tuchman in her well-known article with the striking title, 'The Symbolic Annihilation of Women by the Mass Media' (1978):

> From children's shows to commercials to prime-time adventures and situation comedies, television proclaims that women don't count for much. They are underrepresented in television's fictional life – they are 'symbolically annihilated.' ... The paucity of women on American television tells viewers that women don't matter much in American society.
>
> (1978: 10–11)

It wasn't just a problem of numbers, either. Tuchman asserts that those women who *were* shown to be working were portayed as 'incompetents and inferiors', as victims, or having 'trivial' interests. Even in women's traditional domain of the home, men were shown solving both emotional and practical problems – leaving women with little value in the TV world (1978: 13–14).

A decade later, the book *Boxed In: Women and Television* (Baehr and Dyer, 1987) reported a mixture of the sexist legacy described above, and changing times:

> Television [in the mid-1980s] is increasingly taking women seriously, and there are a number of programmes, or types of programme, that feature women in a more central way ... Women's issues have arrived on the media agenda – documentaries, discussion programmes and dramas on female topics such as infertility, cervical and breast cancer, rape, etc.
>
> (Dyer, 1987: 7)

From today's perspective it seems a bit sad that women would have been particularly *grateful* for the addition of a few worthy programmes on these serious subjects. The idea that they are 'female topics' is not ideal either (surely men *and* women are affected by these issues?). Elsewhere, TV remained stubborn, with game shows not bothering to change their 'degrading and trivialising views of women', sports programming remaining 'the preserve of men' and news programmes accused of tokenism or 'window dressing' by including some women in key positions whilst retaining a male-dominated culture (Dyer, 1987: 7–8).

The situation in 1980s TV drama was more complex. Gillian Dyer observed that the number of women in central roles in police and crime series had increased, but found a new reason for discomfort:

This development, although in many ways refreshing, raises new contradictions in the portrayal of power and gender for, ironically, 'strong' women policewomen, lawyers, etc. are invariably shown enforcing the patriarchal laws which oppress them.

(1987: 10)

This criticism seems a little unfair. Female TV cops would, like their male counterparts, usually be seen investigating murders or robberies, the laws against which are not notably 'patriarchal' or oppressive to women. The other kind of serious crime which TV detectives might investigate is, of course, rape and sexual abuse, and the introduction of female characters into these investigations clearly *did* make a difference. (See *Cagney and Lacey*, *The Bill*, *Juliet Bravo* and other police series at the time, and parallel stories in *LA Law*). Although perhaps it could be called 'tokenism', the rape storyline was typically an opportunity for programme makers to build drama around the feminist critique of police attitudes, and for female characters to clash with the 'old guard' who might not treat rape very sensitively.

WOMEN AND MEN IN MOVIES

Unsurprisingly, women and men's roles in the movies were generally very similar to their TV counterparts. Here we'll gallop briefly through recent decades, mentioning films which were amongst the most prominent and successful at the time (see box office and other information at www.imdb.com). This broad-sweep approach, taking in movies that the largest number of people will have seen, is a deliberate alternative to the method typically seen in film studies, where single films – often selected for their uniqueness – are studied in depth. Books such as *Women and Film* (Kaplan, 1983), *Screening the Male* (Cohan and Rae Hark, 1993), *You Tarzan: Masculinity, Movies and Men* (Kirkham and Thumim, 1993), *Me Jane: Masculinity, Movies and Women* (Kirkham and Thumim, 1995), *Feminism and Film* (Humm, 1997) and *Working Girls: Gender and Sexuality in Popular Cinema* (Tasker, 1998, as noted in the previous chapter) offer detailed analyses of gender representations in particular films. These pieces are often intriguing and insightful – although the reader is haunted by concern that each film discussed may be atypical, telling us little about gender in the *majority* of popular films. Here I will assume that you have seen a few films from the past and will have your own idea of how gender was typically shown; this is just an attempt to summarise, and jog the memory.

In the 1950s, the most popular films included *High Noon* (1952), *12 Angry Men* (1957), *Bridge on the River Kwai* (1957), *Touch of Evil* (1959), as well as Hitchcock classics such as *Strangers on a Train* (1951), *Rear Window* (1954), *North by Northwest* (1959). The films almost always focused on male heroes. These men typically made the decisions which led the story, and were assertive, confident and dominant. Women had important roles in many films but were far more likely than men to be shown as frightened, in need of protection and direction, and offering love and support to the male lead character(s). The stylishness of the gentlemen at the heart of Hitchcock's thrillers, say, can seem more 'feminine' than the grunting macho heroes of 1980s action films, but it was tied to a buttoned-down, statesmanlike, quick-thinking masculinity which contrasted with the feminine beauty and lack of assertiveness of key women characters. *Some Like it Hot* (1959) played with the performance of gender, but only hinted at a challenge to masculine and feminine roles.

The 1960s gave us hits like *Lawrence of Arabia* (1962), *The Manchurian Candidate* (1962), *Dr Strangelove* (1964), *The Sound of Music* (1965), *Doctor Zhivago* (1965), *2001: A Space Odyssey* (1968). Gender roles, on average, did not differ greatly from the previous decade. The 1960s may have been 'swinging', to some extent, but the impact on film scripts, in terms of gender roles, seems quite minimal. As before, it would be wrong to suggest that all women characters were shown as inept, or were always cast as housewives, but male characters were consistently more intelligent, more assertive – and much more prevalent.

In the 1970s, Leia in the decade's top hit *Star Wars* (1977) was pretty good at shooting stormtroopers, but she was also the prized princess that the heroic boys had to rescue, and win the heart of. Ripley in *Alien* (1979), though, was a superior female interplanetary survivor. Other popular films of the 1970s such as *The Godfather* (1972), *The Sting* (1973), *The Exorcist* (1973), *Jaws* (1975), *The Deer Hunter* (1978) and *Superman* (1978) fit within the model described for previous decades. Although Lois Lane in *Superman* is a successful reporter, for example, it is still the (super-)heroic man who leads the story and saves the world. Woody Allen found success with films like *Annie Hall* (1977) and *Manhattan* (1979), featuring intelligent women who captured the eye of the famously witty but neurotic and un-macho leading man – which was, at least, somewhat different to the norm.

The 1980s saw Ripley become stronger in *Aliens* (1986), and Sarah Connor was courageous in *The Terminator* (1984), even if patronising future-people did send a man back in time to save her. An executive with an instinct for equal opportunities green-lighted *Supergirl* (1984) but forgot to make it a good film. Meanwhile, the reliable heroic male still featured prominently in most films, including the *Indiana Jones* series (1981, 1984, 1989), the *Rambo* series (1982, 1985, 1988), *Crocodile Dundee* (1986), *Die Hard* (1988), and many more. The likeable, funny guys in comedies like *Ghostbusters* (1984) and *Back to the Future* (1985) didn't have any strong female competition. *Three Men and a Baby* (1987) – despite being based on the idea that whilst one woman can readily deal with a baby, even as many as *three* men are going to have trouble – at least gave us something different to contemplate.

This quick skim over films from the 1950s to the 1980s is, it must be admitted, rather simplistic. As the film studies books mentioned at the start of this section show, masculinity and femininity in films is often rather precarious. Characters are made more interesting by being imperfectly masculine, or slightly-different-to-what-you-might-expect feminine, and the nuances of these gender characterisations are often worthy of some examination. The character of Indiana Jones, to take one example, is the typical macho action-adventure hero on the one hand, but we see him being tender with women in each film, acting as a father to Short Round in the second picture, and responding as a son to his dad in the third. We can, no doubt, spot homoerotic elements in the films. We can note that things often go wrong for Indy – his plans are not flawless, and his attractive body may be damaged. *Nevertheless:* as with almost all male heroes in almost all films, Indiana Jones is basically reliable and decisive and victorious. We may find some imperfections or quirks, but he's basically *outstanding* as a hero, and unquestionably masculine.

Women's roles, also, have much more complexity and value than my summary suggests. The history of movies is no doubt full of remarkable female characters in supporting roles. Even in a straightforward action hit like *Raiders of the Lost Ark* (1981), to continue the previous example, Karen Allen is not simply a 'love interest' for the hero, but is a spunky, assertive and intelligent character in her own right. *Nevertheless*, she doesn't lead the story, she doesn't make the central decisions, she doesn't repeatedly save her male colleague. And she's not the star of the film. And this, we have to note, has typically been the place of women in films.

Feminist critics have put it even more starkly. In 1973, Marjorie Rosen asserted that 'the Cinema Woman is a Popcorn Venus, a delectable but insubstantial hybrid of cultural distortions' (1973: 10). Rosen charted the changing representations of women in Hollywood films, noting backlashes against working women in the 1940s and 1950s, and against female sexual emancipation in the 1960s and 1970s. The representation of women as 'sex objects' varied in *style* but was otherwise constant throughout (Rosen,

1973). The early 1970s also saw the launch of a journal, *Women and Film*, in the first issue of which Sharon Smith declared:

> Women, in any fully human form, have almost completely been left out of film ... The role of a woman in a film almost always revolves around her physical attraction and the mating games she plays with the male characters. On the other hand a man is not shown purely in relation to the female characters, but in a wide variety of roles.
>
> (1972: 13)

A decade later, E. Ann Kaplan (1983) felt able to be just as sweeping:

> In Hollywood films, then, women are ultimately refused a voice, a discourse, and their desire is subjected to male desire. They live out silently frustrated lives, or, if they resist their placing, sacrifice their lives for their daring.
>
> (pp. 7–8)

And at the start of the 1990s, Kathi Maio – in a book of her film reviews – observed that Hollywood's ideas about gender were 'often reprehensible' (1991: vii). As a jobbing reviewer, Maio had sat through many popular films of the 1980s (in happy contrast to those film *theorists* who sometimes seemed to have avoided mainstream films altogether). She was not impressed (1991: 2):

> Women are not only given less screen time, when we're up there on the screen we are likely to be portrayed as powerless and ineffectual ... Where are the *triumphant* women heroes to match the winner roles men play constantly?

Maio is pleased to find a few exceptions, and notes the roles for resourceful females in *Dead Calm* (1989) and *Heathers* (1989). 'Strong, victorious women [do] exist in film', she says. 'Just not often enough, and generally not in movies that get much play' (p. 4).

In her best-selling book *Backlash: The Undeclared War Against Women* (1991), Susan Faludi went one step further, arguing that films of the 1980s such as *Fatal Attraction* (1987) and *Baby Boom* (1987) were part of a wider backlash against women's liberation and women's careers. She also noted women being 'reduced to mute and incidental characters or banished altogether' in action movies like *Predator* (1987), *Lethal Weapon*

JAMES BOND AND CHANGING TIMES

The long-running series of James Bond films span the decades, and so give us a chance to see gender roles develop. But in truth, they don't develop much. The charming, tough, self-reliant Bond seen in *Dr No* (1962) had not changed much 40 years and 20 films later, in *Die Another Day* (2002), although the character was at his most patronising to women during the Roger Moore era (1973–85). His AIDS-aware reincarnation as Timothy Dalton was relatively monogamous in *The Living Daylights* (1987), but this didn't go down so well with audiences. Next time round, in *Licence to Kill* (1989), Dalton's Bond had extinguished all charm and was as romantic as an iceberg.

Recast as Pierce Brosnan in *Goldeneye* (1995), Bond faced his most difficult clash with modernity. His boss, 'M', was now Judi Dench, an authoritative woman who told him: 'You are a sexist misogynist dinosaur, a relic from the Cold War.' Bond wasn't used to this kind of thing. Even the age-old flirtation between Bond and Moneypenny took a new turn as she mentioned – albeit not seriously – that 'this kind of behaviour could qualify as sexual harassment'. Later, in a rare introspective scene, Izabella Scorupco asked Bond, 'How can you be so cold?' He says, 'It's what keeps me alive', but she tells him: 'No. It's what keeps you alone.' In the three subsequent Brosnan films, however, it was business as usual, and Bond seemed to be a masculine archetype again.

That was before the release of *Casino Royale* (2006), however. Critics were almost universally thrilled to welcome a back-to-basics, 'hard' Bond – and magazines for both male and female audiences agreed. Daniel Craig's tough performance was compared favourably with Pierce Brosnan, who was now typically described as 'bouffant' and a bit wet. This may or may not reflect a change of tide in terms of gender imagery; or might indicate a post-9/11 public mood, where terrorism should be met with a ruthless and steely response.

Although Bond does not change that much, we can note that the female characters have become more resourceful as the series progressed. In 1985's *A View to a Kill*, for example, not-very-frightening Christopher Walken has superstrong Grace Jones to protect him. Michelle Yeoh is a martial arts ace in *Tomorrow Never Dies* (1997); Denise Richards shows that Bond-girl good looks don't stop you being a nuclear scientist in *The World is Not Enough* (1999); and *Die Another Day* (2002) seemed to toy with the idea of treating special agent Halle Berry as Bond's equal, and featured her on the poster in a strong gun-pointing pose matching Brosnan's.

(1987) and *Days of Thunder* (1990) (p. 169). Even the tough Ripley in *Aliens* is criticised because her motivation to defend the little girl Newt is 'maternal' (p. 145). Faludi marshals an impressive array of evidence to show that the backlash against women stretched throughout popular media and political culture. Some of the examples seem rather exceptional – even the archetypal 'backlash' film, *Fatal Attraction*, was rather unique and not representative of many other movies. Nevertheless, Faludi leaves the reader in no doubt that these 'backlash' tendencies were certainly in circulation.

WOMEN'S MAGAZINES IN THE PAST

Today there is a well-known, comical stereotype of the ways in which women's magazines and adverts used to address women as simpering housewives whose dream was to impress their authoritative, working hus-bands by using the latest kitchen accessory or washing powder. The advice offered to women was not about how to fulfil their own potential, but was instead focused on bringing happiness to their family. Unlike some stereo-types, this one is based on reality: these mags and ads really did exist. (Lifestyle magazines for men, incidentally, did not really take off until the 1990s, and so this book does not contain a parallel *historical* section about magazines for men – but see the discussions of modern men's magazines below.)

Betty Friedan's *The Feminine Mystique* (1963) was the first major assault on these images of 'the happy housewife heroine'. As a former contributor to women's magazines, Friedan had become troubled by the image of bliss-ful domesticity she was helping to propagate. She considers a typical issue of *McCall's* magazine, from July 1960:

> The image of woman that emerges from this big, pretty maga-zine is young and frivolous, almost childlike; fluffy and feminine; passive; gaily content in a world of bedroom and kitchen, sex, babies, and home. The magazine surely does not leave out sex; the only goal a woman is permitted is the pursuit of a man. It is crammed full of food, clothing, cosmetics, furniture, and the physical bodies of young women, but where is the world of thought and ideas, the life of the mind and spirit?
>
> (1963: 32)

From the 1940s to Friedan's present (the 1960s), women's magazines had focused on this feminine, home-bound image – but they did not trivialise it;

on the contrary, the emphasis was on the great *importance* of this role, in both societal and personal terms. The social value of the housewife was often celebrated and praised. On the other side of the coin, fear of deviance was also fostered. Friedan reports that in the 1940s:

> All the magazines were echoing Farnham and Lundberg's *Modern Woman: The Lost Sex*, which came out in 1942, with its warning that careers and higher education were leading to the 'masculinization of women with enormously dangerous consequences to the home, the children dependent on it and to the ability of the woman, as well as her husband, to obtain sexual gratification.'
>
> (1963: 37)

In the 1950s, concerns that women may have had about their lack of a career were countered with the promotion of 'Occupation: Housewife', one of the most crucial roles in society. The senior staff on women's magazines were mostly men – but these men had a clear idea of what women wanted. As Friedan recalls:

> Writing for these magazines [in the 1950s], I was continually reminded by editors that 'women *have* to identify'. Once I wanted to write an article about an artist. So I wrote about her cooking and [shopping] and falling in love with her husband, and painting a crib for her baby. I had to leave out the hours she spent painting her pictures, her serious work – and the way she felt about it. You could sometimes get away with writing about a woman who was not really a housewife, if you made her *sound* like a housewife, if you left out her commitment to the world outside the home, or the private vision of mind or spirit that she pursued.
>
> (1963: 46)

We should note that the 1950s seem to have been a particularly low point for aspirational women; magazines from the 1930s and early 1940s were not afraid to talk about career women – although, ideally, these women's 'feminine' qualities would be emphasised as well (Friedan, 1963). However, it is worth noting that according to Tuchman (1978), some magazines of the 1950s – *Glamour*, *Mademoiselle* and *Cosmopolitan* – assumed that women would work *until the birth of their first child*, and accordingly stressed 'the joys of achievement and power' for women in work (p. 22).

However, finding a man to marry and have those children with was still a primary – and seemingly inevitable – goal.

The 1960s saw the seeds of change, sparked, in part, by the publication of Friedan's book, but the world of magazines was not transformed overnight. Indeed, the traditional titles such as *Family Circle, Ladies' Home Journal, Woman's Own* and *Woman's Weekly* continued to do well, flourishing *alongside* the less traditional titles which slowly emerged. *Ms*, for example, was launched from New York in 1972, the first US national monthly 'by women, for women' to have been inspired by the women's liberation movement (Phillips, 1978). From the start, the magazine focused on politics, women's achievements outside the home, global current affairs and feminist issues – and was successful (although a circulation of 380,000 by 1975 did not exactly compare with *Family Circle*'s figure of eight million). Barbara Phillips (1978) observed that the 'heroines' featured in *Ms*'s articles were not women who had become millionaires – the traditional model by which American men would be judged a success – but rather were women who had helped to bring important political, social or cultural changes. Therefore, it could be argued – as Phillips does – that women were still being praised for their selfless virtue – a 'feminine' trait. This seems unduly picky though, especially as a magazine which simply applied so-called 'male' values to women would be criticised too, for not challenging the accepted models of what makes a person successful or important.

In 1987, Janice Winship's book *Inside Women's Magazines* was published. This was notable because Winship, who felt connected to and sympathetic with the women's movement, dared to break some unwritten feminist rules by admitting that she found women's magazines enjoyable, by suggesting that they could sometimes be engaging and useful, and by noting that magazines were changing in the 1970s and 1980s to take account of women's changing position in society. Winship explains at the start that feminist friends and colleagues had seemed to think that studying women's magazines was unimportant: 'Surely we all know women's magazines demean women and solely benefit capitalist profits. What more is there to say?' (p. xiii). But Winship was undeterred:

> I continued to believe that it was as important to understand what women's magazines were about as it was, say, to understand how sex discrimination operated in the workplace. I felt that to simply dismiss women's magazines was also to dismiss the lives of millions of women who read and enjoyed them each week.
>
> (p. xiii)

Winship's case studies take in the traditional, such as *Woman's Own*, which in the 1980s was still offering the familiar regular sections on home, fashion, beauty, cookery, knitting and fiction. Winship observed that the magazine was apolitical, casually racist, and assumed that its readers are married or would like to be. So far, so predictable. But Winship is willing to admit that in the 1980s, not all women's magazines were the same, and her case study of *Cosmopolitan* is more interesting.

THE *COSMO* FACTOR

Where had the magazine come from? *Cosmopolitan* in its modern form, confident about being sexy and single, had been launched in America in 1964 when Helen Gurley Brown – author of the best-selling *Sex and the Single Girl* – took over the editorship of the 'long-established but moribund' magazine (Winship, 1987: 106). The title was launched in the UK in 1972, and was able to assert a strong sexual identity from the outset. Its readers represented a new generation, and a new kind of reader:

> More of them than ever before had gone away to college, and often on to the pill, and with high expectations of a world at their feet they were set, if nothing else, on ensuring they didn't have to forsake womanly delights, as their spinsterly and not to be envied schoolteachers had, in order to take a public place in the world.
>
> (p. 107)

Cosmo girl might have owed a lot to feminism, but she was unlikely to identify with it; she just wanted to get out there and enjoy her independence. Winship says that the idea of the typical *Cosmo* article being 'How to get a man into bed', whilst not completely off the mark, rather misses the point of the magazine's sexual agenda – for *Cosmo* was playing *Playboy* at its own game, seeing sexual pleasure as important, and suggesting that women were entitled to it. *Cosmo*'s assertion of women's right to enjoy sex, and to talk about it, was quite radical, and this new discourse brought other changes – men, for example, were no longer treated with reverence, but could be seen as inadequate, or the butt of jokes.

Examining several issues from the early 1980s, Winship finds that *Cosmo* does not bother being consistent: one article would encourage readers to be happy with their body size, whilst another would encourage slimming; men are given both sympathy and criticism; marriage might be endorsed or condemned; romance and fidelity might be good, or bad, depending on the article; and the style might be serious or silly. This pluralism of contradictions is no accident. *Cosmo*'s editor of the time, Deirdre McSharry, tells Winship that it is her job 'to get the balance right' (p. 100). More challenging articles are countered by more 'reassuring' ones, but 'the clever thing is to always offer a very strong element which will surprise [the readers], and that's really what keeps them going', McSharry explains. It is not surprising that the *Cosmo* woman cannot escape contradiction, as she is expected to be so many things: sexy, successful, glamorous, hard-working; sharp and relaxed in social settings, powerful and likeable at work. Looking over the magazine's idealised photographs which accompany articles about relationships, as well as fashion, Winship observes:

> [*Cosmopolitan* is aware] firstly, that being a woman involves constantly adjusting one's own image to fit time and place in an ever-changing game of images; and secondly, that 'real life' is constantly thought through '(dream) images'.
>
> (p. 101)

This complex mix of aspirational dreams and multiple realities is a minefield which *Cosmo* celebrates, and tries to help readers with. The possibilities suggested by the magazine are not infinite, of course – *Cosmo*'s dreams are almost always heterosexual, for instance; they don't have much tolerance for the imperfect or the unsexy; and they usually require you to spend a certain amount of money on beauty products. Critics such as Susan Douglas (1995) see this as a triumph of the capitalists, managing to turn feminism into something narcissistic which you have to spend lots of money on, and – in line with L'Oreal's 'Because I'm worth it!' tagline – even feel pleasure and liberation in doing so. *Cosmo*'s selling of arguably rather narrow fantasy lifestyles may certainly be of concern; but we should also not forget Winship's point that *Cosmo* was, at one time at least, a vehicle for liberation and change, giving voice to ideas and perspectives which had not previously been in mass circulation.

Cosmopolitan spawned many imitators and variants, of course, including *Over 21, Glamour, Working Woman* and *Company*. The late 1980s saw the launch of even more sex-obsessed magazines like the UK's *More!*, which stripped out much of the more 'mature' stuff about lifestyle and work, and gave young readers even more of the glamour, problem pages, handsome hunks and sex – most obviously in the notorious 'position of the fortnight' feature – which they seemed to crave.

GENDER IN ADVERTISING

The stereotypes in advertising have been similar to those in women's magazines, and other media, described above, although they have often been slower to change with the times. Friedan's (1963) critique of women's magazines runs alongside a similar assessment of advertising; the stereotypes reproduced by the housewife's journals were the same as those exploited by advertisers. And Tuchman's (1978) argument about 'the symbolic annihilation of women' is based on an analysis of advertising as well as other media.

Again, Gunter (1995) provides a useful guide to the many empirical content analysis studies which have been conducted. The studies show that women in magazine adverts prior to the 1970s were rarely shown to be in paid work, and when they were it would usually be a stereotypical role (the smiling secretary or hairdresser). The number of 'housewife' images began to decline slowly after the 1950s, but the image was still common in the 1960s and 1970s (Gunter, 1995: 34). Content analyses of advertising on *television* in the early 1970s found strong evidence of stereotyping: of all ads featuring women, three-quarters were for kitchen and bathroom products. Women were more than twice as likely as men to be seen inside the home, and when seen in a paid work environment, they were more often than not subservient to men. Men were most likely to be seen in authority roles, and were ten times more likely than women to provide the dependable voice-over (ibid.: 35). Studies in the later 1970s and early 1980s saw a continuation of these trends, with men most often shown at work, and women as housewives and mothers at home. Nevertheless, it became somewhat more common for men to be shown at home as well, in the role of husband or father; and the range of women's occupations increased (ibid.: 36–37).

In a study of TV ads, Scheibe (1979) included an assessment of what male and female characters were shown to be *concerned* about – an astute addition to the usual enumeration of role and location. Women in ads were found to be more concerned about beauty, cleanliness, family and pleasing others. Men were only more concerned about achievement and having fun. So even if women and men are shown in more unusual settings, these stereotyped concerns can come shining through. Other studies found strong similarities in gender representations from country to country, and particular sexism in adverts aimed at children (Gunter, 1995: 44–50). In the 1980s, TV advertising did start to take on the idea of the busy working woman – but often by offering solutions to the working woman who, it was assumed, would still have to perform cooking and cleaning chores in the household.

By the start of the 1990s, a study of 500 prime-time TV ads in the UK, by Cumberbatch (reported in Strinati, 1995: 186), found that advertisers had seemingly become wary of showing women doing housework (which was seen in 7 per cent of the ads). For the first time, it was found that men were shown cooking more often than women – but these would be supposedly impressive 'special occasions', in contrast to the more routine cookery duties of women which had traditionally been shown. In other respects, little had changed: women in ads were more likely to be young and attractive; men were twice as likely as women to be shown in paid employment; work was seen as central to men's lives, whereas 'relationships' were shown to be more important to women; and 89 per cent of the ads used a male voice-over.

Unsurprisingly then, gender representations in ads have been similar to those in other media, usually affirming the same old stereotypes. However, as Macdonald notes, 'Advertisers generally lagged behind women's magazines in the cultivation of new modes of address, even when the evidence suggested that commercial advantages could be gained from modernising their approach' (1995: 89–90). The advertising industry has often been accused of a quiet conservatism, and a fear of challenging certain elements of what it thinks the audience needs and expects. Representation of gender roles seem to have been, for many years at least, one of the areas where advertisers were often reluctant to do anything very different.

Adverts, therefore, found themselves on the front line of feminist counter-attack. Partly because advertising was seen as a pernicious case of capitalists exploiting gender-related insecurities, and partly because billboards were easier to interfere with than movies and TV broadcasts, feminists in the 1970s and 1980s took their message to the streets – and their spray-paints to the adverts. Ascerbic comments were painted onto billboard ads, such as a Fiat ad with a woman reclining on the vehicle receiving the new tagline, 'When I'm not lying on cars I'm a brain surgeon' (Macdonald, 1995: 87), and the delightfully acerbic one where an ad showing a woman carving a lover's message into a tree, with the printed slogan 'Renew his interest in carpentry', was supplemented by the helpful suggestion, 'Saw his head off' (Posener, 1982).

SUMMARY

We have seen, unsurprisingly, that the mass media used to be very stereotyped in its representations of gender. As well as showing men being more active, decisive, courageous, intelligent and resourceful, television and movies showed a much greater *quantity* of men, compared to women, as well. There were exceptions, of course – it's not hard to think of the odd clever, brave or challenging female character from the past – but these remained exceptions to the norm. Magazines and adverts aimed at women also tended to reinforce the feminine and housewifely stereotypes. The emergence of *Cosmopolitan*, though, with its contradictory but generally forthright, assertive and sexually frank approach, heralded the changes which we would see develop in more recent media – as covered in the next chapter.

Chapter 4

REPRESENTATIONS OF GENDER TODAY

IN THE PREVIOUS chapter, we established that the media of the past was, pretty much, just as stereotyped as we probably tend to imagine it was. But in the past couple of decades, things have been changing quite considerably. Men and women are seen working side by side, as equals, in the hospitals, schools and police stations of television-land. Movie producers are more wary of having women as screaming victims, and have realised that kick-ass heroines can do better business. Advertisers have by now realised that audiences will only laugh at images of the pretty housewife, and have reacted by showing women how to be sexy at work instead. Gay characters have slowly started to be more prominent on TV and in the movies, and discussions of the rights of marginalized groups have also surfaced within popular culture. This chapter considers each of these things in turn.

CONTENT ANALYSIS: DO IT YOURSELF

Representations on TV change from year to year. Although a proper content analysis study should ideally take in many hours of broadcast television, and be performed using rigorous measures, you can still do a simple version yourself. Pick a slice of popular, mainstream programming and count up the number of main characters who are female, and those who are male. Note their roles, concerns and leadership. The more programmes you include, the more (roughly) reliable your figures will be.

GENDER AND TV: TURNING THE CORNER IN THE 1990s?

During the 1990s and into the new century, gender roles on television seemed to become increasingly equal and non-stereotyped – within some limits – although the majority of lead characters were still male. (As throughout this book, our main emphasis here is largely on popular, prime-time programmes from the USA and the UK.)

There have been fewer content analysis studies of gender representations published during, and since, the 1990s – although we should also note that academics are often embarrassingly slow to get their findings into print. One key study of the portrayal of women in prime-time TV shows during the 1992–93 season, by Elasmar, Hasegawa and Brain, was not published until six years later, in 1999. Another major study of women in prime-time series during the 1995–96 season, by Lauzen and Dozier, was published in the same year. Both studies offer some interesting statistics, although the lack of comparable figures for *men* on TV in some cases makes the findings difficult to interpret – for example, Elasmar *et al.* report the numbers of TV women who are employed, and who care for children, but we cannot really interpret these figures without knowing the parallel figures for male characters in these positions, which they failed to record. Remember, too, that all of these findings are now well over a decade old. Nevertheless, it is worth noting that:

- In prime-time TV shows, 1992–93, men took 61 per cent of the total number of speaking roles, with women having the other 39 per cent. The 1995–96 study found that men took 63 per cent of the speaking roles, with women having the other 37 per cent.
- The 1992–93 study found a startlingly small number of the major characters were female – just 18 per cent – and of this meagre group, more than two-thirds were the stars of domestic situation comedies. However, the 1995–96 study (which examined a greater range and number of popular programmes) found that 43 per cent of major characters were female – a much greater proportion, although still less than half.
- The 1992–93 study found that only 3 per cent of women were represented as housewives as their main occupation – a massive decrease from the 1970s. An additional 8 per cent of women were shown as 'homemakers', but without knowing the number of male homemakers it is difficult to interpret this properly.
- The 1995–96 study examined the roles of women and men in

conversations on screen, recording the degree of control they exerted over dialogue, the power of their language use and the frequency with which they gave direct advice. It was found that on a character-by-character basis, females and males were equal in these respects.

- Overall, the 1992–93 study found that 'the woman on prime time TV in the early 1990s was young, single, independent, and free from family and work place pressures' (Elasmar et al., 1999: 33).

These studies show a growth in gender equality on screen, although by the mid-1990s there was still some distance to go. The researchers noted that they were observing trends which were seeing women on television becoming gradually more emancipated and equal. Maybe, however, they had already reached a disappointing plateau.

TV GENDER RATIOS TODAY

A more recent study by Lauzen et al. (2006) – the same people, basically, that did the 1995–96 study above – suggests that, in terms of the basic numbers at least, not much has changed in a decade. The researchers conducted a content analysis of characters in situation comedies, dramas and reality programmes that were broadcast on the six US broadcast networks (ABC, CBS, NBC, WB, UPN) during the 2004–05 prime-time season. One episode of each series was randomly chosen for analysis, from a total of 129 programmes, and every person that appeared on-screen and spoke at least one line was included. (One episode from each series may not sound like much, but over 129 different shows this adds up to a pretty thorough analysis.) They found that 61 per cent of characters were male, and 39 per cent were female. Unscripted 'reality' programmes featured a slightly higher proportion of women – 42 per cent – than the scripted drama and comedy shows, where women were 38 per cent of the speaking characters. Therefore, little appears to have changed since 1992.

Furthermore, the researchers had hypothesised that the presence of women working in powerful behind-the-scenes roles would result in greater on-screen representation of female characters, and representations of conflict and its resolution which were 'more egalitarian' (by which they mean co-operative and non-aggressive rather than competitive or violent). However, they found that this was not necessarily the case:

> On scripted programs, the employment of at least one woman as a writer or producer was positively related to the percentage of female characters and their involvement in a common plot

device: conflict and its resolution. Further, the presence of women storytellers on scripted programs was positively related to the more egalitarian use of conflict resolution strategies by both female and male characters. In contrast, on reality programs, the employment of at least one woman as a writer, executive producer, or editor was negatively related to the percentage of female characters and their involvement in conflict resolution.

(Lauzen *et al.*, 2006: 453)

The ratio of women to men on television has barely changed in a decade, then, and the presence of women in production teams does not *necessarily* mean that women will be better represented. Perhaps it will help to think about some concrete examples.

TELEVISION CHARACTERS SINCE THE 1990s

It could be said that in the 1990s, to a certain extent, programme makers arrived at comfortable, not-particularly-offensive models of masculinity and femininity, which a majority of the public seemed to think were OK. Producers thus seemed to give up on feeling that they might need to challenge gender representations. Take for example the internationally popular sit-com *Friends* (1994–2004). The three men (Ross, Chandler and Joey) fit easily within conventional models of masculinity, but are given some characteristics of sensitivity and gentleness, and male-bonding, to make things slightly refreshing. Similarly, the three women (Rachel, Monica and Phoebe) are clearly feminine, whilst being sufficiently intelligent and non-housewifey to seem like acceptable characters for the 1990s. The six were also, of course, originally all characters with a good set of both male and female friendships – i.e. each other – and the friendship circle was a refreshing modern replacement for the traditional family. (It was not long, of course, before the producers squashed this concept by getting the characters to couple up – although the relationship between Chandler and Joey remained interesting to the end.) This model of equal, if somewhat different, genders appeared in many other shows from the 1990s onwards, including *ER*, *Dawson's Creek*, *Frasier*, *The West Wing*, and indeed the majority of dramas, reality TV shows and current affairs programmes. Nevertheless we can also note that many series – including most of those named in the previous sentence – may have an ensemble cast of equals but are still often seen to revolve, first and foremost, around one or more male characters.

Some shows, of course, put successful professional women at the forefront, and have focused on their quests for sex, pleasure and romantic love.

Ally McBeal (1997–2002) and *Sex and the City* (1998–2004) did this in rather different ways. Ally McBeal was a very good lawyer, but – more stereotypically – was quite desperate to find a husband. As played by Calista Flockhart, she also inhabited an alarmingly anorexic-looking body. Oddly, she was probably the weakest main character in the show. Ally's colleagues Ling (Lucy Liu) and Nelle (Portia de Rossi) were tougher, and both had been out with men from the law firm who were typically portrayed as rather geeky and lacking self-assurance. The show sided with the women, and often showed them making fun of the men – a characteristic taken further by *Sex and the City*, in which male sexual performance was subject to laughter and scathing review. Mulling over the huge popularity of this show in a British newspaper, Madeleine Bunting (2001) noted:

> [*Sex and the City*'s Carrie, Miranda, Samantha and Charlotte] discuss every kind of sex – masturbation, dildos, telephone sex and blowjobs – comparing experiences, offering advice and encouragement. Nothing is out of bounds, sex is an adventure playground which doesn't necessarily have much to do with love ... The sex stuff works because it turns on its head the age-old female sexual victimhood. The whole rationale of *Sex and the City* is that these women want pleasure, know how to get it and are determined to do so. And the kick is in the assumption that the women are always great in bed, the men more variable.

Bunting later complained that men will still be able to comfort themselves that they remain 'the sole object of any sensible woman's life', but given these women's very high standards, there was little room for men to be complacent. The character of Samantha, played by Kim Cattrall, was particularly notable as a portrayal of a sexually assertive woman in her forties. As Cattrall said in an interview, 'I don't think there's ever been a woman who has expressed so much sexual joy [on television] without her being punished. I never tire of women coming up and saying "You've affected my life"' (Williams, 2002).

Another notable female icon created in the 1990s was, of course, Buffy Summers. *Buffy the Vampire Slayer* (1997–2003) made an indelible impact on teen TV, and also broke new ground by becoming hugely popular within the typically male-dominated world of sci-fi fans (*Buffy* repeatedly won 'Best Television Show' in *SFX* magazine's annual readers poll, for example). It is difficult to think of any contemporary TV character more powerful and heroic than Buffy – even when compared with superheroes. When Superman was relaunched earlier in the 1990s (*Lois and Clark*, a.k.a.

The New Adventures of Superman, 1993–97), he was sweet and insecure and always consulting his small-town parents about emotional turmoil. Which made a nice change. The newer, younger Clark Kent seen in *Smallville* (2001–) is also polite and rather shy. But Buffy is more confident and assertive than either of these incarnations of the Man of Steel – whilst remaining recognisably human. As Polly Vernon has noted (1999):

> Buffy may be styled like Britney Spears on a warm day, but her midriff is very much her own and her whirling intensity, healthy self-irony, and inescapably dark undertones suggests that her main function is not titillation. She's a girl's girl, at once hard as nails and physically confident in a way that's genuinely empowering, and yet warm enough and scared enough not to become some kind of clumsy, shouting, mutated Spice Girl on autopilot … Men who fancy Buffy do it with a healthy degree of awe.

Buffy's creator and driving force, Joss Whedon, adds that Buffy 'is a good role model for not just girls but for everybody, because she has to use her wits and her physical strength to win. Yet, she still has to get high marks in all her courses at school' (www.buffy.com, 2001).

The 1990s also produced one of the richest studies of masculinity and repression ever made, in the form of *NYPD Blue* (1993–2001). The character of Andy Sipowicz (Dennis Franz) was put through the emotional ringer for almost a decade. When the show began, Sipowicz seemed like a stereotypical stout, sleazy, bigoted, divorced, (recovering) alcoholic cop, but over the years viewers saw many layers of complexity and vulnerability rise to the surface of his macho mix. His protective love for his younger professional partners has been a constant, and his grief at the death of his grown-up son, and joy at the birth of his young child Theo, have added depth. Numerous other tests (including the deaths of his wife and some colleagues, and threats to Theo) made him increasingly tightly-wound, upset and angry. The crime episodes were really just vehicles for character development, and so after 261 episodes – 190 hours of continuous drama – this added up to an extremely dense study of a tormented human being, and the division between his gruff exterior and complex emotional core.

Other angles on masculinity have also been offered in *NYPD Blue*. Sipowicz's partners were typically more sensitive but had problems of their own; young Danny Sorenson, for instance, whilst a confident man most of the time, had nervous bursts and a fear of 'getting stirred up'. Their colleague Greg Medavoy – a rather anxious and clumsy figure – was also generally presented seriously, rather than as a mere 'joke' character. During one

GENDER AND VIDEO GAMES

In video games, the representation of men and women is more stereo-typed. By their nature, video games are typically about action rather than reflection, and male characters in games are often brutal gang-sters or grunting soldiers. Female *player* characters are not weak – which would make for boring gameplay – but are usually fighters who are meant to have a particular 'sexy-feminine' allure (Jansz and Martis, 2007). Other women are represented less favourably – most famously the prostitutes who can be picked up in *Grand Theft Auto: Vice City* (2002–). A study of US college students found that female video game characters were seen as 'significantly more helpless and sexually provocative' compared to male characters, and were not as strong or aggressive (Ogletree and Drake, 2007: 537).

phase of the show (1996–98), Medavoy seemed to be 'trying for size' the more aggressive masculinity worn by Sipowicz, but he didn't really have the self-assurance to carry it through. Whilst Sipowicz could use violence and threats against suspects in order to gain moral victories, Medavoy's attempts – most notably in an episode where he ridiculously cuffed a suspect with a phone book – never paid off, and this was seen as a kind of crisis of self-image for the detective. After that, Medavoy's solid relationship with his newer partner, the younger, more confident Baldwin Jones, helped him to become more self-assured.

Of course, there are so many thousands of TV shows that it would be impossible to consider them all here, so I have merely tried to mention some trends. You will be better acquainted with examples from your own experience. You will probably notice that although things seem roughly 'equal' in gender terms, the main character in a drama series is more often a man; political discussions are dominated by men; and even in a 'trivial' sphere such as the comedy game show, panellists are more often men.

Case study: *Ugly Betty*

The US comedy-drama series *Ugly Betty* was launched in autumn 2006 and quickly became a hit show in over 40 countries around the world. The series won numerous awards including two 2007 Golden Globes (including 'Best Television Series – Comedy or Musical') and a 2007 Writers Guild Award for best new TV series. The show is based on the Colombian

Figure 4.1   Fan websites dedicated to *Ugly Betty*, celebrating its 'inspirational' hero played by America Ferrera

telenovela *Yo soy Betty, la fea* (1999–2001), which had already been adapted into several versions, including Indian, German and Russian productions.

Although we quickly come to take programme titles for granted, it is worth pausing to consider the name of the show, *Ugly Betty*, which introduced the programme into the world with a rather shocking judgement on the appearance of its star. Indeed, every week, moments after fans have been re-introduced to their lovable heroine, big gaudy letters spelling UGLY BETTY appear on the screen. Literal-minded critics might take this to show how insensitive today's TV producers can be. But, of course, it's a bit more complicated than that.

To summarise the basic story, I may as well give you this pitch from the producers themselves (ABC's *Ugly Betty* website, 2007):

> In the superficial world of high fashion, image is everything. Styles come and go, and the only constants are the superthin beauties who wear them. How can an ordinary girl – a slightly plump plain-Jane from Queens – possibly fit in?

If you took a moment to get to know Betty Suarez, you'd see how sweet, intelligent and hard-working she is. But few people do, because in the world of high fashion Betty is the oversized peg in the petite round hole. When publishing mogul Bradford Meade hands the reigns of *Mode*, the bible of the fashion industry, over to his son, Daniel, he specifically hires Betty as his son's new assistant – mostly because she's the only woman in NYC Daniel won't sleep with. Though this 'player' is reluctant to accept her at first, Betty's indomitable spirit and bright ideas will eventually win him over. Neither of them really knows the ins and outs of the fashion world, but the two are a formidable team against those who will do anything to see them fall.

It would be easy to complain that the show has its cake and eats it. It satirises the superficial, glossy world of fashion, full of stick-thin models who are supposedly gorgeous, and at the same time it is able to fill the screen with the glamorous fixtures and fittings of this world, including the stick-thin models who are supposedly gorgeous. Even 'ugly' Betty is actually a conventionally attractive woman with added eyebrows and braces; the producers would not dare to actually have a really rough-looking heroine, with or without the heart of gold. Indeed, the fact that the show itself appears to partly agree with the idea that Betty is ugly, even though she is a *really nice person*, is one of the more difficult aspects of the recipe.

The basic messages of *Ugly Betty* are clichés, then – but nice ones: beauty is only skin deep; don't judge a book by its cover. These themes are perfectly conventional, but we should not forget that they can be powerful messages for a top-rated show to carry. They also make a notable change from other core TV drama themes, such as the ever-present threat of terrorism and murder. The actress America Ferrera, who plays Betty, said in a 2007 interview:

> Just last weekend, I read a letter from a young girl. I did the cover of *Cosmo Girl*, and she was thanking the magazine for putting me on the cover, because, 'When I watched Ugly Betty, it was the first time in my life that I felt beautiful.' That was overwhelming for me. All you can ever hope to do in this business is touch one person, and yet I'm sure there were others.
>
> (quoted in Strachan, 2007)

The show's network, ABC, sponsored an outreach campaign for girl empowerment, 'Be Ugly '07', in association with the advocacy group Girls

Inc (www.girlsinc.org), 'inspiring all girls to be strong, smart and bold' (ibid.). The above quote from Ferrera, and this campaign, could easily be dismissed as opportunistic, self-serving ways of promoting a television programme. However, if we look on the internet, we can see a wide range of voices who have been inspired by *Ugly Betty*. For instance, one fan writes:

> If you have ever felt out of place or the ugly duckling, *Ugly Betty* proves week after week where true beauty lies. Beyond the designer labels, the layers of makeup, and yoyo dieting, the true self is achieved through intelligence, heart, and soul.
>
> ('Ajla' at Yahoo TV, 2007)

A 21-year-old female blogger from Sydney, Australia, comments:

> *Ugly Betty* is not only a good show because Betty is inspiring, but because she is real. Things are not easy for her, and though she is a hero because she is strong enough to be an individual and doesn't conform to the world's cruel rules, she struggles, she gets hurt, confused, disappointed with herself ... but she doesn't back down, and to me that is inspiring. She learns to accept who and what is without the approval of everyone else around her.
>
> ('Babygirl_Gigi', 2007)

When America Ferrera won her Golden Globe for Best Actress, her speech seems to have touched many viewers:

> Her teary speech about being a role model for young women was inspiring, especially since it is so rare to see a working-class, Mexican-American character in such a prominent role on TV, particularly a normal-looking, smart young woman whose father is an illegal immigrant!
>
> (Nicole Cohen at the Shameless blog, 2007)

Similarly, in an 'open letter' to America Ferrera posted at the website of Women in Media and News, feminist activist Olivia Ortiz was moved to write:

> I found myself openly weeping with you as you took the stage to accept your Golden Globe award for 'Best Actress' on Monday night. From your acceptance speech, I quote: 'I hear from

WHAT ABOUT REPRESENTATIONS OF GENDER ONLINE?

As noted at the start of Chapter 3, the internet and World Wide Web are central providers of the information and images that we receive about the social world, and the impact of this should be considered alongside all of the other sources of ideas about gender covered in this chapter and elsewhere.

However, it is not straightforward to provide a meaningful analysis of 'representations of gender online' because the internet is necessarily diverse, and any two individuals could spend years on it without ever looking at the same stuff. Of course, many people use the same search services, but their journeys on the Web are likely to be unique.

Nevertheless, there are some 'hot' points where millions of people do end up. One of these is YouTube, which at the time of writing is the world's most popular website that's not primarily a search site (Alexa.com, 2007). It's easy to see what's popular here: the list of 'most viewed' videos of all time is one click away from the top page. Here we can see, for instance, that (as of June 2007) the most popular clip in YouTube's history is a performance by a male comedian, 'The Evolution of Dance' (50 million views). The second most popular is the video for Avril Lavigne's hit single, *Girlfriend* (2007), with 38 million views, in which she asserts her desires quite forcefully. So the top two YouTube videos are a man being funny and a woman being feisty.

Seemingly in keeping with internet stereotypes, the fourth most popular video is entitled 'Porn XXX', but has presumably disappointed almost all of its 23 million viewers by showing seven seconds of a potential sex scene before declaring 'Shame on you! Now you watch *My Little Pony*!' – which is what viewers get for the remaining four minutes. They should have known better, as YouTube does not allow pornography.

Looking through the most-watched videos, it is difficult to discern any kind of gender pattern – except that you could say there *really isn't a pattern*. YouTube videos tend to be short, amusing items, or pop videos. Apart from general entertainment-seeking it would be impossible to claim that YouTube videos had any kind of overall message. The ideology they lean most towards is one of general silliness. If we look at the 'Directors' channel on the site, though, we can see which material made especially for YouTube is reaching the masses. Again, it is a diverse collection of things. Perhaps because they spend much of their time making funny little videos for the internet, most of YouTube's stars are rather sweet, nerdy and ironic. At the time of writing, the most popular channel contributors of all time are Smosh (with 6.2 million views in June 2007), two 19-year-old guys who make comic, knowingly-amateurish music videos. They are appealingly harmless, and less macho than almost anything on television. Close behind at 5.6 million views is Brookers, a 21-year-old woman who, again, makes short comic, often musical, videos. Her success stems from her quirky humour and not, refreshingly, from being an 'internet hottie'.

It may be possible to conclude, then, that online outlets for personal expression such as YouTube reflect a level of diversity which we do not see in mainstream media. The representations of women and men on YouTube are less glossy and stereotypical, and are correspondingly more real, varied and imaginative. Those people who predicted that internet-based media would quickly become just the same as mainstream broadcast or print media didn't anticipate this unfiltered flood of people power.

young girls on a daily basis how Betty makes them feel worthy and loveable and how they have more to offer the world than they thought.' As a young Latina feminist, I wanted to shout from the rooftop of my building my congratulations to you and to say thank you – thank you for exemplifying the class, ethnic and body ideals of this woman and of real women the world over.

(WIMN's Voices, 2007)

You can find hundreds more opinions about *Ugly Betty* online, of course. As always, it is difficult to 'prove' that a particular television show is 'actually' challenging or inspirational; but if a lot of people have been moved to spontaneously write about it in blogs, websites and forums, then it is fair to take this as evidence that this programme can move and inspire viewers.

GENDER IN MOVIES SINCE THE 1990s

In the previous chapter we saw that films in the past had tended to give men all the primary clever and resourceful roles, which made them the lead character(s), whilst women usually got to be love interests and helpers. There were exceptions, of course, but this was the general picture. But what of representations in the 1990s and the new century? Maggie Humm's *Feminism and Film*, published in 1997, certainly didn't seem to think that anything had changed. The book begins with the assertion that:

> Film ... often and anxiously envisions women stereotypically as 'good' mothers or 'bad', hysterical careerists. [In the past, and] today, every Hollywood woman is someone else's Other.
>
> (1997: 3)

This kind of bold assertion is good for prompting discussion, but doesn't *really* have much connection with today's films. Where are all those 'bad, hysterical careerists'? Humm only mentions one film, *Fatal Attraction*, from back in 1987, though we can probably think of a couple more (such as 1994's *Disclosure*). 'Good mother' stereotypes are not overwhelming either; we might think of Jodie Foster protecting her child in a tough, resourceful and assertive way in *Panic Room* (2002) and *Flightplan* (2005), but these roles are hardly negative representations.

Fiesty mothers have been joined by a greater number of good fathers. Susan Jeffords (1993) notes how Arnold Schwarzenegger's evil *Terminator* (1984) comes back in *Terminator 2: Judgment Day* (1991) as a protective father-figure to nice little Ed Furlong. Jeffords sees this as part of a 1990s trend of reinventing masculinity as fatherhood and caring (1993: 245):

> What Hollywood culture is offering, in place of the bold spectacle of male muscularity and/as violence, is a self-effacing man, one who now, instead of learning to fight, learns to love. We can include here such [box office hits] as *Field of Dreams* (1989), *Robin Hood* (1991), *The Doctor* (1991), *Regarding Henry* (1991), even *Boyz N the Hood* (1991).

The 1990s, of course, did not entirely turn out like that. Looking through the list of hit movies of the past ten years or so, we can find examples of standard male action figures doing pretty much the same old thing: from *The Rock* (1996) and *Air Force One* (1997) to *Batman Begins* (2005), *Shooter* (2007), and *Die Hard 4.0* (entitled *Live Free or Die Hard* in the US) (2007). The difference with some 1980s action movies may be that the male hero is today more cynical, weary, and perhaps aware that violence may not be the solution to everything. But it usually is the solution to *this* thing. Meanwhile there are many other hit films where the male action hero works alongside a more-or-less equally powerful female action hero. Examples from around the 1990s included *The Matrix* (1999), *Tomorrow*

Never Dies (1997), *X-Men* (2000), *The Mummy Returns* (2001) and we can even throw in *Speed* (1994), *Titanic* (1997) and *Shrek* (2001). More recent examples include the *Fantastic Four* movies (2005, 2007) – although three of the Four are men, *Dawn of the Dead* (2004), *Mr & Mrs Smith* (2005), and perhaps *The Da Vinci Code* (2006) and the *Pirates of the Caribbean* trilogy (2003, 2006, 2007).

There have also been several films centred around leading female action-hero roles, including *Tank Girl* (1995), *The Long Kiss Goodnight* (1996), the *Scream* trilogy (1996–2000), *Alien Resurrection* (1997), *Mulan* (1998), *Crouching Tiger, Hidden Dragon* (2000), *Charlie's Angels* (2000) and *Charlie's Angels: Full Throttle* (2003), *Tomb Raider* (2001) and *Lara Croft Tomb Raider: The Cradle of Life* (2003), *Underworld* (2003) and *Underworld: Evolution* (2006), *Aeon Flux* (2005), *Ultraviolet* (2006) and three *Resident Evil* films (2002, 2004, 2007). These are a small minority of all action films, of course.

Jeffords's point about the demise of machismo did not turn out to be wrong, exactly, but a little overstated. Men in Hollywood films today tend not to be the seamlessly hard-masculine heroes which we saw in the 1980s; they more often combine the toughness required of an action hero with a more sensitive, thoughtful or caring side, typically revealed at certain (often quite brief) points in the movie. Meanwhile, female roles have definitely become tougher – not least of all because executives have realised that the audience of movie-going young men, in general, do not insist on their action heroes being male. On the contrary, if the traditional thrills of the action genre can be combined with the sight of Jessica Alba saving the world in tight clothing, for example, then the deal is sealed.

Case study: *Charlie's Angels*

It's not a recent case study any more, but the movie *Charlie's Angels* (2000) appeared on the crest of a 'girl power' flavoured wave, and it's still worth looking at its reception by audiences and critics. Based on the 1970s TV series of the same name, *Charlie's Angels* starred Cameron Diaz, Drew Barrymore and Lucy Liu as the detective trio, who are employed by an unseen millionaire, Charlie, to solve mysteries, look good and kick baddies in the face. The film was directed by McG, making his feature debut after a career in music videos, and Drew Barrymore was one of the producers. *Charlie's Angels* was a big commercial hit, taking over $170 million in its first three months (imdb.com), and was followed by a somewhat less successful sequel, *Charlie's Angels: Full Throttle* (2003).

Just because people went to see the movie doesn't mean it was necessarily adored, or influential, of course. In fact its reception was split between an 'old guard' who complained that it was an exploitative, stupid movie, and another audience who enjoyed seeing the women 'kick ass'. Those who publicly criticised it were not (necessarily) women and feminists, however – they were the mainstream, mostly male, film critics. Some just didn't like it. Max Messier at *Filmcritic.com* found it 'just plain dumb' in both story and execution. Mick LaSalle of the *San Francisco Chronicle* despaired at this 'utter debacle' (3 November 2000). Richard Schickel at *Time* magazine noticed its cheerfulness but found it 'a waste of time' (3 November 2000). America's celebrated critic Roger Ebert dismissed it as 'eye candy for the blind' (*Chicago Sun-Times*, 3 November 2000), and went on to express concern about its use of women:

> Barrymore, Diaz and Liu represent redhead, blond and brunet respectively (or, as my colleague David Poland has pointed out, T[its], A[ss] and Hair). Sad, isn't it, that three such intelligent, charming and talented actresses could be reduced to their most prominent component parts?

Michael Thomson of *BBC Online* (24 November 2000) was similarly upset by the women's glamour and pouting, saying that the film's message was 'by all means be feisty, but never forget to be feminine'. Many male reviewers (and some women) at the internationally well-known Internet Movie Database (www.imdb.com) made similar complaints, including the occasional note that the women are 'bimbos'.

However, the women are hardly shown as brainless – on the contrary, they are amazingly multi-skilled: they are forensic scientists and electronic engineers, espionage and surveillance specialists, racing-car drivers and superhuman fighting machines. They also defeat their enemies without using guns (at Barrymore's insistence). The film does knowingly showcase the women's physical attractiveness, but their success comes from their use of their brains, and their athletic skills. Nobody ever called Indiana Jones a 'bimbo' just because Harrison Ford took his shirt off, or because he sometimes used his seductive looks and charm to get what he wanted. With *Charlie's Angels* there may be more of a fear that the film will feed existing stereotypes, but we are hardly always rolling our eyes at the number of women on screen who can hack into high-security computers, speak several languages, skydive, reprogram missiles *and* beat up a posse of henchmen singlehanded.

So I would argue that some of the male reviewers are using this 'concern' about the representation of the *Angels* as a cover for their own disinterest in this happy, fizzy-pop 'post-feminist' celebration of a film. Their other complaints seem to reveal a feeling that pleasure in films comes from suspense and intricate plotting, and not from watching empowered young women get their way in a somewhat camp, jolly entertainment. The film clearly counters a lot of stereotypes about women's abilities. And whilst the filmmakers seem to enjoy the women's glamorous looks – in a knowing way which is meant to give pleasure to both women and men in the audience – the characters themselves are confident and independent, only sometimes using their looks to trick stupid, weak men. *Charlie's Angels* has an effervescent 'girl power' zing which had not been seen since the Spice Girls went down the dumper.

Female reviewers seemed more likely to embrace the movie: Susan Stark in the *Detroit News* (3 November 2000) found it to be 'immensely entertaining', and noted approvingly that 'Diaz, Liu and Barrymore obviously get a huge charge from having the chance to play Bond (as opposed to Bond Girl)'. Cindy Fuchs in the *Philadelphia City Paper* found 'excitement' and 'much adorable girl-bonding' (2 November 2000). Kamal Larsuel at *3BlackChicks.com* 'loved it'. And back in the Internet Movie Database, where thousands of filmgoers have rated *Charlie's Angels* from one to ten, we find that in every age group, women consistently rated the film higher than men. In the year following its release, the film got an average score of 6.6 from men and 7.3 from women; amongst females aged under 18, the film was rated even higher, at an average of 8.2 (compared to 7.3 from the under 18 males).[1]

This is not an attempt to show that *Charlie's Angels* is either good or bad; the point is that although several (not-so-young) male critics claimed that the film was generally rubbish but might provide some thrills for adolescent boys, in fact those boys were less keen than their female counterparts, who enjoyed the bubbly 'girl power' exuberance on offer. As one female IMDB reviewer writes about why women enjoy *Charlie's Angels*:

> I think it [is because of] the fact that we so rarely get to see female action heroes, particularly ones we can like. We had Trinity at the beginning of *The Matrix* before the movie quickly found a man to focus on, and we have Max and Buffy on television. It's a sign, though, that even silly movies featuring women kicking butt are so popular among, well, women. We need this. We need strong females in leading roles, even in silly movies. And this is a very silly movie, make no mistake. I also think it intends to be that way. Each scene has its own cartoon feel, and

DOES GIRL POWER LEAD TO GIRL VIOLENCE?

A study by psychologists Muncer *et al.* (2001) responded to growing media concern about 'ladettes' – young women with the assertive/aggressive attitudes usually associated with 'lads'. Their survey asked female students whether acts such as drinking, swearing, fast driving and graffiti-painting were as acceptable in women as in men. The women were also asked to indicate how aggressive they were in their own lives. It was found that women who agreed with the non-sexist view were *not* likely to be more aggressive than other women. In other words, support for 'girl power' ideas does not mean that women will necessarily be more violent themselves. This entirely unsurprising finding is described by the psychologists as 'unexpected'.

the movie itself is like a comic book come to life. There are some very nice and admirable touches, added at Drew Barrymore's insistence. We see the Angels eating heartily, we see the Angels use martial arts abilities instead of guns, we see the Angels saving gentlemen in distress.

(1 April 2001)

It may be flawed, but *Charlie's Angels* seemed to be making some valiant attempts at role-reversal within the blockbuster mainstream. The final complaint from this film's detractors is usually that these supposedly independent women remain *Charlie's* women. But what does Charlie do? Apart from being rich, he is totally impotent. He redistributes his wealth to three women in whom he has absolute trust. In other words, he's a Marxist and a feminist. There can be only one explanation: Charlie's Engels.

GENDER AND THE MOVIES: A FEW MORE EXAMPLES

Spider-Man 3 (2007)

The *Spider-Man* movie series (2001, 2004, 2007) is perhaps typical of contemporary blockbusters, in gender terms, in both positive and negative ways. We must begin by noting that it's another celebration of a *male* superhero, who must use physical action to achieve his goals. That is entirely traditional, and is in line with other recent hits such as *Batman Begins* (2005), *Superman Returns* (2006) and – although James Bond is not technically a 'superhero' – *Casino Royale* (2006). There is no point protesting that these movies have female-led equivalents, in the form of *Catwoman* (2004) and *Elektra* (2005), as these films were not only unsuccessful but seemed almost *designed* to be so, with lower budgets, poor scripts and lacklustre marketing. Reviews for both films were exceptionally bad (see www.rottentomatoes.com). Hollywood still puts its money on male heroes. Furthermore, the *Spider-Man* series does not present very strong female characters. Mary Jane, played by Kirsten Dunst, is independent and intelligent, but doesn't get to *do* much, and story-wise needs to be saved from peril by Spider-Man. Both *Batman Begins* and *Superman Returns* similarly gave their leading women little to do.

So far, so traditional. However, in his role as Spider-Man's alter ego, Peter Parker, Tobey Maguire presents a humane and multilayered representation of contemporary masculinity. He is sensitive and emotional; he is appealing but not a little geeky; he tries hard and does not always succeed. In *Spider-Man 2* especially, he is thoroughly torn between his desire for love and happiness, and his sense of 'duty' to protect the people of New York. In *Spider-Man 3*, possession by an alien goop leads Peter to explore a more masculine 'dark' side, but this is played as a parody of idiotic machismo. Mary Jane is profoundly unimpressed, and it is clear that this version of Peter – without his sensitivity and sweet good nature – is laughably inferior.

Meanwhile, our hero ends up having to fight three different bad guys. The villains in the *Spider-Man* series, though, are not randomly 'evil' creatures who must be predictably killed in the climax; and the third film is especially generous in this department. The new Green Goblin, Harry Osborn, is forgiven and redeemed as he gives his life to save his former friends; the Sandman, Flint Marko, is shown to have been driven to desperate measures as he wanted to save his daughter's life, and is also forgiven; and Eddie Brock is seen to be just a little misguided, and was taken over by the alien goop against his will. In other words, nobody here is 'actually' bad; they are just understood to have been overcome by events and misunderstandings.

Fantastic Four: Rise of the Silver Surfer (2007)

It's worth noting another Marvel Comics movie from the same summer – one which features a female superhero. *Fantastic Four: Rise of the Silver Surfer*, like its predecessor, *Fantastic Four* (2005), features Jessica Alba as

Sue Storm (also known as the Invisible Woman), alongside Ioan Gruffudd as Reed Richards (Mr Fantastic), Chris Evans as Johnny Storm (the Human Torch) and Michael Chiklis as Ben Grimm (The Thing). Obviously in terms of numbers, that's a bit unfair – three men and one woman. I am also aware that anything one might say about Jessica Alba's role in this, and perhaps any, film may be scoffed at by traditional feminists and other critics who could never allow that such an 'airbrushed beauty' kind of woman might represent any kind of reasonable role model. On the other hand, it wouldn't be fair to hold appearances against her, as feminists well know.

In the film, macho soldiers want to kill the Silver Surfer with guns and missiles, but Sue makes the crucial discovery that the Surfer is not the real enemy. The contrast of the masculine but stupid military with Sue's intelligent feminine empathy is arguably a sexist stereotype, but it's one which credits women with the superior role. Sue also plays a crucial role in saving the day during various action sequences. The military commander tries to dismiss the Fantastic Four as science geeks and 'freaks', but is shown to be ignorant and wrong. As in *Spider-Man 3*, the movie shows the film's supposed main villain, the Surfer, to be a misunderstood, fundamentally kind-hearted figure who only did bad things because he wanted to

Figure 4.2 The Silver Surfer seen here flying through the London Eye, and feeling misunderstood

be reunited with his loved one. The overall message, then, is about team-work and understanding as opposed to macho violence and prejudiced judgements.

Knocked Up (2007)

Apparently a very different kind of film, but playing to the same mainstream audience, the 'surprise' hit *Knocked Up* was very warmly received by critics and audiences alike. In the story, a condom misunderstanding during a one night stand between Ben and Alison leads to an unexpected pregnancy. Ben is clearly well-meaning, but immature; as the movie unfolds, he (unsurprisingly) realises he has to rise to the new challenge in his life. Meanwhile Alison is the sensible one, and holds all the cards, being seen by the other people in the film as superior to Ben in terms of looks, prospects and everything else. Nevertheless, a sweet friendship/partnership develops between the two characters, unusual in mainstream comedies.

Figure 4.3   Posters advertising *Knocked Up*, asking 'What if this guy got you pregnant?'

Thankfully Alison does not have to 'teach' Ben to grow up; he learns those lessons for himself. In gender terms, then, the film makes interesting assumptions: men are idiots, basically; not thuggish idiots, but just rather sweet, hopeless idiots who don't have much of a clue about life or responsibilities. The challenge of being a woman in a world with men like this is also taken seriously. There's no grand statement about gender roles here, but it's interesting to see some unusual complexities – and certainly no celebration of how fantastic men are – in a hit comedy film.

Click (2006)

Like *Knocked Up*, the Adam Sandler vehicle *Click* was a summertime hit featuring both 'gross' humour and touching emotional scenes (or Hollywood sentimentalism, depending on your view). Sandler plays an architect, Michael, who says he would like to spend more time with his wife and children, but repeatedly prioritises his work, believing that gaining promotions will be good for them all in the long run. Spooky Christopher Walken gives him a 'universal remote control' which can be used to *literally* control his universe. Michael is particularly taken with the fast-forward feature, which enables him to skip bits of his life such as family meals and arguments with his wife. Ultimately, in the style of *It's a Wonderful Life* (1946), this high-concept plot device enables Michael to learn that it is the small, special moments with his family which are important, not working every hour available in the hope of future benefits. The movie also confronts the imperfect bond between fathers and sons, underlined in an upsetting scene where Michael fast-forwards to a point where his father has died, then rewinds to the last time he saw him alive, and discovers that he was dismissive and rude to the old guy, but cannot change what has already happened.

The 'family comes first' message – which is spelt out rather clunkily in the film (not least of all by having a character say the phrase as his dying words) – might be seen as roll-your-eyes predictable for a Hollywood movie. It's a curious one, though: surely evil capitalist ideology should say that working all day for the corporate system comes first? *Click* argues the opposite: working all day for the corporate system is a waste of time – you should spend your time with the people you love.

The movie is, therefore, interesting in gender terms: on the one hand, Sandler plays the familiar all-American guy, whose instincts upon receiving the 'universal remote' are to use it to watch busty female joggers in slow-motion. On the other hand, Sandler is the focus of a narrative which emphasises the richness of love and emotion and family life, and is therefore not in favour of superficial laddish behaviour, nor even grown-up male hard-working behaviour. Conventional masculinity is therefore challenged within a conventional-looking comedy.

Summary

I've only mentioned a handful of movies here, to remind you of a few trends. You can think about films you've seen yourself in the light of these suggestions. My main point is that representations of gender in movies may have certain predictable trends, but are quite diverse. Any critic or theorist who tries to suggest that films are 'all the same' in terms of gender representation is simplifying to the point of meaninglessness.

To summarise some key points: women and men tend to have similar skills and abilities in films today, but if you look at any bunch of films on release and identify the one leading character in each, there's likely to be more men than women. Male characters are also more likely to find themselves able to save a woman in a heroic moment. Leading women have to be attractive, within our recognised conventions of what makes women attractive; but, to be fair, we should note that leading men also have to be attractive, within the recognised conventions for males. Men can get away with being older, however, and there are far more leading men in their forties, fifties and sixties than there are leading women in this age group. (There are too many examples to list here, but look at the careers of Mel Gibson, Harrison Ford, Sean Connery, Michael Douglas, Bruce Willis . . .)

GENDER IN CONTEMPORARY ADVERTISING

In advertising today, the representation of women and men isn't *usually* very conspicuously sexist. Sometimes it is, but then we sit up and comment. In the first edition of this book, in 2002, I noted that 'there are also a smallish number of cases where advertisers seem to have decided that it is OK to show women as housewives after all; and even in the twenty-first century, rather amazingly, the UK supermarket chain Iceland was still using the slogan "That's why mum's go to Iceland"'. Even more incredibly, in 2007 they were still using it. Where the modern dad buys his groceries remains unclear. So, some advertising is unapologetically sexist, and is presumably used because it is felt that the message 'works' for the target audience, even if it might surprise and offend some others. The fact that this doesn't happen all the time does not necessarily show that advertisers take their social responsibilities very seriously, but probably *does* show that they have learned that it is not good business to offend their customers with sexist stereotypes.

Although the gender relationships shown in adverts may usually seem equal, content analyses still find uneven numbers of men and women. A study of over 750 prime-time TV ads from spring 1998 conducted by Bartsch *et al.* (2000) found that, as in earlier studies, women were twice as likely as men to be in commercials for domestic products, and men were twice as likely as women to appear in ads for non-domestic products. Such a basic count-up of men and women does not take into account the story, message or joke within each advert, or the manner of representation of these males and females, but does appear to reflect a basic lack of fundamental change. An analysis of nearly 1,700 TV commercials from 1992–94 by Coltrane and Messineo (2000) also found that characters in the ads 'enjoy more prominence and exercise more authority if they are white, or men'. Another study of 1,337 prime time TV commercials from 1998 by Ganahl, Prinsen and Netzley (2003) concluded that:

> The commercials in this sample maintained the exact same percentage of underrepresentation for women who were primary characters as was found by Bretl and Cantor (1988). In the present study, the character ratio was 46.4% female and 53.6% male for the 1,281 primary characters. These findings were inconsistent with the population ratio provided by the 2000 U.S. Census Bureau, which is 51.2% female and 48.8% male ... Women are still cast as younger, supportive counterparts to men, and older women are still the most underrepresented group. Television commercials perpetuate traditional stereotypes of women and men.
>
> (Ganahl *et al.*, 2003: 547, 545)

More recently, a study of 400 prime-time TV commercials broadcast in Spain in 2005 found that there was a balance of male and female characters, almost but not quite matching the actual population – 50.6 per cent men and 49.4 per cent women on TV ads, 49.3 per cent men and 50.7 per cent women in reality (Valls-Fernández and Martínez-Vicente, 2007: 694). However, when it came to providing the authoritative voiceover, 68 per cent of ads used a man and only 20 per cent used a woman (in ads with a single narrator). Women were twice as likely to be shown doing housework or child care, whilst men were twice as likely to be shown doing work outside the home (ibid.: 697).

Very recent data for different countries is patchy, but following the considerable changes in representation between the 1970s and the 1990s, things seem to have reached a plateau. Certainly, the very obvious stereotypes from the past have mostly gone (although today's sexism may just be more subtle). The woman we *expect* to see in ads these days is the busy, confident, attractive success, in control of her professional and social life, and a kitchen slave to no-one. Men do not tell her what to do; instead, she sometimes gets to have a laugh at the expense of a man. Occasionally, 'ironic' adverts patronise female characters in a knowing way which is meant to be funny, though this may not always be successful. Macdonald (1995: 90) summarises the changes from the late 1980s and through the 1990s:

> Believing both that feminism's battles had been won, and that its ideology was now harmless by virtue of being out of date, advertisers invented 'postfeminism' as a utopia where women could do whatever they pleased, provided they had sufficient will and enthusiasm.

Feminist discourses were thus cunningly 'co-opted' by the advertising industry and used to sell stuff to women. The notions of 'freedom' and 'liberation' had, in the 1970s, been part of a revolutionary slate of changes sought by feminists who wanted to escape the oppression of patriarchy. By the 1990s, 'freedom' and 'liberation' were things offered by the manufacturers of sanitary products, to women who wanted to escape the oppression of periods.

Selling beauty

Sometimes it is unclear why gendered messages in *advertising* are singled out for particular attention by researchers – there are more publications on women in advertising than there are on women in TV programmes, for example – when TV series take up more of our time and attention than the ads which fly by every day. But the make-up adverts referred to above remind us of a concern uniquely applicable to advertising – that it is produced by capitalists who want to cultivate insecurities which they can then sell 'solutions' to. Germaine Greer put the case strongly in her book *The Whole Woman* (1999):

> Every woman knows that, regardless of her other achievements, she is a failure if she is not beautiful ... The UK beauty industry takes £8.9 billion a year out of women's pockets.[2] Magazines financed by the beauty industry teach little girls that they need make-up and train them to use it, so establishing their lifelong

reliance on beauty products. Not content with showing pre-teens how to use foundations, powders, concealers, blushers, eye-shadows, eye-liners, lip-liners, lipstick and lip gloss, the magazines identify problems of dryness, flakiness, blackheads, shininess, dullness, blemishes, puffiness, oiliness, spots, greasiness, that little girls are meant to treat with moisturisers, fresheners, masks, packs, washes, lotions, cleansers, toners, scrubs, astringents ... Pre-teen cosmetics are relatively cheap but within a few years more sophisticated marketing will have persuaded the most level-headed woman to throw money away on alchemical preparations containing anything from silk to cashmere, pearls, proteins, royal jelly ... anything real or phony that might fend off her imminent collapse into hideous decrepitude.

(pp. 19, 23)

Of course, this argument has been an important part of the feminist case for decades, but Greer reminds us that the beauty industry thrives today. (In the decade since she wrote this, little has changed, except that the industry's scientists have found even more amazing 'solutions' to previously unidentified skin and hair problems.) Indeed, Greer asserts that things have got worse since she wrote *The Female Eunuch* in the late 1960s: 'Women who were unselfconscious and unmade-up thirty years ago', she says, are now 'infected' with the need to conform to certain images of beauty (pp. 23–24). Greer also reminds us of the booming cosmetic surgery industry, which promises to make women look more like some mediated ideal, but is expensive, exploitative and dangerous.

The beauty ideal is often a substantial pressure on women, then. But this obsession with looks affects *people*, not only women. For example, Greer observes: 'Thirty years ago it was enough to *look* beautiful; now a woman has to have a tight, toned body, including her buttocks and thighs, so that she is good to touch, all over' (p. 22). This is true, for an 'ideal' woman at least, but it's worth noting that it is true for the 'ideal' man as well. Today, men are also expected to spend time in the gym, working to develop 'tight, toned' bodies. Women who have these well-toned bodies are likely to expect – equitably enough – that men will put in a similar effort. Every male film star today has to have a good body, just as women have to. So you might say that it's a pressure that our culture puts on *people* these days, but it's not just limited to women. In *The New Feminism*, Natasha Walter (1998) quotes surveys to suggest that today's women are more-or-less happy with how they look, whereas a vast majority of men felt unsatisfied with their own appearance. 'If ... only 4 per cent of men think they are attractive, we should not be too quick to argue that only women feel cast down by the pressures of beautiful ideals', she notes (p. 101).

Greer (1999), nevertheless, reminds us that there is much more pressure on women to impress with their make-up, high heels and wonderbras. This is true. But Walter (1998) complicates the picture by pointing out that many women *enjoy* fashion and adornment. Walter is a feminist, but she refuses to see fashion and beauty advertising as a conspiracy to keep women down. She argues that the use of beauty products, fashion and decoration are a source of pleasure which should not be denied – for women *or* men – and which, in any case, do not seem to have a huge impact upon how successful people are in the world. More attractive people *do* earn more than their plain colleagues, a study found in 1993, but the difference was larger for men than for women (Walter, 1998: 101).

Nevertheless, Walter may have been looking at an unusual set of statistics. In 2001, a survey produced by the Social and Public Health Sciences Unit at the University of Glasgow found that women were up to ten times more likely than men to be unhappy with their body image. This perception persisted even when women were a healthy weight for their height. The study's main author, Carol Emslie, said that 'Images are still of very thin women as desirable body shapes. There is still an association that beautiful women are thin. For men there is still more of a range of images' (BBC Online, 2001b). This seems to be true, despite the fact that other surveys have shown that men do not find the ultra-skinny look to be especially attractive. For example, a survey of English adolescents by Dittmar *et al.* (2000) found that teenage boys said that an ideal woman should be 'voluptuous', whereas girls did not. Nevertheless, both sexes felt that ideal women *and* ideal men should be thin.

To put things into perspective, though, a 2003 study by Hargreaves and Tiggemann (2003) asked Australian boys aged 13–15 to rank a list of ten characteristics which they would use when choosing a partner or girlfriend. 'Personality' and 'sense of humour' came out top, followed by 'attractiveness', 'similar interests' and 'manners'. 'Slim figure' was behind all of these in the rankings, at number six.

We can also note that whilst magazines for *women* celebrate the very thin look, magazines for men favour a more curvaceous and not-particularly-skinny look. *Loaded* magazine even put it into words: rejecting a female academic's assertion that 'women have the difficulty of living with the male idea of beauty shown on the catwalk', John Perry responds:

> No, men fancy models because they have beautiful faces, not because they look like they've been fed under a door. Sleeping

with a supermodel would be about as pleasurable as shagging a bicycle. The truth is, it's women themselves who see these freaks as the epitome of perfection.

(*Loaded*, July 2001: 95)

One could say, though, that the relative levels of skinniness are irrelevant: almost all of the 'beautiful women' in both women's and men's magazines are thin, not fat, and this must have an impact. Men are ideally required to be thin and well-toned too, but can get away with imperfections as long as they can compensate with charm or humour.

EMERGING ALTERNATIVE SEXUALITIES ON TV

Lesbians, gay men and bisexuals remained hidden from view, in mainstream television shows, for decades. As recently as 1990, even the sight of two men sitting in bed together talking, with no physical contact – in the US drama series *Thirtysomething* – prompted half the advertisers to side with homophobic campaigners and withdraw their support, reportedly losing the ABC network over a million dollars (Brooke, 1997; Miller, 2000). Even in 1997–98, Ellen DeGeneres's coming out as a lesbian in her sitcom *Ellen* (as well as in real life) caused an even bigger controversy, with advertisers fleeing, and ABC/Disney dropping the popular show after one 'lesbian' season. (Advertisers claim that it is not the content which scares them away, but controversy of any kind; this excuse is supported by the fact that several advertisers have dropped support for the radio and TV broadcasts of 'Dr Laura' Schlessinger, whose anti-gay views have been widely criticised (Wilke, 2000).) Astonishingly, it was not until May 2000 that teen soap-drama *Dawson's Creek* included 'what is considered to be the first male-male romantic kiss on a prime-time [US] TV program' (Wilke, 2000).

To get an overview of the sluggish emergence of gays into mainstream

---

QUEER TV

An excellent database of gay, lesbian and bisexual characters on television shows in the USA, Canada, Britain, Australia and elsewhere, from the 1960s to the present, appears at http://home.cc.umanitoba.ca/~wyatt/tv-characters.html.

media, we will have to rewind a few decades. The first serial drama to feature recurring gay characters was probably Australia's *Number 96* (Network Ten, 1972–77), a deliberately controversial story of life in and around a block of flats in Sydney. Regular characters included Don, a gay man who had several partners during the show's run, Karen, a lesbian and Robyn, a transsexual. The series was adapted by NBC for America in the early 1980s, but the gay characters were cut. In the 1970s a handful of other serials featured gay characters in minor roles, or as stereotypical gays played for laughs in sitcoms, but otherwise – as we can see from David Wyatt's excellent online guide (see 'Queer TV' box) – television gays were few and far between.

In the 1980s, glamorous US soap *Dynasty* included the regular gay character of Steven Carrington (1981–86), and although he would never be seen kissing or being especially intimate with a man, the story followed his struggle to get the family – in particular his father, arch patriarch Blake Carrington – to accept his sexuality. In the UK, the BBC's most popular show, the 'gritty' soap *EastEnders*, went further with the character of Colin Russell from 1986–89, a gay graphic designer who was probably more marginalized for owning a yuppie Filofax than for his sexuality. Colin was seen falling in love with Barry, a working-class gay man; they moved in together, and although their physical relationship as shown on screen was often rather stilted and distant, they were allowed some moments of intimacy including a controversial kiss (1987). The UK's other 'issues' soap of the time, *Brookside*, also featured a young gay character, Gordon Collins (1985–90), who was bullied about his sexuality in one storyline, and eventually found a lover. Elsewhere in the 1980s, gay characters remained scarce on TV, as marginal bit-players or comic relief – or in the 'other world' of the British aristocracy, as in *Brideshead Revisited* (1981) and *The Jewel in the Crown* (1984).

In the 1990s, lesbians became more visible as leading characters in television series (as opposed to rare appearances as deviants). In Britain, the decade began with the outstanding screen adaptation of Jeanette Winterson's lesbian coming-of-age novel *Oranges Are Not the Only Fruit* (1990). In 1993, *Brookside* pioneered the first lesbian kiss in a mainstream soap opera, and went on to show the relationship develop for a few months, on the knowingly controversial Channel Four. The characters, Beth and Margaret, were young, ordinary attractive women, which may have helped to dispel ignorant stereotypes of what lesbians might look like; although Beth had previously been a victim of sexual abuse, and Margaret later fell in love with a male priest – but that's soaps for you. The previously rather conventional ITV countryside soap *Emmerdale* had a young female character, Zoe, come out in the same year. (*Emmerdale* deserves credit for keeping this character for 12 more years, until 2005, giving her meaningful relationships with a series of non-stereotyped lesbian partners (first screen kiss: 1995), and not having the character return to heterosexuality.) In 1994, the BBC jumped on the lesbian soap bandwagon in *EastEnders*, where the relationship between a white woman and a black woman, Della and Binnie – both young and attractive, again – was prominent for a while, but didn't last long. Everyday lesbians began to appear in other British drama serials such as *Medics* (ITV, 1994) and *Between the Lines* (BBC, 1993–95). By 2000, the British public were open-minded enough to *almost* let lesbian ex-nun Anna win the reality gameshow *Big Brother* (C4), and the following year it was a gay man, Brian, who won the prize.

In the USA, a fleeting kiss between women in *LA Law* (1991) and a one-off lesbian kiss for *Roseanne* (1994) were noisily discussed but did not really rock the boat; and the shockwaves of *Ellen*'s outing (1997–98), mentioned above, might have put American broadcasters off lesbian central characters for a while. In teen hit *Buffy the Vampire Slayer*, Buffy's reliable sidekick, Willow, fell in love with fellow witch Tara in 2000. Their onscreen physical connection was never more than quick kisses on the cheek, but the relationship was sensitively developed. In the internationally popular *ER*, grouchy doctor Weaver began to explore her desire for women in the same year. And James Cameron's sci-fi series *Dark Angel* (2000–02) gave the lead cop an assertive lesbian sidekick. A small number of other lesbians could be found in supporting or background roles.

The 1990s saw gay men become more commonplace on British TV; for example, in *EastEnders* the young gay couple Simon and Tony (1996–99) were allowed to kiss without the BBC switchboard exploding with irate calls. The BBC even included a gay art teacher in its long-running drama for children, *Grange Hill* (1993–98). BBC2's *This Life* (1994–96) featured gay males Warren and Lenny, as well as bisexual Ferdy, in its twentysomething ensemble. The UK's Channel Four financed the production of the San Francisco-based *Tales of the City* (1993), which was followed by *More Tales of the City* (1998) and *Further Tales of the City* (2001). Most spectacularly of all, the same channel commissioned and heavily promoted *Queer as Folk* (1999–2000), the story of the lives of three gay men (and various friends) in Manchester, extremely well-written by Russell T. Davies. The series was notable for its non-judgemental treatment of interesting gay lives, its gay sex scenes, its emotional depth and its refusal to get bogged down with unhappy 'issues'. When Davies revived the classic series *Doctor Who* in 2005, he stirred into the mix a regular character, Captain Jack Harkness, who is openly bisexual; coming from the fifty-first century, he regards any notions of sexual orientation as 'quaint'. Captain Jack's attraction to men was quite challenging for a BBC 'family' programme, but the character was popular, even becoming the star of the spin-off series *Torchwood* (2006–).

Queer as Folk, meanwhile, boosted the TV visibility of gay men in the USA and Canada as well, in its remade form produced by cable channel Showtime (2000–2005). The show was the topic of numerous newspaper stories from coast to coast, and ran to many more episodes than the UK original (83 episodes over five seasons, compared to just ten UK episodes). The premiere scored Showtime's best ratings in three years (Miller, 2000). Although cynics had predicted that its transfer across the Atlantic would lead to a more bland production, the US *Queer as Folk* was surprisingly bold and frank.

The 1990s weren't especially kind to gay men on US TV, though. On *Northern Exposure*, occasional characters Ron and Erick operated a bed-and-breakfast, and got 'married' in 1994 – although two TV stations refused to transmit this episode. In the same year, a gay kiss was cut from *Melrose Place* because 'it would cost $1 million in ads' (DeWolf, 1997). ABC's daytime soap *All My Children* featured a few gay characters, including a high school history teacher, whose presence in the classroom led to 'gay teacher' controversy in the storyline (1995–98). Carter, one of the Mayor's staff in sitcom *Spin City*, is a gay activist (1996–2002). *Tales of the City* appeared on PBS in 1994, but *More Tales* did not appear until 1998, on Showtime, after PBS had abandoned it. The Fox network allowed gay characters to appear in its teen shows *Beverley Hills 90210* and *Party of Five* (as well as *Melrose Place*, mentioned above) but in each case the characters became marginalized over time (Hart, 2000). By 1998 the sitcom *Will and Grace* (1998–2006) dared to include a gay man – Will – as a lead character. The show was US network TV's fourth-highest rated programme – just below *ER*, *Survivor* and *Friends* – in March 2001 (Wilke, 2001), indicating a growing acceptance of gay characters. *Will and Grace* got through two seasons without showing a same-sex kiss, however, allowing *Dawson's Creek* to steal that crown, as mentioned above.

More recently, viewers have become more used to seeing representations of gay men and lesbians as 'regular' characters, where their sexuality is taken for granted as commonplace, rather than shocking. Notable examples include David Fisher in *Six Feet Under* (2001–05), who ultimately married his partner Keith Charles, and adopted two boys; Kevin Walker in *Brothers and Sisters* (2006–), who has had a number of relationships; and *The L Word* (2004–), which features a whole cast of lesbian and bisexual characters. Meanwhile reality television producers found a way to turn gay stereotypes into positive virtues, arguably, with *Queer Eye* (2003–2007) – originally *Queer Eye for the Straight Guy* – in which a 'fab five' of stylish gay

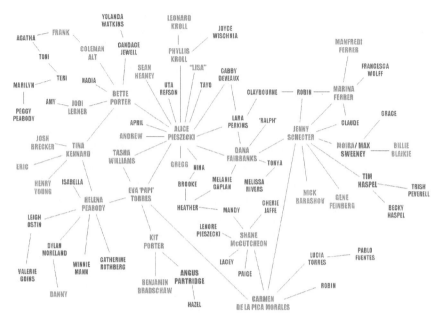

Figure 4.4   'The chart' from *The L Word*, illustrating the complex network of relationships on the show

men give less fashionable (generally heterosexual) individuals a makeover encompassing grooming, fashion, diet, interior design and social interaction. (See www.glaad.org for latest tracking of lesbian, gay and bisexual characters on US TV.)

Finally, a small but growing number of TV advertisements have included gay characters – often based around a joke where a woman finds a man to be very attractive but he turns out to be gay, or vice versa. Details of such ads can be found on the website 'The Commercial Closet: The World's Largest Collection of Gay Advertising', at www.commercialcloset.org.

Overall, television broadcasters have been cautious about their use of non-heterosexual characters. For years, lesbians and gays were invisible, and even now, although some reasonable examples are listed above, these instances are exceptional and the majority of TV programmes have featured, and continue to feature, a seemingly all-straight set of characters. Bisexuals, and transsexuals, except in a few memorable cases, have been excluded altogether.

GAYS ON FILM

In mainstream movies, there have been very few lesbian or gay *leading* characters. The major examples – such as *The Adventures of Priscilla Queen of the Desert* (1994), *The Birdcage* (1996), *Beautiful Thing* (1996), *Bound* (1996), *Boys On the Side* (1995), *Desert Hearts* (1985), *Flawless* (1999), *Go Fish* (1994), *Jeffrey* (1995), *Kiss of the Spider Woman* (1985), *Priest* (1994), *Torch Song Trilogy* (1988), *Velvet Goldmine* (1998) – tend to be thought of as 'gay-themed films' or 'alternative' anyway, which may detract from their general impact on society. Some literary stories of English aristocratic homosexuality in the past – *Maurice* (1987), *Another Country* (1984) and *Wilde* (1998) – may have slipped under the radar of more conservative audiences with their attractive 'costume drama' production values. And of course there are a few other exceptional examples, such as *But I'm a Cheerleader* (2000), a teen comedy that makes fun of 'gay rehabilitation' centres. Of course, mainstream filmmakers are increasingly happy to have non-heterosexuals in *supporting* roles – often the familiar 'gay best friend' character, wise and sensitive, who can help to guide the main character towards happiness. See for example *True Identity* (1991), *Four Weddings and a Funeral* (1994), *Clueless* (1995), *My Best Friend's Wedding* (1997), *As Good As It Gets* (1997), *The Object of My Affection* (1997), *Primary Colors* (1998), *Billy Elliot* (2000).

The most highly-praised movie centred on gay characters in recent years, and therefore probably of all time, is *Brokeback Mountain* (2005). The story of repressed and hidden love between two cowboys won three Oscars, four Golden Globes and four BAFTA awards, and was much lauded by critics. This reception appeared to suggest that Hollywood had 'officially' decided to embrace alternative sexualities. Other recent films with sympathetic central gay or lesbian characters include *Imagine Me & You* (2005), *Capote* (2005) and *Running with Scissors* (2006).

Prior to films like these, the best-remembered image of a gay man in the movies was probably Tom Hanks dying of AIDS in *Philadelphia* (1993). This well-intentioned Oscar-winner nowadays looks like a patronising, bland and overly polite attempt to have a gay character accepted as 'normal' by a 'normal' audience: Hanks is seen as part of a loving family, adores opera, is always polite and pleasant, and never shocks anyone with physical displays of affection for his male partner. The characterisation in *Philadelphia* was the antithesis of that in the TV series *Queer as Folk* (see above), where gay men were actually allowed to be seen as interesting and funny and different – and not having to imitate middle-class, middle-aged heterosexuality in order to be accepted.

Some other films convey a pro-gay message without necessarily having gay characters as the stars. The *X-Men* trilogy (2000, 2003, 2006), discussed below, can be seen to have done this by way of analogy. *V for Vendetta* (2006) was more explicit, depicting a Britain where an ultra-conservative dictatorship enforces a Christian, heterosexual way of life, with 'social deviants' being tortured, experimented upon or killed. Perhaps offended by the film's view of religious zealots as intolerant, Ted Baehr, chairman of the Christian Film and Television Commission, called *V for Vendetta* 'a vile, pro-terrorist piece of neo-Marxist, left-wing propaganda filled with radical sexual politics and nasty attacks on religion and Christianity' (Baehr, 2006) – which must have delighted the film's producers.

OTHER 'OTHERS': THE QUEER CASE OF THE *X-MEN*

Some of the most interesting treatments of sexual minorities have been done by allusion (although campaigners would rightly assert that this should not replace better representation of characters who 'actually' do have unconventional sexualities). For example, the blockbuster *X-Men* (2000) showed the 'mutants' as a misunderstood minority, whose human rights were being attacked by politicians and society. The sequels continued these themes: *X2: X-Men United* (2003) involved a human plot to exterminate all the mutants, and *X-Men: The Last Stand* (2006) concerned the discovery of a 'cure' which may be forcibly administered to the mutants.

The different mutant factions in the films have an obvious parallel with the anti-racist civil rights movement in America: peaceful Charles Xavier and his heroic 'X-Men' team represent Martin Luther King and his followers, whilst Magneto and his more militant supporters represent the Malcolm X wing. Both groups are threatened by the conservative anti-mutant humans, represented in the first film by the character of Senator Kelly, who is seen campaigning against the mutants using language which very clearly echoes the rhetoric of anti-gay speakers. The film-makers even set up a spoof website, *Mutant Watch* (www.mutantwatch.com), which matches the style and argument of anti-gay websites such as *National Association for Research and Therapy of Homosexuality* (www.narth.com), the *American Family Association* (www.afa.net), the *Family Research Council* (www.frc.org) and *Morality in Media* (www.moralityinmedia.org). This comparison also gives us a chance to take a minor detour into the cultural battlefield of homophobic sexual politics.

The *Mutant Watch* site includes an introduction from Senator Kelly entitled 'Protecting Our Children' which begins:

America is built on the strength of its families. The question is, what are families built on? The answer is people. Ordinary people. Lawyers and doctors, steel workers and schoolteachers. People like you. People like me. As I speak, there is a new and ominous danger facing our families. It is a danger facing every man, woman and child.

Kelly goes on to describe the threat to American families posed by these 'genetic aberrations', and encourages his supporters to 'preserve our heritage'. In another article on the site, Kelly discusses the problem of mutants in the school classroom, and there are links to 'independent scientific studies' which provide medical evidence about the abnormal mutants. There is also an online poll which asks whether unborn children should be tested for 'advanced genetic mutation'.

All of these perspectives and discourses can be seen in the websites of those organisations who feel that it is their duty to stamp out homosexuality to protect 'American families'. At the time of *X-Men*'s release, a 'position statement' on the website of the Family Research Council stated:

By upholding the permanence of marriage between one man and one woman as a foundation for civil society, the Family Research Council consequently seeks to reverse many of the destructive aspects of the sexual revolution, including no-fault divorce, widespread adultery, and abortion. The council also, however, considers the increased acceptance of homosexuality as a part of that tragic mix. We do not consider homosexuality an alternative lifestyle or even a sexual 'preference;' it is unhealthy and destructive to individual persons, families, and society. Compassion – not bigotry – compels us to support the healing of homosexuals who wish to change their destructive behavior. In addition, we challenge efforts by political activists to normalize homosexuality and we oppose attempts to equate homosexuality with civil rights or compare it to benign characteristics such as skin color or place of origin.

(Family Research Council, 2001)

To clarify – although the *Mutant Watch* site was a spoof tied to the first *X-Men* movie, the Family Research Council is a very real organisation based in Washington DC, lobbying politicians and the media. Its vigorous activity continues: in 2006–07 it was especially concerned with fighting gay marriage (setting up a special website, www.protectmarriage.org), and stopping schoolchildren from hearing about non-heterosexual lifestyles, or Charles Darwin. It produces a range of pamphlets warning parents of the homosexual threat. Senator Kelly in *X-Men* warned that mutants might infiltrate schools, and use their super-powers to gain an advantage in public debate. The FRC booklet *Homosexuality In Your Child's School* has similar concerns:

> This pamphlet describes how pro-homosexual activists work their way up from seemingly innocent-sounding 'safe schools' programs (which treat traditional values as being equivalent to racism), to one-sided 'training' of teachers and students, to injecting homosexuality into every subject in the curriculum. Their final step is the active punishment of those who dare to express disapproval of homosexual behavior. This pamphlet will equip you to oppose this promotion of homosexuality in your child's school.
>
> (Family Research Council, 2007)

Young people concerned that they may have been 'affected' by homosexuality are directed to Exodus Youth (www.exodusyouth.net) – a trendy-looking website, which also has an outpost on MySpace – which offers resources to help people 'overcome' their homosexual feelings and gain 'freedom from homosexuality'.

In *X-Men*, Senator Kelly has a smooth presentation style – authoritative and reassuring – which matches that of all the organisations mentioned above (and indeed there are many more 'family institutes' just like them, across the United States in particular). They all share the desire to appear as respectable policy and research centres. The National Association for Research and Therapy of Homosexuality, for example, has the smart website that befits a national organisation, and its compassionate language aims to suggest that they are offering a helpful service. A more extreme agenda seems to lie beneath the surface, however. An article on the site explains, 'We don't hate gays; we simply desire to live free of homosexuality' (Davies, 2007), a seemingly unselfconscious echo of the reasoning given by fascists in the past. The article outlining 'Our purpose' quickly moves from 'concern' for homosexuals, to presenting them as a threat to the 'natural' way of life:

> Fifty years ago, researcher C.D. King offered a very useful definition of 'normal' ... Normality, he said, is 'that which functions according to its design'. As clinicians, we have witnessed the

intense suffering caused by homosexuality, which many of our members see as a 'failure to function according to design'. Homosexuality distorts the natural bond of friendship that would naturally unite persons of the same sex. It threatens the continuity of traditional male–female marriage – a bond which is naturally anchored by the complementarity of the sexes, and has long been considered essential for the protection of children.

All three *X-Men* movies satirised these types of discourse – the conservative majority's fear of a 'different' minority – within the form of successful blockbusters. When highly regarded director Bryan Singer dropped out of directing the third instalment, *X-Men: The Last Stand* (2006), fans suspected that bland replacement Brett Ratner would gently drop the political themes. In the event, though, the plot concerning a mutant 'cure' presented a clear analogy with those who seek to 'save' people from homosexuality. The authority figures in the film are reassuring, saying, 'This cure is voluntary – nobody's talking about extermination.' But Eric Lensherr (Magneto), played by Ian McKellen, doubts this account:

> No one ever talks about it. They just do it. And you go on with your lives, ignoring the signs all around you. And then one day, when the air is still and the night is fallen, they come for you … Only then do you realize that while you're talking about organizing and committees, the extermination has already begun. Make no mistake, my brothers, they will draw first blood. They will force their cure upon us. There is only one question you must answer: Will you stand and fight? Or wait for the inevitable genocide?

The third film was, therefore, quite clear in its message. It was also enormously successful (taking $122 million on its opening weekend alone). We don't know, however, whether members of organisations such as the National Association for Research and Therapy of Homosexuality or the Family Research Council will have recognised themselves in its portrayal of intolerance.

SUMMARY

Representations of gender today are more complex, and less stereotyped, than in the past. Women and men are generally equals in the worlds of today's TV and movies, although male characters are still often to the fore.

Women are seen as self-reliant heroes quite often today, whilst the depiction of masculinity has become less straightforward, and more troubled. Advertising, and the broader world of stars and celebrities, promotes images of well-toned and conventionally attractive women and men, which may mean that *everyone* is under pressure to look good, although women are additionally coerced about make-up, and subjected to even greater paranoia about looking thin. Meanwhile, gay and lesbian characters have started to gain a certain amount of acceptance within the TV mainstream, but remain relatively uncommon in movies.

Overall, then, modern media has a more complex view of gender and sexuality than ever before. The images of women and men which it propagates today may be equally valued, but remain different, and diverse. To see how people deal with these ideas and images in their everyday lives, we will now turn to some more theoretical perspectives concerning self-identity.

Chapter 5

GIDDENS, MODERNITY AND SELF-IDENTITY

IN THIS CHAPTER, and the next two, we consider some theoretical approaches which provide us with ways of looking at how people form their sense of self and identity. This will be fleshed out in the discussions of actual media, and actual audiences, in the subsequent chapters. Here, we look at the work of Anthony Giddens on how people understand and shape their self-identity in modern societies, and how the media might feed into this. We begin with some background to his approach, to provide some context.

CLASSICAL AND MODERN

Anthony Giddens combines an old-school, 'classical' sociological style with a contemporary awareness of changes in society, and he is happy to mix new theories with more established sociological perspectives. He was born in 1938, but has kept up with the rolling ball of social change. He hasn't tried to marginalise the impact of feminism in his understanding of society, for instance, and considers change in gender relations to be important. Some commentators criticise him for being too eclectic and for not going into things in enough depth, but those people are normally trying to turn their own narrowness into a virtue, and therefore might not be entirely trustworthy. In interviews, Giddens seems pleasant and self-effacing, which is nice because he has been so prolific that you wouldn't expect him to have had time to develop social skills.

Giddens manages to continue the grand sociological traditions, whilst dealing with the issues of today. The 'founding fathers' of sociology, Durkheim and Weber, cast shadows across his work. The other 'founding father' is, of course, Marx, whom Giddens finds less significant for contemporary sociology. Although Giddens had published analyses of Marx in the 1970s, his textbook, *Sociology* (several editions from 1989), shocked the world of sociology teachers by barely mentioning him – especially in contrast with other sociology textbooks, which had previously been obliged to outline a Marxist perspective on every area of sociology. This reflects a frustration with the simplistic arguments of left-wing sociology; whilst it is easy to say that capitalism has ruined everything, Giddens indicates that we need to look for more thorough and sophisticated theories about how the world works today.

ANTHONY GIDDENS: QUICK FACTS

- Giddens enterprisingly co-founded Polity Press in 1984, to exercise more power in academic publishing.
- Giddens was a lecturer at the University of Cambridge from 1969, but the institution rejected Giddens's applications for promotion to a readership for ten years – 'I think this was a record', he says – before finally making him a Professor in 1987, after he had published 13 books.
- In 1996, Routledge published a four-volume set entitled *Anthony Giddens: Critical Assessments*, which discussed his work over some 1,800 pages.
- Giddens's notion of a 'Third Way' – which sought to avoid the traditional certainties of left- and right-wing politics – was said to be an intellectual inspiration to New Labour in the UK, and he was given a life peerage in June 2004, as Baron Giddens of Southgate.
- In recent years, Giddens has correspondingly turned to writing more hands-on political books such as *Europe in the Global Age* (2006) and *Over To You, Mr Brown: How Labour Can Win Again* (2007).
- His impact on New Labour may have been patchy, however. David Blunkett's famously self-serving diaries reveal him dismissing a Giddens speech in 1998 – when Blunkett was Secretary of State for Education and Employment – as 'all very entertaining', but 'an insult' to those who had been developing a 'third way' within politics for the previous 15 years (Blunkett, 2006: 93).

KEY THEMES

The main Giddens themes, of concern to us here, are:

- The fusion of individual actions and grand social forces in one theoretical approach ('structuration').
- The impact of 'late modernity' – where all activity is the subject of social reflection – on social actors, relationships and institutions.
- The consequent 'democratisation' of everything from big organisations to intimate relationships.

Giddens has a number of other related interests, such as globalisation, the state and the 'third way' in politics, but these are not so central to the present discussion.

LEFT AND RIGHT

Giddens would not deny that Marx was very important in the development of social science, and his instincts seem to be the nice-to-other-people ones which can be found at the theoretical heart of 'the left'. But he is frustrated at the left/right divide in social analysis, and became identified as one of the architects of the 'third way', which Tony Blair, Gordon Brown and Gerhard Schroeder were supposedly interested in – although Giddens's idea of it seems to be more original and complex than, say, Blair's mix of left and right traditions (see Giddens's *The Third Way: The Renewal of Social Democracy* (1998), *The Third Way and Its Critics* (2000)).

In sociology there has been a long-standing divide between those theorists who prioritise 'macro level' studies of social life – looking at the 'big picture' of society – and those who emphasise the 'micro level' – what everyday life means to individuals. Giddens always had an interesting relationship with this dichotomy. He seemed to admire Durkheim's preference for broad statements about society and sociology itself (his 1976 treatise on methodology even bore the cheekily grand Durkheimian title *New Rules of Sociological Method*). But Giddens rejects Durkheim's idea that we should be able to identify laws which will predict how societies will operate, without looking at the meanings understood by individual actors in society. Giddens is here much closer to the other 'grandfather' of sociology, Weber, who argued that individuals' own accounts of social action were paramount. But Giddens recognised that both perspectives had value – and since the 'macro' and 'micro' levels of social life naturally feed into each other, you shouldn't have to choose between them. So he came up with the theory of 'structuration', which bridges this divide.

THE THEORY OF STRUCTURATION

Giddens's theory of structuration notes that social life is more than random individual acts, but is not merely determined by social forces. To put it another way, it's not *merely* a mass of 'micro'-level activity – but on the other hand, you can't study it by only looking for 'macro'-level explanations. Instead, Giddens suggests, human agency and social structure are in a relationship with each other, and it is the repetition of the acts of individual agents which reproduces the structure. This means that there *is* a social structure – traditions, institutions, moral codes and established ways of doing things; but it also means that these can be changed when people start to ignore them, replace them or reproduce them differently.

In the book *Conversations with Anthony Giddens* (Giddens and Pierson, 1998), we find Giddens untroubled by his critics' efforts to find problems in the detail of how this might actually work. His 'oh, you're making it very complicated, but it's perfectly simple' attitude might frustrate some, but you can't really argue with it, because the whole idea of structuration is perfectly straightforward, and makes sense.

STRUCTURATION

Human agency (micro level activity) and social structure (macro level forces) continuously feed into each other. The social structure is reproduced through repetition of acts by individual people (and therefore can change).

SOCIAL ORDER AND SOCIAL REPRODUCTION

But if individuals find it difficult to act in any way that they fancy, what is the nature of those invisible social forces which provide resistance? Giddens finds an answer by drawing an analogy with language: although language only exists in those instances where we speak or write it, people react strongly against others who disregard its rules and conventions. In a similar way, the 'rules' of social order may only be 'in our heads' – they are not usually written down, and often have no formal force to back them up – but nevertheless, people can be shocked when seemingly minor social expectations are not adhered to. Harold Garfinkel's sociological studies in the 1960s showed that when people responded in unexpected ways to everyday questions or situations, other actors could react quite angrily to this breach of the collective understanding of 'normal behaviour' (see Garfinkel, 1984 [first published 1967]).

In the case of gender this form of social reproduction is particularly clear. When a boy goes to school wearing eyeliner and a dash of lipstick, the shockwaves – communicated through the conventions of punishment and teasing – can be powerful. And yet he only supplemented his appearance with materials which are used by millions of women every day. Women who choose not to shave their legs or armpits may be singled out in a similar way, treated as deviants for ignoring a social convention about feminine appearance.

People's everyday actions, then, reinforce and reproduce a set of expectations – and it is this set of *other people's expectations* which make up the 'social forces' and 'social structures' that sociologists talk about. As Giddens puts it, 'Society only has form, and that form only has effects on people, in so far as structure is produced and reproduced in what people do' (Giddens and Pierson, 1998: 77).

But why should we care about maintaining this shared framework of reality? Would it matter if other people were surprised by our actions? Giddens argues that people have 'a "faith" in the coherence of everyday life', which is developed very early in life – when we have to place absolute trust in our carers – and sustained by our ordinary interactions with others (Giddens, 1991: 38). It is because of this faith – a kind of routine trust, extended without a second thought – that some people are so shaken when others challenge the taken-for-granted consensus about how, say, women and men should behave.

This could explain, for example, why some men are disturbed – even angered – to see other men acting in an 'effeminate' manner: because this behaviour challenges their everyday understanding of how things should be in the world. (TV entertainers in drag, on the other hand, pose no threat as they are just 'entertainment' which can easily be read as a *confirmation* of gender stereotypes.) People have an emotional investment in their world as they expect it, and for some, certain aberrations are most unwelcome. Others, of course, don't mind at all. Unfortunately, this account does not explain exactly why appearance or behaviour which crosses traditional *gender* boundaries can be so much more contentious than other unexpected things, such as unusual forms of hair colour or politeness.

The performance of gender appears here – as it does throughout this book – as something which is learned and policed, and which has to be constantly worked on and monitored.

GIDDENS, LATE MODERNITY AND POSTMODERNISM

We are not in a post-modern era, Giddens says. It is a period of *late modernity*. He does not necessarily disagree with the characterisations of recent social life which other theorists have labelled as postmodern – cultural self-consciousness, heightened superficiality, consumerism, scepticism towards theories which aim to explain everything ('metanarratives' such as science, religion or Marxism) and so on. Giddens doesn't dispute these changes, but he says that we haven't really gone beyond modernity. It has just developed, into late modernity.

So it's inappropriate to call it postmodernity. Giddens is undoubtedly right that postmodernity isn't a completely new era – although to be fair, we can note that most major theorists of postmodernity, such as Jean-François Lyotard, did not actually say that postmodernity replaced, and came after, modernity, anyway. Nevertheless, the focus on modernity is useful because the most important contrast for Giddens is between pre-modern (traditional) culture and modern (post-traditional) culture. The phenomena that some have dubbed 'postmodern' are, in Giddens's terms, usually just the more extreme instances of a fully developed modernity. Furthermore, studies such as my Lego identity study (Gauntlett, 2007, discussed below and in Chapter 11) have shown that the postmodernist claim that identities are 'fragmented' these days does not match people's actual experience: individuals may think of their identities as *complex*, and *multi-faceted*, but they still understand their identity as all one thing, and not fragmented at all.

POST-TRADITIONAL SOCIETY

It is important for understanding Giddens to note his interest in the increasingly *post-traditional* nature of society. When tradition dominates, individual actions do not have to be analysed and thought about so much, because choices are already prescribed by the traditions and customs. (Of course, this does not mean that the traditions can never be thought about, or challenged.) In post-traditional times, however, we don't really worry about the precedents set by previous generations, and options are at least as open as the law and public opinion will allow. All questions of how to behave in society then become matters which we have to consider and make

Figure 5.1   Anthony Giddens, reflecting on late modernity

decisions about. Society becomes much more *reflexive* and aware of its own precariously constructed state. Giddens is fascinated by the growing amounts of reflexivity in all aspects of society, from formal government at one end of the scale to intimate sexual relationships at the other.

Modernity is post-traditional. A society can't be fully modern if attitudes, actions or institutions are significantly influenced by traditions, because deference to tradition – doing things just because people did them in the past – is the opposite of modern reflexivity. Because of this, Giddens (1999) suggests that societies which try to 'modernise' in the most obvious institutional sense – by becoming something like a capitalist democracy – but which do not throw off other traditions, such as gender inequalities, are likely to fail in their attempt to be successful modern societies.

MODERNITY AND THE SELF

In modern societies – by which we mean not 'societies today' but 'societies where modernity is well developed' – self-identity becomes an inescapable issue. Even those who would say that they have never given any thought to questions or anxieties about their own identity will inevitably have been compelled to make significant choices throughout their lives, from everyday questions about clothing, appearance and leisure to high-impact decisions about relationships, beliefs and occupations. Whilst earlier societies with a social order based firmly in *tradition* would provide individuals with (more or less) clearly defined roles, in *post-traditional* societies we have to work out our roles for ourselves. As Giddens (1991: 70) puts it:

What to do? How to act? Who to be? These are focal questions for everyone living in circumstances of late modernity – and ones which, on some level or another, all of us answer, either discursively or through day-to-day social behaviour.

The prominence of these questions of identity in modern society is both a consequence and a cause of changes at the institutional level. Typically, Giddens sees connections between the most 'micro' aspects of society – individuals' internal sense of self and identity – and the big 'macro' picture of the state, multinational capitalist corporations and globalisation. These different levels, which have traditionally been treated quite separately by sociology, have influence upon each other, and cannot really be understood in isolation.

Take, for example, the changes in intimate relationships which we have seen in the last 60 years – the much greater levels of divorce and separation as people move from one relationship to another, the substantially increased openness about sexuality, and much more conspicuous sexual diversity. These changes cannot be understood by assuming they were led by social institutions and the state, not least of all because conventional thinking on both left and right has been that both capitalism and the 'moral authorities' of the state would prefer the population to have stable monogamous family lives.

But these changes cannot be explained by looking only at the individual

FEATURES OF LATE MODERNITY

- The self is not something we are born with, and it is not fixed.
- Instead, the self is reflexively made – thoughtfully constructed by the individual.
- We all choose a *lifestyle* (even if we wouldn't call it one).
- Relationships are increasingly like the 'pure relationship' of equals, where everything has to be negotiated and there are no external reasons for being together.
- We accept that all knowledge is provisional, and may be proved wrong in the future.
- We need *trust* in everyday life and relationships, or we'd be paralysed by thoughts of unhappy possibilities.
- We accept *risks*, and choose possible future actions by anticipating outcomes. The media adds to our awareness of risks.

level, either: we couldn't just say that people spontaneously started to change their minds about how to live. A serious explanation must lie somewhere within the network of macro and micro forces. The changes in marriage, relationships and visible sexuality are associated with the decline of religion and the rise of rationality – social changes brought about by changes in how individuals view life, which in turn stem from social influences and observations. These developments are also a product of changes in the laws relating to marriage and sexuality (macro); but the demand for these changes came from the level of everyday lives (micro). These, in turn, had been affected by the social movements of women's liberation and egalitarianism (macro); which themselves had grown out of dissatisfactions within everyday life (micro). So change stems from a mesh of micro and macro forces.

The mass media is also likely to influence individuals' perceptions of their relationships. Whether in serious drama, or celebrity gossip, the need for 'good stories' would always support an emphasis on change in relationships. Since almost nobody on TV remains happily married for a lifetime – whether we're talking about fictional characters or real-life public figures – we inevitably receive a message that monogamous heterosexual stability is, at best, a rare 'ideal', which few can expect to achieve. We are encouraged to reflect on our relationships in magazines and self-help books (explicitly), and in movies, comedy and drama (implicitly). The news and factual media inform us about the findings of lifestyle research, and actual social changes in family life. This knowledge is then 'reappropriated' by ordinary people, often lending support to non-traditional models of living. Information and ideas from the media do not merely *reflect* the social world, then, but contribute to its shape, and are central to modern reflexivity.

THE REFLEXIVE PROJECT OF THE SELF

If the self is 'made', rather than inherited or just passively static, what form is it in? What is the thing that we make? Giddens says that in the post-traditional order, self-identity becomes a reflexive project – an endeavour that we continuously work and reflect on. We create, maintain and revise a set of biographical narratives – the story of who we are, and how we came to be where we are now.

Self-identity, then, is not a set of traits or observable characteristics. It is a person's own reflexive understanding of their biography. Self-identity has continuity – that is, it cannot easily be completely changed at will – but that continuity is only a product of the person's reflexive beliefs about their own biography (Giddens, 1991: 53). A stable self-identity is based on an account of a person's life, actions and influences which makes sense to themselves, and which can be explained to other people without much difficulty. It 'explains' the past, and is oriented towards an anticipated future. This narrative can always be gently revised, but an individual who tells conspicuously different versions of their biography to friends may be resented and rejected, and acute *embarrassment* is associated with the revelation that one has provided divergent accounts of past events.

> The existential question of self-identity is bound up with the fragile nature of the biography which the individual 'supplies' about herself. A person's identity is not to be found in behaviour, nor – important though this is – in the reactions of others, but in the capacity *to keep a particular narrative going*. The individual's biography, if she is to maintain regular interaction with others in the day-to-day world, cannot be wholly fictive. It must continually integrate events which occur in the external world, and sort them into the ongoing 'story' about the self.
>
> (Giddens, 1991: 54)

A self-identity is not an objective description of what a person is 'like', and we would not expect it to be. Take, for example, a middle-aged man who has recently left his wife and moved in with his new lover, a younger woman. His biography covering these events might say that he was the victim of a failed and ultimately loveless marriage, and that his rational move into this new relationship has brought the happiness which he always sought and, indeed, deserved. His wife's biography, on the other hand, might assert that she did everything she could to make the marriage work, but her pathetic husband was enticed by younger flesh. And the younger woman's account might view her lover as misunderstood, or exciting, or something else. None of these views is 'correct', of course – they are merely interpretations of a situation. Nevertheless, each person's own view is true as far as they are concerned, and they retain pride in their self-identities.

The ability to maintain a satisfactory story, then, is paramount: to believe in oneself, and command the respect of others, we need a strong narrative which can explain everything that has happened and in which, ideally, we play a heroic role. This narrative, whilst usually built upon a set of real events, needs to be creatively and continuously maintained. Pride and self-esteem, Giddens says, are based on 'confidence in the integrity and value of the narrative of self-identity' (1991: 66). *Shame*, meanwhile, stems from anxiety about the adequacy of the narrative on which self-identity is based – a fear that one's story isn't really good enough.

These theories about identity have previously been rather difficult to explore empirically (in the real world). Giddens himself relies mostly on the power of his own philosophical assertions, references to other theorists, and some novels and self-help books. In the Lego identity study which I've mentioned already (Gauntlett, 2007), I sought to make identity issues more tangible – literally – by asking 79 diverse individuals to build metaphorical *models* of their identities in Lego (the full process is outlined in Chapter 11). The study found that the participants did indeed have a sense of personal identity as a story – a true story, as far as they were concerned, although they knew that others might see the same story differently. In particular, they went somewhat further than Giddens, as we will see later, seeing their own story in the light of the multitude of other stories which we encounter in everyday life (such as movies, soaps, news, anecdotes and adverts). Rather than the theory of the 'reflexive project of the self' being an academic abstraction, the study suggested that it was a commonly accepted part of everyday life (although, of course, everyone understood it in their own way, and would not use Giddens's terminology as such).

ROMANTIC NARRATIVES

The notion of constructed biographies is, again, all very *modern*. Giddens links the rise of the narrative of the self with the emergence of romantic love. Passion and sex have, of course, been around for a very long time, but the discourse of romantic love is said to have developed from the late eighteenth century. 'Romantic love introduced the idea of a narrative into an individual's life', Giddens says (1992: 39) – a story about two individuals with little connection to wider social processes. He connects this development with the simultaneous emergence of the novel – a relatively early form of mass media, suggesting ideal (or less than ideal) romantic life narratives. These stories did not construct love as a partnership of equals, of course – instead, women were associated with a world of femininity and motherhood which was supposedly unknowable to men. Nevertheless, the female protagonists were usually independent and spirited. The masculine world, meanwhile, was detached from the domestic sphere, both emotionally and physically, and involved a decisive sense of purpose in the outside world.

Whilst passionate affairs might come and go rather unpredictably, the more long-term and future-oriented narrative of romantic love created a 'shared history' which made sense of two lives and gave their relationship an important and recognised role. The rise of this 'mutual narrative biography' led individuals to construct accounts of their lives, so that, even if the relationship with their partner went awry, a story still had to be maintained.

And so now the biography of the self has taken on a life of its own, encouraged by a range of narratives suggested by popular media. Feature films, for example, often include the story of two people who are 'destined' to be together – they have found 'the one', and are happily united as the credits roll. Soap operas, on the other hand, almost always feature characters who move from one relationship to another, and sometimes even back again, because of the demands of the continuous serial form. Lifestyle magazines, as we will see in Chapters 8 and 9, have yet another vocabulary for relationships, which places a heavy emphasis on sexual fulfilment. These sources suggest a (potentially confusing) mix of ways of considering oneself and one's relationships.

THE REFLEXIVE SELF AND SEXUALITY

Freud famously argued that society sought to repress sexuality. Foucault later suggested that sexuality was not repressed but was more of a social obsession – any efforts to 'repress' sex reflected a fascination with it, and would always create even more awareness and talk about it. (More on this in the next chapter.) But Giddens argues that neither of these views is particularly satisfactory. His own argument is that during the nineteenth and twentieth centuries, sexual behaviour became 'hidden away' not because of prurience, but because it was being connected to the newly emergent sphere of intimate relationships – partnerships characterised by love and trust (which, we are told, were not common features of marriages in earlier times). 'Sexual development and sexual satisfaction henceforth became bound to the reflexive project of the self,' Giddens says (1991: 164). This is really a view shared with Foucault, although Giddens's emphasis here is more on the recent development of intimate relationship discourses which are fitted into autobiographical narratives (whereas Foucault's emphasis is more on discourses of the individual sexual body).

With sexuality and sexual identity being regarded, in modern societies, as so central to self-identity, issues in this area take on a profound level of importance. The question of one's sexual orientation, for instance, is of much more fundamental concern to us than taste in music or preference for certain kinds of foods. To have a 'problem' in the sexual department can lead people to declare that they no longer feel like a complete man or woman. And of course, this is heightened because sexual feelings are the subject matter of a huge number of songs, films, books, dramas and magazine articles. Other topics of everyday concern, such as food, shopping, pollution, work and illness, do not feature in anything like as many popular media products.

CONSUMERISM AND IDENTITY

Modernity does not, of course, offer up an unendingly diverse set of identities for citizens, newly freed from the chains of tradition, to step into. Many social expectations remain – although these are perhaps the remnants of the traditions which modernity is gradually shrugging off. But in addition, there is *capitalism*. Here, think not of the dirty factories we associate with Marx's critique, but of fashion and glamour, must-have toys, blockbusting bands and movies, fine foods and nice houses. As Giddens puts it, 'Modernity opens up the project of the self, but under conditions strongly influenced by the standardising effects of commodity capitalism' (1991: 196). The stuff we can buy to 'express' ourselves inevitably has an impact upon the project of the self.

Advertising promotes the idea that products will help us to accent our *individuality*, but of course the market only offers us a certain range of goods. The project of the self is redirected, by the corporate world, into a set of shopping opportunities. Giddens sees this as a corruption of, and a threat to, the true quest for self. At the same time, he notes that people will react *creatively* to commodification – they will not be compelled to accept any particular product in one specific way. Nevertheless, he says that the reflexive project of the self 'is in some part necessarily a struggle against commodified influences' (1991: 200), since the identities which are directly 'sold' to us are, by their very nature, similar to the fixed identities of tradition, which the reflexive citizen will question.

LIFESTYLE

Consumerism is one of the clearest ways in which we develop and project a *lifestyle*. Again, this is a feature of the post-traditional era: since social roles are no longer handed to us by society, we have to make choices – although the options are not, of course, unlimited. 'Lifestyle choices' may sound like a luxury of the more affluent classes, but Giddens asserts that everyone in modern society has to select a lifestyle, although different groups will have different possibilities (and wealth would certainly seem to increase the range of options). 'Lifestyle' is not only about fancy jobs and conspicuous consumption, though; the term applies to wider choices, behaviours and (to greater or lesser degrees) attitudes and beliefs.

Lifestyles could be said to be like ready-made templates for a narrative of self. But the choice of one lifestyle does not predict any particular type of life story. So a lifestyle is more like a *genre*: whilst movie directors can choose to make a romance, or a western, or a horror story, we – as 'directors' of our own life narratives – can choose a metropolitan or a rural lifestyle, a lifestyle focused on success in work, or one centred on clubbing, sport, romance, or sexual conquests. The best-known lifestyle template must be that of the 'yuppie', perhaps because this model emerged in the 1980s as the first radically post-traditional professional identity, based on the individualistic desire to amass personal wealth. This lifestyle stemmed from particular occupations, but also came complete with a handy set of accessories by which would-be yuppies could identify themselves: mobile phone, braces and hair gel (for men), and a conspicuous designer wardrobe. Identifiable yuppie apartments made it easy to decide where to live, and yuppie wine bars gave them somewhere to go in the evening. (Yuppies were effectively satirised by Brett Easton Ellis in *American Psycho* (1991) – and by Mary Harron in the film of the novel (2000) – in which the protagonist finds he can get away with satisfying any desire, including killing people, because no-one will challenge his smooth designer-label identity.)

Lifestyle choices, then, can give our personal narratives an identifiable shape, linking us to communities of people who are 'like us' – or people who, at least, have made similar choices. The behaviour associated with our chosen lifestyle will likely have practical value in itself, but is also a visible expression of a certain narrative of self-identity.

The choices which we make in modern society may be affected by the weight of tradition on the one hand, and a sense of relative freedom on the other. Everyday choices about what to eat, what to wear, who to socialise with, are all decisions which position ourselves as one kind of person and not another. And as Giddens says, 'The more post-traditional the settings in which an individual moves, the more lifestyle concerns the very core of self-identity, its making and remaking' (1991: 81).

An identity fitted into a lifestyle is not entirely free-floating. A lifestyle is a rather orderly container for identity, each type coming with certain expectations, so that particular actions would be seen as 'out of character' with it (Giddens, 1991: 82). However, an individual might have more than one 'lifestyle', each one reserved for certain audiences. Giddens calls these '*lifestyle sectors*' – aspects of lifestyle that go with work, or home, or other relationships.

The importance of the media in propagating many modern lifestyles should be obvious. Whilst some ways of life – rural farming lifestyles, for instance – are not reflected too often on television, and will mostly be passed on by more direct means, ideas about other less traditional ways of life will be disseminated by the media – *alongside* everyday experience, of course. For example:

• A young person interested in dance music and clubbing might 'learn' about this scene first of all from the glossy dance music magazines; then real-life experience might lead this view to be adapted or replaced – but the magazines would still exert an influence over associations of the lifestyle with glamour, or drugs, or whatever.

- A young schoolteacher's idea of what it means to be a teacher will mostly be based on their real-life training, experience and observation – not on something they've seen in some TV drama about teachers. Nevertheless, a meaningful part of their ideal notion of what a teacher *could* or *should* be like may be based on 'inspirational' films or dramas about teachers such as *Dead Poets Society* (1989), *Wonder Boys* (2000) or *Freedom Writers* (2007).
- People who have moved into a social group which they were previously unfamiliar with – such as a working-class woman who suddenly lands a job on Wall Street – may (initially, at least) try to acquire some of the personal styles, and possessions, which the media typically associates with them.

The range of lifestyles – or lifestyle *ideals* – offered by the media may be limited, but at the same time it is usually broader than those we would expect to just 'bump into' in everyday life. So the media in modernity offers possibilities and celebrates diversity, but also offers narrow interpretations of certain roles or lifestyles – depending where you look.

THE BODY, AGENCY AND IDENTITY

Just as the self has become malleable in late modernity, so too has the body. No longer do we feel that the body is a more or less disappointing 'given' – instead, the body is the outer expression of our self, to be improved and worked upon; the body has, in the words of Giddens, become 'reflexively mobilized' – thrown into the expanding sphere of personal attributes which we are required to think about and control.

In *The Presentation of Self in Everyday Life*, Erving Goffman (1959) wrote about 'impression management' as the means by which a person may adjust their facial expressions, posture or clothing to suit a particular situation. In every interaction with another person or group, each of us routinely fosters more or less of an illusion (which may or may not reflect how we 'really' feel) designed to give the 'right impression' to our 'audience'. Goffman's argument should apply to human interactions at any point in history – even cavemen must have adjusted their faces and apparel to encourage feelings of affection, admiration or fear, in those they met.

So in what way is the 'reflexive mobilization' of the body a new feature of late modernity? Giddens would suggest that it is to do with the ways in which all aspects of the body are now 'up for grabs' to a previously unheard-of extent. At the grandest of extremes, operations can now make people taller, slimmer and bustier. Even sex can be changed. On a more commonplace level, we assume that anyone these days can adopt a regime which will make them look more slim, or athletic, or muscular. Whilst we have to admit that different regimes of the body have existed for thousands of years, in different forms, the diversity of the different bodily manipulations available today – and in particular the amount of *thought* we put into these regimes – may be unique. Certainly the level of media coverage of these possibilities, in magazines and guidebooks, must be unprecedented. As we will see in Chapters 8 and 9, almost all lifestyle magazines for both women and men contain advice on how readers can change their appearance so that they can 'feel good' personally, and be more attractive to others.

Curiously, Giddens is unhappy with Foucault's account of the body and how we present ourselves in society. Foucault 'cannot analyse the relation between body and agency' – the relationship between our outer display and our inner consciousness – 'since to all intents and purposes he equates the two' (Giddens, 1991: 57). In other words, since Foucault sees people as all 'surface' – with no true 'inner self' (that's nothing but discourse, Foucault suggests, all that talk about your inner self) – he is unable to conceive of an inner consciousness driving the external presentations of self. For Foucault, Giddens complains, 'the body plus power equals agency. But this idea will not do, and appears unsophisticated when placed alongside the standpoint developed prior to Foucault by Merleau-Ponty, and contemporaneously by Goffman' (ibid.).

It's funny that Giddens suggests that Goffman is more sophisticated than Foucault, because everybody normally thinks of Foucault as being at the height of sophistication and complexity, whereas Goffman's theatrical metaphor for everyday life – 'all the world's a stage', basically, with everybody presenting a performance for their various audiences – is simple and almost obvious (which doesn't mean it's actually wrong, of course). Foucault's argument is relatively difficult to pin down, whereas Goffman presents his case clearly and in detail, with lots of well-observed examples. Giddens is unimpressed by the challenging vagueness of Foucault and (refreshingly, perhaps?) plumps for the down-to-earth sociological reportage of Goffman.

The problem with *The Presentation of Self in Everyday Life*, though, is that it is very difficult to see what might lie *behind* all of the displays of self. Apart from the idea of the inner self being basically a cynical actor who wants to get on comfortably with everyone, in any given situation, Goffman doesn't give us much to go on. One is reminded, again, of Bret Easton Ellis's *American Psycho* (1991), where the narrator of the title, Patrick Bateman, says:

> There is an idea of a Patrick Bateman, some kind of abstraction, but there is no real me, only an entity, something illusory, and though I can hide my cold gaze and you can shake my hand and feel flesh gripping yours and maybe you can even sense our lifestyles are probably comparable: *I simply am not there.* . . . I am a noncontingent human being. . . . But even after admitting this – and I have, countless times, in just about every act I've committed – and coming face-to-face with these truths, there is no catharsis. I gain no deeper knowledge about myself, no new understanding can be extracted from my telling.
>
> (1991: 376–377)

Bateman is troubled by the apparent lack of a coherent 'self' at his core – 'Is evil something you are? Or is it something you do?' he wonders (ibid.) – and, like the reader of Goffman, is aware of his own successful performances, but doesn't know where any of them come from. Since Giddens sees people, in a rather 'common sense' way, as thoughtful actors making choices, he is able to skip past this problem.

THE TRANSFORMATION OF INTIMACY

In the post-traditional society, as mentioned above, relationships are entered into for the mutual satisfaction of emotional needs – unlike in the marriages of traditional cultures, which (we are told) were primarily for economic and symbolic convenience. Even if love was an element of such a marriage, the partnership would not be disbanded just because one or both parties felt that it was not bringing them complete fulfilment. By contrast, post-traditional relationships are consciously constructed, analysed, or broken up, according to how the participants are feeling. This is what Giddens calls *the transformation of intimacy*, in which an intimate, democratic partnership of two equal 'soulmates' becomes important for members of modern society. The traditional idea of 'marriage for life' is here replaced with the 'pure relationship', in which communication between equal partners (of whatever sex) ensures the couple are always oriented towards mutual satisfaction. The pure relationship is typical of reflexive modernity, where people's actions are oriented towards the achievement of personal satisfaction. Lest this seem extreme, Giddens admits (1998: 124) that the pure relationship is an 'ideal type', and that in real life today there is still a strong pull of tradition, as well as a consideration for the feelings of others.

Giddens is interested in sexuality and intimacy *within* – importantly – the contexts of modern everyday life. He criticises Foucault, for example, for putting too much emphasis on sexuality, while failing to come up with adequate accounts of gender, romantic love and the family (Giddens, 1992: 24), all of which are linked with sexuality in different ways. He also suggests that Foucault isn't that great on sexuality either. The Frenchman's account doesn't really explain the explosion in sexual awareness within the past century, for example: how did we get from the dry texts written and studied by a small number of male doctors at the start of the twentieth century, to the mass appeal of sizzling sex specials in popular magazines at the start of the tewnty-first? Giddens, in typically sensible and sociological mode, points to the arrival of effective contraception as an important turning-point: once sex was separated from reproduction, sexual pleasure and variety could come to the fore. Reliable birth control paved the way for the 'sexual revolution', women's liberation and the emergence of 'plastic sexuality' – sexuality you can play with.

Whilst contraception (in the days before AIDS) had a direct impact on heterosexual sex, it had a knock-on effect on homosexual lives and sexuality generally, as the idea of sexual pleasure in society became more open and less riddled with anxiety. Furthermore, although in traditional societies the important function of reproduction was necessarily focused on heterosexual couples, in more modern times, once reproduction had come under human control, heterosexuality lost its primacy. This, Giddens suggests, is part of the long march of modernity; more and more areas of life come under social control, and so choice and diversity may prosper. (This may be optimistic, and Giddens admits that a point of blithe sexual diversity has not yet been reached – lesbians and gay men still face prejudice, abuse and violence, generally from those people we rightly call 'unreconstructed'.)

The media has continually reflected – and may have partly led – the changing status of different sexual activities, attitudes and sexualities, spreading awareness of different expectations, and the existence of diversity. The private world of sex, however hidden or visible it had been at different points in the past, has certainly been thrown into the popular public domain in the past two or three decades, by the mass media, in a way which is quite unprecedented. Formal studies of the changing face of sexuality, alongside the representations of sexuality in films, magazines, news reports, pop videos, websites, soap operas and so on, all form part of what Giddens calls the *institutional reflexivity* regarding sex – society talking to itself about sexuality. This greater openness about sex has meant that there is a greater awareness of sexual skills, techniques and possibilities; and as examples of 'good sex' and 'bad sex' become more conspicuous, so sexual performance becomes more central to relationships overall, and a factor in whether they thrive or fail. Consequently, magazines, books and TV shows contain more sex advice than ever before. Even magazines for men, which were previously happy to admire women's bodies and assume that the male readers would know how to show the women a good time, are now full of advice for men on how they can impress women in and out of the bedroom (see Chapter 8).

SELF-HELP, POPULAR CULTURE AND THE IDEAL SELF

Self-help books are another source of lifestyle information in the modern world. These populist guides would usually be sneered at by academics, but Giddens has studied them to gain some insight into the more popular ways in which modern living is discussed. (I will be discussing self-help books, too, in Chapter 10.) In one such book, *Self-Therapy* by Janette Rainwater (1989), Giddens finds support for his idea that therapy is basically about helping individuals to sort out a strong self-identity based on a coherent and fully understood narrative of the self: a thoroughly modern and reflex-ive 'methodology of life-planning' (Giddens, 1991: 180). But the language of self-help offers new elements, too, such as 'being true to oneself', which means that the reader has to construct an ideal self which they can then try to be 'true' to. Self-help books are typically about self-actualisation (fulfill-ing personal potential), and so the self, and the narrative of the self, then has to be directed towards particular *goals* which, of course, have to be selected. So, from self-help books we acquire a picture of the self as based on a quest for particular achievements, seeking happiness, and trying to put together a narrative in which obstacles are overcome and fulfilment is ulti-mately reached.

Self-help books, of course, are only the most explicit purveyors of life advice. Many other forms of popular media offer images of what good rela-tionships look like, what constitutes attractiveness, and what makes life worth living. Characters in films usually have clear goals, which we are expected to identify with. Magazines offer specific advice on how to impress and succeed. Game shows, as well as some dramas, equate wealth with hap-piness (although the dramatic cliché that money brings misery is also popular). If we all have an 'ideal self' which is the aspirational heart of self-identity, and which informs our construction of narratives of self-identity, then the mass media must surely play a part in its development in modern societies. Therefore we will consider actual media examples and their relationship with the construction of self-identity in Chapters 8, 9 and 10.

STORY STRUCTURES

Another influence of the media might be found not in the *content* of stories, but in the promotion of coherent stories themselves. We come to expect strong, clear narratives, where the motivations of different characters can be identified. For example, Giddens says of soap operas: 'The form is what matters rather than the content; in these stories one gains a sense of reflexive control over life circumstances, a feeling of a coherent narrative which is a reassuring balance to difficulties in sustaining the narrative of the self in actual social situations' (Giddens, 1991: 199).

In his book *Story*, Robert McKee (1999) sets out a template for the structure of a satisfying mainstream movie. Maybe this will show us the archetypal story which people connect with, and which they would want to live their own lives by? The point of the book is not to tell screenwriters what their movies should be *about*, but describes the general way in which a well-told story should unfold. The model can be applied to any story, from a domestic period drama to a sci-fi action thriller. Whilst McKee welcomes all kinds of variations, he suggests that the 'classic' kind of story involves an initially reluctant protagonist who is drawn into a world of challenges, faces various crises, gets to a point where all seems lost, but ultimately arrives at a climax (beginning 20 minutes before the end, please) where the hero and/or the situation is changed forever. We can see that this is the basic structure of many popular movies, old and new, from *The Battleship Potemkin* (1925) and *The Wizard of Oz* (1939) to *Music and Lyrics* (2007) and *Hot Fuzz* (2007). Whether you have Ioan Gruffudd as bendy-limbed Mr Fantastic in *Fantastic Four: Rise of the Silver Surfer* (2007) or Ioan Gruffudd as anti-slavery campaigner William Wilberforce in *Amazing Grace* (2007), this story structure remains present and correct.

In a book from the same screenwriting shelf, *The Writer's Journey*, Hollywood 'story consultant' Christopher Vogler (1999) draws on ancient and supposedly 'universal' myths and archetypes to suggest a rather more precise sequence of elements which should make a successful film – one which is able to touch hearts around the world. The 'Hero's Journey' described by Vogler, drawing upon the work of mythologist Joseph Campbell, comes in 12 stages. A hero is introduced in their everyday environment (the 'ordinary world'), where they receive a 'call to adventure', which is refused. Encouraged by a mentor, however, they enter the 'special world' of the story, and encounter tests, allies and enemies. The hero approaches the heart of the story, and has to survive a traumatic (ideally, life-threatening) ordeal. They get a reward, but are pursued on 'the road back' to the ordinary world. Finally the hero experiences a transformative 'resurrection', and returns with a prize which will benefit the ordinary world.

Although this may look like a very prescriptive formula, Vogler insists that there is no fixed order for these elements, and that they can be applied to any kind of story. Vogler is not providing a *new* recipe for shaping stories, but rather feels that he is distilling the story elements which have been present in many super-popular stories in the past, from ancient myths and fairy tales to the *Star Wars* saga (1977–2005) and almost every other blockbuster.

But what do these Hollywood story tips have to do with our discussion? Both Robert McKee and Christopher Vogler consider the connections between popular stories and everyday life to be strong. McKee suggests that 'our appetite for story is a reflection of the profound human need to grasp the patterns of living, not merely as an intellectual exercise, but within a very personal, emotional experience' (1999: 12). He quotes Kenneth Burke's assertion that stories are 'equipment for living'. Vogler goes even further:

> I came looking for the design principles of storytelling, but on the road I found something more; a set of principles for living. I came to believe that the Hero's Journey is nothing less than a handbook for life, a complete instruction manual in the art of being human.
>
> (1999: ix)

The key story elements described by the two authors do not appear as a result of coincidence or chance. Indeed, George Lucas has acknowledged the influence of Joseph Campbell's studies of mythology upon the *Star Wars* plots, and director James Cameron accounted for the phenomenal international success of his *Titanic* (1997) by noting that it 'intentionally incorporates universals of human experience that are timeless ... By dealing in archetypes, the film touches people in all cultures and of all ages' (quoted in Vogler, 1999: 243).

Whether truly 'universal' or not, these 'classic' story structures and character types do certainly seem to be appealing and meaningful to many people around the world. They are stories which we can relate to, and which we enjoy. The international success of certain stories seems to confirm this – for instance, the examples we discussed in Chapter 4, *Ugly Betty* (2006–) and the *Spider-Man* movie series (2001, 2004, 2007), have been incredibly successful in diverse countries around the world, presumably because they tell of a good 'everyman'/'everywoman' kind of character who struggles with extraordinarily testing situations but is eventually victorious. It seems likely, then – to return to the Giddens terminology – that we would borrow from these stories when shaping our narratives of the self.

As mentioned above (p. 109), the Lego identity study (Gauntlett, 2007) found that individuals do indeed use story frames in their understanding of their own lives. The analysis of the Lego identity models drew upon the work of French philosopher Paul Ricoeur, who argued that narratives provide their audiences with the opportunity to consider ethical questions. Ricoeur suggests that literature – which we can take to mean all kinds of fictional narrative – is 'a vast laboratory for thought experiments in which the resources of variation encompassed by narrative identity are put to the test of narration' (1992: 148). In other words, all possible ways of living life are played out in the stories that are told in a culture, and we learn from stories of greed, lust, hate, love, kindness and heroism, and develop our own narrative of self in relation to these templates. Popular media obviously provides us with many such narratives every day, including television drama and soaps, movies, comics, video games, and even the 'true' narratives about celebrities and reality TV stars which appear across a range of media. Such narratives give people the chance to think about what constitutes a 'good life' or a desirable identity. The Lego study found that individuals sought to construct a story of identity – often building on the common narrative frame of a *journey* – which was unified and drew in other elements of the story-frames suggested by popular media (Gauntlett, 2007: 194–195; and see Chapter 11).

THE ANTI-GIDDENS: STJEPAN MEŠTROVIĆ

Much of the appeal of Giddens's work rests on his belief in people's own capacities – he sees people as rational agents, in control of their lives, who have the ability to evaluate received ideas and creatively bring shape to their own lives. I should perhaps note, or admit, that – although I happened not to have studied Giddens properly until preparing the first edition of this book – my own work has also always favoured this approach. For example, in previous books – based on empirical research – I have emphasised the ability of people to resist media messages (Gauntlett, 1995, 1997, 2005, Gauntlett and Hill, 1999), the ability of young people to make their own creative media texts (1997), the ability of audiences to make television programmes relevant to their own lives (Gauntlett and Hill, 1999) and the ability of ordinary people to make expressive websites (Gauntlett, 2000; Gauntlett and Horsley, 2004). It seems preferable to assume that people are thoughtful and creative beings, in control of their own lives – not least of all because that is how most people surely see themselves. A sociology which disagrees with this view of people, and claims to 'know better', would seem to be almost inhuman.

Here, then, it is instructive to look at Stjepan Meštrović's critical polemic, *Anthony Giddens: The Last Modernist* (1998). The author implies that it is Giddens who is inhuman because his model of social life is far too rational, and excludes emotions and sentiment. The continuing popularity of nationalism, leading to violence and genocide, in many parts of the world, shows that people do not act on a purely rational basis. Nationalism, Meštrović suggests, is just one of many unruly and irrational emotions which people harbour – and which have deadly consequences – and which Giddens's model of the sophisticated, thoughtful, rational actor is unable to explain.

> [Giddens's] glib optimism, popular sociology rhetoric, and shallow treatment of theory resonate with the current climate of feel-good-optimistic ideology in sociology ... Giddens and many other mainstream sociologists have been singing a merry tune of global democratisation even as genocide raged in Bosnia, Russians expressed a nostalgia for Communism, the European Community began unravelling almost as soon as it was formed, and 'ethnic cleansing' became a metaphor for our times.
>
> (Meštrović, 1998: 4–5)

Meštrović suggests that Giddens offers an account of social life which is appealing to comfortable, middle-class Western sociologists, but which is weak when faced with the plight of the poor and the dispossessed. Giddens's more recent, more directly 'political' books (e.g. 1999, 2000, 2006, 2007) show awareness of, and discomfort about, ethnic conflicts and social problems, but Meštrović would no doubt say that his solutions are simplistic, optimistic and unconvincing.

A judgement about whether Giddens or Meštrović are right or wrong about this may ultimately rest on whether one agrees with Giddens's hope for optimism or Meštrović's inclination towards pessimism. Meštrović makes the surprising mistake of confusing his own interpretation of modernity with Giddens's use of the term. Meštrović understands modernity in the usual sociological way, as the time following the Enlightenment, which means we have been living under modernity for a couple of centuries at least. But Giddens, as we have seen, uses the term rather differently as part of his opposition between tradition and modernity, where tradition still plays a (decreasing) role in contemporary society. So Meštrović thinks that

Giddens's account of modernity is flawed because it cannot account for irrational nationalist feelings, but actually Giddens is fine on this point because he wouldn't count those nationalist sentiments as part of modernity anyway – they are remnants of tradition which have not yet been discarded. (We could also note that nationalists no doubt feel themselves to be rational, and will have rational-sounding arguments to support their views.) So Giddens does have grounds for optimism, on his own terms, because we can see that tradition is in decline and that modernity is a more tolerant way of living. The kinds of oppression that concern Meštrović, whether they stem from tradition, and/or irrational thought, should cease to occur as rational modernity gets an even firmer grip.

Meštrović has no sympathy for this rational model, however. 'Giddens's agent is all mind and no heart', he says (1998: 78). 'Giddens's knowledgeable human agent is ultimately a rationalist, a modernist caricature of what it means to be human' (ibid.: 80). The discussion of how people can creatively engage with their emotional lives through contemporary resources such as self-help books and other media, in *The Transformation of Intimacy* (Giddens, 1992), had seemed to me to be a liberating analysis of modern living. But for Meštrović it is quite the opposite:

> Previously, modernists got as far as Fordism and the assembly line in applying the machine model to social life. Giddens goes a step further: in *The Transformation of Intimacy* and other works, he advocates the self-diagnosis of emotional problems and the remedy to such problems in much the same manner that one would fix a faulty carburettor.
>
> (Meštrović, 1998: 7)

Whilst the machine analogy seems to be an effective put-down, it isn't really clear what is wrong with the idea that people can try to heal their own affairs of the heart. Meštrović clearly reads Giddens as unemotional and 'heartless', but I find Giddens to be refreshingly willing to consider emotions and feelings within his sociology. The 'pure relationship', for example, could cynically be seen as a selfish and rational approach to partnerships, where a person stays attached to another only when it is rewarding to do so. But on the other hand, it is a model concerned with people following their *feelings*, staying together if they are in love, or seeking an alternative if they are not – an honest, emotional approach.

Meštrović rejects Giddens's belief that people typically know what they are doing, and can account for their actions, asserting instead that people 'most of the time function as if they were on auto-pilot' (ibid.: 34). Both scholars could, no doubt, point to bits of empirical evidence which appear to back up their claims; so it becomes a question of taste. Personally, I prefer Giddens's model of the thoughtful, self-aware modern individual, to Meštrović's idea of the unreflexive conformist. Nevertheless, readers who feel seduced by Giddens's upbeat sociology – dismissed as 'a processed "happy meal" of social theory' by Meštrović (ibid.: 212) – should find it useful to at least consider the latter's arguments.

SUMMARY

In this chapter we saw that with the decline of traditions, identities in general – including gender and sexual identities – have become more diverse and malleable. Although sometimes limited by vestiges of tradition, modern lives are less predictable and fixed than they were for previous generations, and identities today are more 'up for grabs' than ever before. Everyone has to choose a way of living – although some people feel more enabled to make more unusual choices than others. The mass media suggests lifestyles, forms of self-presentation and ways to find happiness (which may or may not be illusory). To interpret the choices we have made, individuals construct a narrative of the self, which gives some order to our complex lives. This narrative will also be influenced by perspectives which we have adopted from the media. Our relationship with our bodies, our sexual partners and our own emotional needs, will all also be influenced by media representations, but (of course) in complex ways which will be swayed and modified by our social experiences and interactions.

FURTHER READING

Conversations with Anthony Giddens: Making Sense of Modernity (Giddens and Pierson, 1998) is a very readable introduction to Giddens's ideas on self-identity and modernity, as well as other matters. The most important book on these issues is *Modernity and Self-Identity* (Giddens, 1991), which offers an excellent detailed discussion, whilst *The Transformation of Intimacy* (Giddens, 1992) further develops some of those ideas. Ulrich Beck and Elisabeth Beck-Gernsheim have pursued related interests in their book *Individualization* (2002).

There are two good and readable introductions to Giddens: *Anthony Giddens and Modern Social Theory* by Kenneth Tucker (1998) and *Anthony Giddens: An Introduction to a Social Theorist* by Lars Bo Kaspersen (2000). See also *Theorising Modernity: Reflexivity,*

Environment and Identity in Giddens' Social Theory edited by O'Brien *et al.* (1999) and *The Contemporary Giddens: Social Theory in a Globalizing Age* edited by Bryant and Jary (2001).

Those interested in seeing what happens when Lord Giddens gets to grips with the nitty-gritty of everyday politics and policy can get an overview of his ideas in *Over to You, Mr Brown: How Labour Can Win Again* (2007).

Chapter 6

MICHEL FOUCAULT
Discourses and lifestyles

MICHEL FOUCAULT IS an elusive figure. Not in the literal, physical sense – he was buried in Vendeuvre, France, in 1984, after a shortish life of 57 years. And not in the sense that nobody talks about him – his influence in sociology, cultural studies, politics and literature has been enormous, and he was clearly one of the most-discussed scholars of the twentieth century. But Foucault's arguments can't really be reduced to a clear-cut list of assertions; the power of Foucault's work stems more from the way he suggests we look at things – which itself is often more implicit than explicit. In this chapter I will attempt to give a relatively straightforward introduction to Foucault's ideas about the self, identity and sexuality, and show how these, and his interest in 'modes of living', can help to develop our understanding of identities and the media in modern society.

The study of Foucault's thought is made additionally difficult because his ideas developed and changed over time. This means that it's best to understand his ideas as different (but related) bodies of thought associated with each of his different major publications. Thus the Foucault who wrote *Madness and Civilisation* (1961 in France) did not have quite the same set of ideas as the Foucault who wrote *The Archaeology of Knowledge* (1969 originally); and the Foucault who wrote *The History of Sexuality* (1976–84) was thinking something rather different again. It's important to know this, or else you get confused by people talking about an era of Foucault that's different to the one you'd just been thinking about. Of course, there's nothing wrong with Foucault changing his approach; in a 1982 interview, he remarked that 'When people say, "Well, you thought this a few years ago and now you say something else," my answer is … [laughs] "Well, do you think I have worked like that all those years to say the same thing and not to be changed?"' (2000: 131). This attitude to his own work fits well with his theoretical approach – that knowledge should transform the self. When asked in another 1982 interview if he was a philosopher, historian, structuralist or Marxist, Foucault replied 'I don't feel that it is necessary to know exactly what I am. The main interest in life and work is to become someone else that you were not in the beginning' (Martin, 1988: 9).

If we can be a little simplistic, though, we can divide the work broadly into an earlier and a later phase. In his earlier studies, Foucault was concerned with the ways in which the discourses of institutions, and their formally recognised 'experts', worked to constrain certain groups – limiting their opportunities by promoting certain views about them. (For 'discourses', read 'ways of speaking and thinking' about something.) The clearest example of this is in his first book *Madness and Civilisation*, where Foucault shows how the discourses of psychiatrists, from the seventeenth century to the start of the nineteenth, served to define and confine those people seen as mad. Other works such as *The Birth of the Clinic* (1963) also look, albeit somewhat more obliquely, at how historical changes in the 'expert' understanding of the human body had effects on the treatment of people by the state and its agents.

In his later works, on the other hand, Foucault shifted emphasis away from the ways that external forces and discourses might constrain people, towards a focus on how discourses might bring people to *police themselves*. At the turning point between these approaches was *Discipline and Punish* (1975), which might have originally been about how prisoners and criminals were defined by experts and institutions, but also came to describe how the disciplines and surveillance of prisoners affected their own behaviour. Subsequently, *The History of Sexuality* (1998) was concerned with ways in which social constructions of sexuality were internalised by people, leading them to see sexuality as the (possibly shameful) 'truth' about themselves, at the core of identity. Sexuality then did not have to be actively regulated by the state, as such, because people would be very careful to monitor their own behaviour themselves.

Foucault's emphasis changed, then, from a world constructed from *without* – external discourses imposed on people – to a world constructed from *within* – the individual's own dynamic adaptation to their surroundings. Note that the wider social environment remains significant; but Foucault had, perhaps, become more interested in people's subjective responses to it, both as internalised constraint, and more creative resistance.

FOUCAULT'S PARIS

Paris offers a range of treats for the discerning follower of Foucault. At www.theory.org.uk/foucault, there is an illustrated *Foucault's Paris* walking tour, which takes tourists to several key Foucault locations. Starting on the south side, at the Bibliothèque du Saulchoir – where the philosopher worked on volumes II and III of the *History of Sexuality* during the last five years of his life – the walk takes in various cafes which he 'probably' visited; the École Normale Supérieure where Foucault both studied and taught; and the Collège de France, where Foucault was elected to a special Chair in the 'History of Systems of Thought' in 1969. It would be fitting to end the tour at Foucault's grave, but that's 200 kilometres away in Normandy.

Figure 6.1   Square Michel Foucault in Paris

In general the Foucault tourism opportunities have been poorly exploited by the French; *Foucault's Paris* suggests they should get top bald actor Patrick Stewart to record highlights of Foucault's works to CD for sale in a nice *Boutique de Foucault* somewhere near the Eiffel Tower.

FOUCAULT ON POWER

To understand why Foucault's model of power caught the attention of many scholars and activists, it helps considerably to remind ourselves of *what had come before*. Prior to Foucault, power was largely seen as a 'thing' which was 'held' by certain dominant groups. For Marxists, and people on the Left generally, power was seen as something held by the dominant class, the bosses, the owners of the means of production. The workers, in this system, were powerless, because in order to earn money to live they had to surrender to their exploitation by the dominant class. For feminists, it was men in patriarchal society who had the power; women were the powerless.

Foucault's understanding of power is quite different. For Foucault, power is not an asset which a person can *have*; rather, power is something *exercised* within interactions. Power *flows through* relationships, or networks of relationships. You couldn't really say that someone was powerful, *per se*, then; but you could say that they frequently found themselves in a powerful position, or had many opportunities to exercise power.

Foucault's clearest description of power occurs in *The History of Sexuality, Volume One: The Will to Knowledge* [1976: pt 4, ch. 2]. Here he says:

> Power is everywhere; not because it embraces everything, but because it comes from everywhere ... Power is not an institution, and not a structure; neither is it a certain strength we are endowed with; it is the name that one attributes to a complex strategical situation in a particular society.
>
> (1998: 93)

This doesn't mean that everybody has equal access to power, though. Foucault falls back on talk of 'force relations' as the general social background of inequality against which all the power interactions are played out. Power, he says, 'is the moving substrate of force relations which, by virtue of their inequality, constantly engender states of power, but the latter are always local and unstable' (1998: 93). This part of the argument seems a little poorly defined – is Foucault trying to sneak back the old idea of power, here, by re-introducing it as 'force relations'? He explains it better elsewhere (Foucault, 2000: 283) when he says that we may find 'states of domination' where power relations have become so entrenched that they can seem entirely one-sided and unchangeable. Nevertheless, Foucault says, such situations can be resisted and changed. The central point remains: power simply cannot be *held* by one group; power is everywhere and plays a role in all relationships and interactions (though this may be to a large or small extent in each case). Power does not exist outside of social relationships; it's exactly *within* these relationships that power comes into play. So it *is* a very different model of power.

But when I was first introduced to this idea, as a student, it was hard to see its value. If power is everywhere, doesn't that mean we can hardly talk about it – or, perhaps, that there's nothing to talk about? And with power slipping and sliding all over the place, it was difficult to see either what this really meant, or what the implications would be.

This view of power also, unsurprisingly, upset those who were attached to the previous model. To see power as a *force* held by a dominant group – as in the traditional view – is valuable, from a political point of view, because it highlights the inequality between the dominant people and everybody else, and it emphasises exploitation. Sometimes it was hard to see what it really *meant*, though, and it was always based on a one-dimensional definition of power. For example, it would seem clear-cut to say that your boss at a workplace has more power than you – they can tell you what to do, and they can even sack you. (The boss can exercise power due to *institutional* arrangements of power, that can be called upon and used.) So that's power, and this simple case alone seems to suggest that the traditional left-wing view – that power is held by bosses and owners of companies – was a strong one. However – to continue the example – maybe your boss would go home and be beaten by their partner, who would dominate their home and make your boss feel miserable and useless – and suddenly, your boss is no longer 'a powerful person' *per se*; we find that the idea of them as powerful only made sense in one particular context.

Similarly, whilst women could point to ways in which patriarchal society supported the continuation of men's power, on the level of individual relationships it would always be easy to find instances where women seemed to have more power than men. In particular, the idea of all men having power, whilst women were united in their global powerlessness, never really worked – especially when a middle-class feminist academic would have much more in common with her male colleagues than she had with a woman living in poverty in the Third World.

So the idea that power is not actually a glorious substance held by dominant groups makes sense. But this is a disappointment if we liked to be able to oppose domination and support minorities; the old model allowed us to jeer at nasty powerful groups, whereas Foucault's model seems to have taken that opportunity away. At the same time, though, we know it makes sense. Whilst it may have been thrilling to condemn all men for their global conspiracy of power, for example, this was always difficult to reconcile with the pathetic examples of men that feminists would encounter in their

FOUCAULT'S FANS AND FOES

In a book entitled *Saint Foucault*, David Halperin makes no secret of his admiration for the late thinker. In 1990, Halperin says, he conducted 'an admittedly unsystematic survey of various people I happened to know who had been active in [AIDS activist organisation] ACT UP/New York during its explosive early phase in the late 1980s'. He asked them to name the one book or resource that had most inspired them, and 'received, without the slightest hesitation or a single exception, the following answer: Michel Foucault, *The History of Sexuality, Volume I*' (p. 16).

Halperin notes that Foucault's popularity with activists would surprise those who felt that his argument that 'power is everywhere' took away the opportunity to criticise injustices or oppose inequality. In the 1980s, Halperin muses, who would have guessed that Foucault 'was about to be canonized as the founding spirit of a newly militant form of popular resistance' (ibid.)?!

Marxist critic Frank Lentricchia, for example, had said that 'Foucault's theory of power, because it gives power to anyone, everywhere, at all times, provides a means of resistance, but no real goal for resistance', and therefore courted despair (Lentricchia, 1982: 51–52). In 1981, Jürgen Habermas had dismissed Foucault, along with other supposed 'antimodernists' such as Jacques Derrida, as a 'Young Conservative' (Halperin, 1994: 22). Edward Said was also frustrated by what he saw as Foucault's circular and self-defeating approach to power (Said, 1983: 245–246).

Halperin has little time for these views. If Foucault was making a covert case for 'political quietism', this was certainly lost on the ACT UP activists who had taken Foucault as inspiration for all kinds of resistant demonstrations and actions (1994: 22–23). Halperin also notes that 'The quietist reading of Foucault is also at stark odds with Foucault's own well-documented practice of political engagement. At the very time that he was crafting formulations about power, in fact, the fifty-year-old philosopher was regularly engaging in street battles with the police', and was very actively involved with campaigns and demonstrations throughout his working life (ibid.).

everyday lives. And meanwhile, Foucault is not saying that there are no inequalities in society, or no marginalised groups. In fact, Foucault himself was quite an activist in support of minorities. Foucault's message, then, is not automatically reactionary just because it proposes a new way of looking at how power works. It doesn't *really* say that you can't jeer at nasty powerful groups, either, but it encourages a more practical and sophisticated approach to examining how that power is exercised. And it doesn't imply that feminism or Marxism are useless, it just forces them to become more interesting, complex and realistic.

POWER AND RESISTANCE

Foucault asserted that wherever power is exercised, resistance is also produced. 'Where there is power, there is resistance' (Foucault, 1998: 95). This is an essential part of his approach to power. Points of resistance are 'everywhere in the power network' (ibid.), and resistance does not (simply) occur at one major point, but all over the place. It might take the form of quiet tensions and suppressed concern, or spontaneous anger and protest. Just as power flows through networks of power relations – 'a dense web that passes through apparatuses and institutions, without being exactly localised in them' (Foucault, 1998: 96) – so the 'swarm of points of resistance' appear all over the place too. (This doesn't mean that resistance would always be dissipated and disorganised – revolutions are possible, Foucault suggests, if enough of these points of resistance can be strategically mobilised.)

This may sound like abstract theory, but it's easy to observe in the real world. We know from experience that wherever power needs to be referred to, to make something happen, then grumbles of discontent accompany it. If a boss has to make menacing reference to the terms of someone's employment, to make them work harder or in a particular way, this creates resentment. If one member of a couple has to allude to all the money they are bringing into the household, in order to get their partner to do something, then resistant feelings will be aroused. If an 'expert' places a contentious label or interpretation on a situation, this will produce oppositional feelings amongst the people involved, or other concerned parties.

These examples help to show why Foucault says that power is *productive*. Whilst the traditional view of power would see it as a negative force, and a dampener on interesting things happening, in Foucault's eyes the exercise of power *might* have positive or negative consequences, but most importantly is productive, bringing things into being – whether as a result of the original action, or the effects of resistance to it, or both. This does not mean that Foucault is saying that acts of power are always 'good', as such – just that they cause things to happen, and are rarely one-dimensional.

This brings us to Foucault's argument in *The History of Sexuality, Volume I*, that it was precisely the discourses about sexuality, in Victorian times and the early twentieth century, which sought to *suppress* certain kinds of behaviour, which simultaneously gave an *identity* to them, and so (ironically) launched them into the public eye:

> There is no question that the appearance in nineteenth-century psychiatry, jurisprudence, and literature of a whole series of discourses on the species and subspecies of homosexuality, inversion, pederasty, and 'psychic hermaphrodism' made possible a strong advance of social controls into this area of 'perversity'; but it also made possible the formation of a 'reverse' discourse: homosexuality began to speak in its own behalf, to demand that its legitimacy or 'naturality' be acknowledged, often in the same vocabulary, using the same categories by which it was medically disqualified.
>
> (Foucault, 1998: 101)

The exercise of power on the one hand – the labelling of 'deviant' sexualities by authority figures – actually *produced* the resistance which would drive gay liberation movements in the twentieth century. The discourses about sex should not be viewed just as a form of domination, then, Foucault suggests, because in fact by making such a fuss about sex they were contributing to the vibrancy of the subject – stoking the fires of sexual discourse, as it were. (One of the broader arguments in *The History of Sexuality, Volume I*, is that far from being a time when no-one could bear to think about sex, the Victorian era was absolutely *obsessed* with sexuality, which is why it was talked about as a problem so much.)

SEX AND IDENTITY

In *The History of Sexuality*, Foucault dismissed the common view that sex had been a freely-expressed, unproblematic part of life throughout history until it had been suppressed and hidden from public view within the last couple of hundred years. Tracing the history of discourses about sex, Foucault argues that sex was brought *into* the spotlight by Christianity in the seventeenth century, when it was decreed that all desires – not just forbidden ones, but all of them – should be transformed into discourse, in the form of the Christian confession. Desires suddenly acquired great importance. This idea of sex as the inner 'truth' about the self spread through Western culture, becoming further reinforced by carefully-worded studies in the eighteenth century, when sex became a 'police' matter, and also rested at the core of the newly-emergent political and economic concern about 'population' (Foucault, 1998: 20–25). Sex became a social and political issue – as it still is today, when teenage pregnancy, AIDS, sex education and pornography, for example, are thrust into the news by interested parties. From the start of the twentieth century, of course, the idea of sex as being at the core of identity was further reinforced by Freudian and psychoanalytic discourses, in which sexual urges and conflicts are the driving force of child development, and at the root of most problems. These ways of thinking about the self are not limited to the readers of Freud's books, or the clients of psychotherapists, but are widely dispersed through the kind of popular general knowledge you gain by reading magazine articles, watching sit-coms or seeing Woody Allen films.

Does it make sense to say that sex is at the heart of identity today? The answer is surely yes, and more so than ever before. As we have seen already, and will consider in more detail in later chapters, the discourses of magazines and self-help books, as well as many screen dramas, make knowing one's sexual identity of crucial importance to inner happiness. The media clearly suggests that in order to be fulfilled and happy, you should:

- understand your own sexuality;
- have sex often;
- seek help for sexual problems;
- have a satisfactory sexual partner – or get a new one.

Talk shows, dramas, magazines, newspaper problem pages and other media, all relay these points. We cannot assume that these messages have a direct impact on people, of course; and it is not necessarily the case that the mass media is *adding* these messages into society – perhaps the media is only circulating ideas which already seem like common sense to many people. But it does circulate them *a lot*, and whatever their origins and power, these notions seem stronger than ever. Between 1961 and 2005, the divorce rate in the UK grew from 27,200 to 155,100 per year (having peaked at 180,000 in 1993 – more than a six-fold increase between the early 1960s and the early 1990s; see www.statistics.gov.uk). Whilst divorce rates are not a perfect indicator – they only tell us about the kind of heterosexual people who are (or were) interested in getting married – this statistic clearly makes the point that people are no longer staying in relationships which no longer satisfy them. (So statistics for *divorce* – where people have made the dramatic step of disbanding a relationship which they previously swore to stay in forever, at a formal ceremony – are particularly telling here.) Whilst a general explanation for these divorces would be oversimplistic, we can say with some confidence that the modern proliferation of discourses of self-fulfilment, in terms of both sex and relationships, are likely to play a part in the termination of these marriages.

The high percentage of divorced people who *re*-marry indicates that these people have not gone off the ideals of romantic love *per se* – they just wanted a better partner, someone who would understand them better, and satisfy their true needs. (In 2005, 40 per cent of UK marriage ceremonies were for couples where one or both of them had been previously married.) Also, of course, marriage itself is in decline, partly because being 'locked' into marriage does not correspond, for a growing number of people, with the modern discourses of self-fulfilment. An official UK *Population Trends* report noted that 'There have been steady trends over the last quarter century, both in the increasing proportion [of couples] cohabiting, and the decline in the relative numbers married – and these trends seem set to continue' (National Statistics, 2001: 15). Indeed, the number of marriages in England and Wales in 2005 was the lowest (244,710) since 1896. Major government surveys have found that two-thirds of the UK adult population agree that 'it is all right for a couple to live together without intending to get married' (ibid.: 7), and those opposed to this idea are clearly shown to be largely clustered within the older generations – those born before 1935 – who are, of course, on the decline.

All in all, we see from these statistics that couples are increasingly unlikely to get married – due in part to an uncertainty that this will bring greater happiness – and that those who *are* married, are today much more likely to divorce in order to continue the quest for self-fulfilment elsewhere. Whilst this does not show that sex itself has become more important than a few decades ago, the popular media discourses of self-fulfilment – which refer to relationships in general but include a heavy emphasis on sexual happiness in particular – are likely to be feeding these trends.

Since the first edition of this book was published, however, a newly-legal phenomenon has suggested a somewhat different story: civil partnerships were introduced in the UK in 2005, as noted in Chapter 1, giving same-sex couples rights and responsibilities identical to civil marriage. These have been popular: 15,672 civil partnerships were formed in the UK between December 2005 and the end of September 2006 (National Statistics, 2006b). On the other hand, this is less than 7 per cent of the record-breakingly low number of heterosexual marriages in the whole of 2005 (a longer period) – and civil partnerships were a new institution that same-sex couples could have been waiting for years to take up. All in all, then, the formal celebration of monogamous partnerships – whether heterosexual or homosexual – still seems to be relatively unpopular.

BACK TO LIFESTYLE: FOUCAULT'S ETHICS

In the previous chapter we discussed Anthony Giddens's interest in *lifestyle* – the idea that in modernity, everyone has to make choices about the shape and character of their lives and identities. A few years before Giddens was publishing in this area, Foucault had come to focus on similar questions, albeit with different emphases, whilst preparing *The History of Sexuality* volumes two and three, in the early 1980s.

In this work, Foucault talks about 'ethics', and it is important to understand that for Foucault this term does not (simply) mean a general moral code; instead, it refers to 'the self's relationship to itself'. To put it another way, ethics here means a person's concern for and care about themselves; the standards they have for how they would like to be treated, and how they will treat themselves. Ethics describes 'the kind of relationship you ought to have with yourself' (Foucault 2000: 263) – the rules one sets for one's own behaviour. These rules, although personal and subjective, are vitally important; as Ian Hacking (1986: 236) notes, 'It is seldom force that keeps us on the straight and narrow; it is conscience.' A person's own ethics will usually *relate* to, but are unlikely to be exactly the same as, well-known sets of morality codes. For example, society says that it is wrong to be unfaithful to your partner, and says that 'being unfaithful' is having sex with another person. But an individual's own ethics might allow them to have sex with someone other than their partner, as long as that partner will not find out, and so cannot (in theory) be hurt by this action. Someone else might deal with this ethical problem in a different way, by shifting their definition of sex – as did Bill Clinton when, as President of the United States, he insisted he had not had 'sexual relations' with the young intern Monica Lewinsky, because they had (as it later transpired) engaged in oral but not penetrative sex.

TECHNOLOGIES OF THE SELF

Another central term in Foucault's later works is 'technologies of the self'. If ethics refers to a person's concern for the self – a set of internal ideas or loose rules – then the 'technologies of the self' are what is actually done about it: the ways that an individual's ethics are manifested in their mindset and actions. Another definition is that 'technologies of the self' refers to the ways in which people put forward, and police, their 'selves' in society; and the ways in which available discourses may enable or discourage various practices of the self.

Summing up what Foucault means by 'technologies of the self' is not straightforward, though. For a few years my website www.theory.org.uk, feeling unsure of the best way to summarise the concept in one sentence, invited users to supply their own attempts. Some of the better entries included:

- 'Technologies of the self are a series of techniques that allow individuals to work on themselves by regulating their bodies, their thoughts and their conduct' (Jennifer Webb, Queensland Art Gallery).
- 'Technologies of the self are methods employed by people resulting in how they will be perceived as "selves" by others and themselves' (Ernst Buchberger, University of Vienna).
- 'Technologies of the self are the specific practices by which subjects constitute themselves within and through systems of power, and which often seem to be either "natural" or imposed from above' (Jason Mittell, University of Wisconsin-Madison).
- 'Technologies of the self are the mechanisms employed by individuals and society, for better or worse, which perpetuate the public consumption of and regulation of individuality' (Jessica Matthews, Sarah Lawrence College).
- 'Technologies of the self are the continuously evolving mechanics of our very "nature" that dictate what we think say and do, based on our daily experiences' (Charlie Webb, UK).

These are all useful summaries of the same idea. At slightly more length, Simon Kweeday of Liverpool Hope University offered this explanation:

> We try to portray our personality in the best possible light, when in fact our personality is not fixed, is always in flux and may not even exist at all, in any realistic sense. Society and its power constraints, rules and regulations, as well as many other contrasting and complementary factors all gel into forming technologies of the self. Our portrayal of these facets from within projected towards society and from outside projected within ourselves determines who we are to ourselves and to other people.

In short, I think we might as well understand technologies of the self as the (internal and external) practice of our (internal) ethics. The ethics are our set of standards to do with being a particular sort of person; the technologies of the self are how we think and act to achieve this. Such acts, though, are not necessarily done 'for show', to give an impression to an audience; they may be practiced for the individual's own sake.

In *The History of Sexuality* volumes two and three, *The Use of Pleasure* and *The Care of the Self*, Foucault explores Ancient Greek and early Christian approaches to ethics, pleasure and technologies of the self. In an interview from 1983, he states most explicitly the meaning of this project and its relationship to the present. He explains, 'What strikes me is that in Greek ethics people were concerned with their moral conduct, their ethics, their relation to themselves and to others, much more than with religious problems' (2000: 255). They were very unconcerned about the nature of the gods, or the afterlife, Foucault asserts, as these were not ethical questions. The Greeks were concerned to 'constitute a kind of ethics which was an *aesthetics of existence*' (ibid., my emphasis) – which, again, has little relation to religion. Furthermore, Greek ethics were cultivated by the individual and were not governed by any formal or institutional regulations. 'For instance', says Foucault, 'the laws against sexual misbehaviour were very few and not very compelling' (ibid.). His studies showed how Christianity brought a different set of technologies of the self, where sexuality was reconceptualised as being closer to the inner self, the soul, and an object of regulation. Desires had to be monitored and understood, and confessed to in a whole new discourse of the 'truth' about oneself which required a person to understand their faults and temptations, in order to be able to confess and therefore cleanse the soul (Foucault, 1980; 2000: 242–243).

To put it very simply, the Greeks wanted to cultivate a decent and beautiful life, in the present, and their ideas of what would make a good life were not bound by universal or normalising prescriptions about sex (such as fidelity to one partner, or a requirement of monogamous heterosexual marriage). The Christians, by contrast, had to worry about maintaining a pure soul, and had to avoid a clear list of sins in order not to be tarnished. The sins, of course, prominently featured sexual desires – not only acts, but mere temptations as well.

Foucault felt that all this is relevant to people in modern Western societies because, with the decline of Christian religion, we find ourselves facing similar questions regarding how to create a satisfactory ethics for living a good life. These are issues which we come up against when we watch *Oprah*, read magazines, view dramas, or try to relate to news stories about the private lives of public figures. In a 1983 interview, Foucault mused:

> I wonder if our problem nowadays is not, in a way, similar to
> [that of the Greeks], since most of us no longer believe that

ethics is founded in religion, nor do we want a legal system to intervene in our moral, personal, private life. Recent liberation movements suffer from the fact that they cannot find any principle on which to base the elaboration of a new ethics. They need an ethics, but they cannot find any other ethics than an ethics founded on so-called scientific knowledge of what the self is, what desire is, what the unconscious is, and so on. I am struck by this similarity of problems.

(2000: 255–256)

Asked whether he thought, then, that the Greeks offered 'an attractive and plausible alternative', however, Foucault was adamant that one cannot find solutions to contemporary problems by copying the solutions of other times or cultures. We can't borrow the ancient Greek lifestyle for use today; we need to address today's problems directly. So it emerges that Foucault was interested in ancient attitudes to life and ways of being – technologies of the self – partly for their own sake (of course), but partly because these histories show people coming to terms with those same questions of identity and lifestyle which keep coming up in this book, namely 'How should I live? Who shall I be? Who should I relate to? Can I find a comfortable self-identity?'.

In fact Foucault, who liked to re-describe his previous work in the light of his current concerns, managed in one 1982 seminar to re-present all of his work as different approaches to self-awareness:

My objective for more than twenty-five years has been to sketch out a history of the different ways in our culture that humans develop knowledge about themselves: economics, biology, psychiatry, medicine, and penology. The main point is not to accept this knowledge at face value but to analyse these so-called sciences as very specific 'truth games' related to specific techniques that human beings use to understand themselves.

(2000: 224)

Here, each of the 'so-called sciences' of human behaviour is seen ultimately as a technology of the self – a way of looking at what it means to be a person. The reason for looking at *several* historical and cultural perspectives on the self is not simply a desire for a bit of variety – it is a means of demonstrating that no particular way of conceptualising the person is fixed or necessarily correct. Today's view of sexuality as an attribute, for example, may seem like common sense to most people here and now, but to the ancient Greeks would not have made sense. Today, we have the idea that you are heterosexual, or homosexual, or perhaps bisexual – and, regardless of whether or not you are comfortable with different sexualities, we expect people to stay within one category. If, for example, you saw your gay friend passionately kissing a person of the opposite sex, there

---

ADVERTISING AND TECHNOLOGIES OF THE SELF

In an article entitled 'Consumerism and "compulsory individuality"', Anne Cronin (2000) argues that the discourses of advertising emphasise *choice* and the power of the individual to transform themselves – through the purchase of certain products. These choices are seen as expressions of our individual identities. Consumerism is a *technology of the self*, then: through purchasing particular products, the adverts tell us, we can become like the liberated, aspiration beings seen in the ads. Nike's 'Just Do It' campaign, for example, suggests a do-it-yourself ethos of bodily regimes and willpower through which one can become a streamlined, fit, independent, self-directed being. Advertising and women's magazines position women, in particular, as both the subject and the object of consumerism, Cronin says (2000: 279):

> Consumerism promises women self-transformation and appears to validate women's choices. Yet, even as subjects, women have faced an impossible imperative 'to be ourselves' through 'doing ourselves' mediated by 'doing' make-up (making yourself up), fashion (fashioning yourself), dieting and exercise (re-forming yourself).

These regimes – these technologies of the self, as Foucault would call them, promoted through the media – remind us of the 'ethical duties to the self' that Foucault discusses in historical times. Advertising and the media often suggest that women have an ethical duty to monitor their appearance, make sacrifices to achieve a better body, and 'treat' themselves to a range of cosmetic treatments and adornments. Cronin warns that these regimes can never make women truly individual; indeed, as more and more messages tell us to 'just be yourself' or 'express yourself', this 'compulsory individuality' takes women further and further away from truly being 'an individual'.

would probably be some confusion – 'Are they still gay? Have they gone straight? Are they now trying "bi"?'. But the Greeks, who (according to Foucault) did not see sexuality as something you 'were' but rather something you 'did' – an activity rather than an identity – would not have had, or even understood, this concern. Foucault would not presume that this was because people in the past were *wrong*; he did not believe that our current forms of knowledge and understanding were necessarily better than any others. (Such a 'different' way of viewing sexuality was not unique to ancient Greece. For example, in his historical study *Gay New York*, George Chauncey (1994) claims that in the early decades of the twentieth century, working-class New York culture did not recognise the categories of 'homosexual' and 'heterosexual' (or 'bisexual', which by meaning 'both' supports the binary division). Although some effeminate men identified as 'fairies' – a subculture well integrated into working-class communities – many other typically masculine men would have sexual relations with other men without this affecting their identity as a 'normal man'. The 'fairies' and 'normal men' were therefore divided by their gender style, rather than sexual activity.)

What Foucault wanted to show was that – not only in relation to sexuality, but many other aspects of social life and living – today's practices are but one option among many, and our ways of 'understanding' ourselves do not necessarily represent the truth, as such; rather they are *strategies* – not necessarily bad ones – for making sense of modern life.

THE ART OF LIFE

Whilst Foucault was indeed interested in a range of different ways of viewing the self, and he was genuinely keen to study them as a way of revealing the divergent possibilities, it is also clear that he preferred some models to others. Whilst he resented being categorised as an anti-psychiatrist, for instance, it is safe to say that Foucault thought that the procedures of early psychiatry were pretty rubbish. The ancient Greek view of life as a work of art, on the other hand, is clearly appealing to him.

> Greek ethics is centred on a problem of personal choice, of the aesthetics of existence. The idea of [one's body, and one's life] as a material for an aesthetic piece of art is something that fascinates me. The idea also that ethics can be a very strong structure of existence, without any relation to [external laws or] a disciplinary structure. All that is very interesting.
>
> (Foucault, 2000: 260)

Foucault is very interested in the idea that there is not necessarily any connection between our personal ways of living – social and sexual ethics – and
the broader functioning of politics and society. Ethics can be 'a very strong
structure of existence' without the need for external laws or disciplinary
structures. Since the self is not 'given' but has to be actively created, then
life itself could be developed and treated as a work of art (pp. 261–262).

But what does 'life as a work of art' really mean? In Foucault's terms, it is
nothing to do with physical appearance – *looking* beautiful; rather, it is
about a beautiful way of living. This does not mean surrounding oneself
with beautiful things, either; it's about behaviour. Foucault seemed to
admire the Greek ethics which led to a control of the self, in particular in
regard to sexuality, where *self-restraint* became an art. Sex acts were not
morally limited in the ways that we would recognise today, but their timing
and quantity was important. (The opposite of this 'beautiful' restraint
would be gross over-indulgence.) Since a variety of sexual practices were
'allowed' – such as sex between men and boys – it was *moderation* and
control of desire that gave a certain beauty to life. As Foucault explains in
The Use of Pleasure (1992: 250–251), the impetus to be

> this self-disciplined subject was not presented in the form of a
> universal law, which each and every individual would have to
> obey, but rather as a principle of stylization of conduct for those
> who wished to give their existence the most graceful and accom-
> plished form possible.

These were suggestions on how to live a fine life, then, but not rules
binding all members of society. As a set of principles that you could opt
into, they were not like (what we now call) traditional morality, but had
more in common with a high-status diet.

Not all aspects of Greek life are admired by Foucault. Although he has
been criticised for not seeming very interested in the lives of Greek women,
he did recognise that they were badly treated in that society (Foucault,
2000: 256–257); and he is not even convinced that sexuality between men
was unproblematic (ibid.). But as we have noted before, Foucault is not
suggesting that modern societies should copy the Greek model. His interest
is in revealing that certain forms of freedom and choice are possibilities, and
that nothing is 'given' from the start.

GAY LIFESTYLE

In the early 1980s, Foucault also became more publicly 'out' as a gay man
(although to a large extent he managed to avoid having his sexuality

turned into an 'explanatory' label – as in 'the gay scholar Michel Foucault'). In interviews conducted during this time, we find Foucault talking about how a gay relationship can be negotiated and created, in the absence of an established lifestyle model for such a partnership. Here, Foucault is concerned with finding a 'mode of life' in which such a relationship could work, and this is very close to Giddens's interest in 'lifestyle' (see previous chapter) developed a few years later. (Like Giddens, Foucault is interested in the idea of people having to forge their own models of sociability – he doesn't actually want to *prescribe* particular models for anybody.) For example, in a 1981 interview for *Gai Pied* (Foucault, 2000: 137–138), he ponders:

> Is it possible to create a homosexual mode of life? This notion of mode of life seems important to me … A way of life can be shared among individuals of different age, status, and social activity. It can yield intense relations not resembling those that are institutionalised. It seems to me that a way of life can yield a culture and an ethics. To be 'gay', I think, is not to identify with the psychological traits and the visible masks of the homosexual but to try to define and develop a way of life.

Here, we see that being gay is of interest to Foucault because it does not come packed with ready-made lifestyle patterns as (to an extent) heterosexuality does; instead it presents the freedom, and the challenge, to develop a meaningful lifestyle. Considering how such a lifestyle might be set out in a public forum, Foucault interestingly picks *magazines* as valuable communicators (2000: 139):

> Something well considered and voluntary like a magazine ought to make possible a homosexual culture, that is to say, [make available] the instruments for polymorphic, varied, and individually modulated relationships.

Magazines seem to be mentioned here because they can playfully make suggestions about lifestyles without being overly prescriptive. Foucault did not want anything as rigid as 'a program of proposals', because it could become a set of laws which would be quite contrary to the openness and creativity needed: 'There ought to be an inventiveness special to a situation like ours and to these feelings.' Warming to his topic, and giving an unusually clear-cut summary of what we might call 'the Foucault project', he asserts:

We have to dig deeply to show how things have been historically contingent, for such and such reason intelligible, but not necessary. We must make the intelligible appear against a background of emptiness and deny its necessity. We must think that what exists is far from filling all possible spaces. To make a truly unavoidable challenge of the question: What can be played?

(pp. 139–140)

Foucault is here emphasising the motivation behind his historical studies, which sometimes is left so implicit (but not explicit) that readers ask of their Foucault paperbacks, 'What's your point? Why are you telling me all this history?' But here it is made clear: the histories of madness, or punishment, or sexuality, are designed to show *why* things were organised a certain way, on the one hand; but on the other hand to show that things didn't *have* to be that way at all.

A text like a magazine – which can be picked up and flicked through in any order, and which is treated in a relaxed, non-reverential way – might indeed offer the best way of exploring 'what can be played', as Foucault puts it, and magazines are discussed in more detail in Chapters 9 and 10. Meanwhile, the idea of giving a *performance* leads us into the next chapter, on queer theory, which directly builds upon Foucault's work.

SUMMARY

Foucault shows that particular ways of talking about things (discourses) shape the way that we perceive the world and our own selves. Today, popular media is obviously a primary channel for the dissemination of prevailing discourses. The ability to influence a certain discourse is a form of power that can be exercised (although power is not a property held by a particular group, but is something that flows through social processes and interactions). The exercise of power always produces resistance, and so in this sense power is *productive* because it causes things to happen (which will not necessarily be the consequences intended by the original agent). The discourses about sexuality and identity are strong ones, enthusiastically spread by the media and consumed by audiences. Sexuality is seen as the key to happiness and knowing your 'true self'. In modern life, Foucault suggests, we have to establish an ethics and a mode of living – not dissimilar to Giddens's ideas about lifestyle – and he hints that the possibilities are virtually endless, but are not always visible to us.

FURTHER READING

Using Foucault's Methods by Gavin Kendall and Gary Wickham (1999) is a surprisingly good introduction to Foucault and how his ideas can be applied to different areas. It's important to read Foucault in his own words, of course. The interviews reproduced in *Ethics: Essential Works of Foucault 1954–1984 Volume 1* (Foucault, 2000) offer the best introduction to his ideas in this sphere, and then *The History of Sexuality, Volume I: The Will to Knowledge* (Foucault, 1998) is very important and reasonably short. See also Bristow (1997), Sarup (1996), Mills (2003), Gutting (2005a, 2005b), Halperin (1994) and Foucault (1980, 1990, 1992).

Chapter 7

QUEER THEORY AND FLUID IDENTITIES

QUEER THEORY, DESPITE one interpretation of its name, is not a theory of homosexuality (although it does have some things to say about that). It is an approach to sexuality and, more generally, identity, which builds on some of the ideas developed by Michel Foucault (see previous chapter). The first and, in my view, the most valuable version of queer theory was put forward by Judith Butler in her book *Gender Trouble: Feminism and the Subversion of Identity* (1990). Butler, born in 1956, is a Professor of Rhetoric and Comparative Literature at the University of California, Berkeley. It should be pointed out that Butler herself didn't label her *Gender Trouble* argument as 'queer theory'. Indeed, in a 1993 interview (Osborne and Segal, 1994) she recalled:

> I remember sitting next to someone at a dinner party, and he said that he was working on queer theory. And I said: What's queer theory? He looked at me like I was crazy, because he evidently thought that I was a part of this thing called queer theory. But all I knew was that Teresa de Lauretis had published an issue of the journal *Differences* called 'Queer Theory'. I thought it was something she had put together. It certainly never occurred to me that I was a part of queer theory.

This really is odd, though, because almost everybody regards Butler as the creator of modern queer theory. She owes a debt to Foucault and other earlier figures, but the thing we call queer theory today definitely starts with

Figure 7.1   Judith Butler

Gender Trouble by Judith Butler. (Also important, within the version of queer theory which is concerned with literature rather than social identities, is the work of Eve Kosofsky Sedgwick, which challenges assumptions about sexuality in literature.)

It is also worth mentioning that Butler is unlikely to win any awards for clarity of writing style. (On the contrary, indeed, she once won an annual international award for having produced the most incomprehensible academic text.) Her prose is unnecessarily dense and long-winded, and almost never fails to use jargon even where much more accessible vocabulary is available. Some people defend this, saying that academics should be allowed to develop complex terminology to express their sophisticated ideas – after all, nobody expects to read journals about rocket science and understand all of it straight away. However, although Butler's writing is like an explosion in a dictionary factory, if one takes time to dig through the rubble one finds that her ideas are actually quite straightforward. So let's get started.

QUEER THEORY SUMMARY

We'll need to look at each of these points in more detail to fully understand their meaning and implications, but here's the simple summary of what queer theory is about:

- Nothing within your identity is fixed.
- Your identity is little more than a pile of (social and cultural) things which you have previously expressed, or which have been said about you.
- There is not really an 'inner self'. We come to believe we have one through the repetition of discourses about it.
- Gender, like other aspects of identity, is a performance (though not necessarily a consciously chosen one). Again, this is reinforced through repetition.
- People can therefore change.
- The binary divide between masculinity and femininity is a social construction built on the binary divide between men and women – which is also a social construction.
- We should challenge the traditional views of masculinity and femininity, and sexuality, by causing 'gender trouble'.

QUESTIONING SEX AS WELL AS GENDER

Butler begins *Gender Trouble* with her concerns about the way that feminism had treated 'women' as a single and coherent group. On the one hand, it is pretty obvious that in order to make its arguments about the domination and mistreatment of women, feminism had to talk about women as one group, who were unfairly treated by the other group – men. The problems with this had been noted before – black feminist bell hooks, for example, had forcefully argued that white middle-class feminists had very insensitively ignored the fact that poor black women tended to have more in common with poor black men than they did with white academic feminists (hooks,

---

QUEER STUDIES

There is a strand of literary and film studies which is related to queer theory, and which entertains itself by 'queering' texts, which generally means coming up with alternative sexualities for the characters in a text. This is perfectly good fun, but – as with all studies which spend time inventing alternative readings of texts which the author probably didn't intend and which most audiences probably won't think of – might be a bit of a waste of time.

In this book we are concerned with queer theory as a tool for thinking about identity which is relevant to everybody.

1982, 2000). The idea that women were united as a group, regardless of race, class or other differences, could be seen as the dream of women who didn't have any other oppressions to worry about. Of course, women might well have unique experiences in common – experiences of childbirth, of menstruation, or of being discriminated against for being female, for example; but it was the feminist implication that being a woman was *the defining factor* in identity that came under fire. This argument does not just apply to sex and gender, but to other axes of identity such as race, class or sexuality, none of which can be broken from its context and singled out as a person's primary identity. Butler says that 'the singular notion of identity [is] a misnomer' (1990: 4). Furthermore:

> By conforming to a requirement of representational politics that feminism articulate a stable subject [i.e. 'women'], feminism thus opens itself to charges of gross misrepresentation.
>
> (Butler, 1990: 5)

Butler asks whether feminism, in seeking to construct 'the category of women as a coherent and stable subject', might actually be performing 'an unwitting regulation and reification of gender relations' (ibid.). To put it another way: one of the initial ideas behind feminism was that we wanted a society where everyone was just treated as an equal person, without their sex making any difference. But by creating a binary 'women versus men' opposition, feminists were confirming the notion of women as a unique species – a notion which, in other contexts, would be seen as sexist. ('Binary' is used here to indicate that something is either one thing or the other – you are either female, or male, and there are no other options.) The emphasis on 'women' as a group has partly worked 'to limit and constrain in advance the very cultural possibilities that feminism is supposed to open up' (ibid.: 147).

Butler notes that feminism and sociology more generally had come to accept a model, which she calls the 'heterosexual matrix', in which 'sex' is seen as a binary biological given – you are born female or male – and then 'gender' is the cultural component which is socialised into the person on that basis. Although Butler herself didn't present it as a diagram, we can draw it like this:

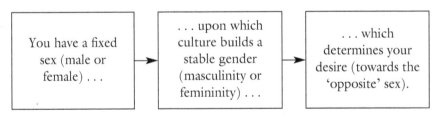

Butler's overall argument is that we should not accept that any of these follow from each other – we should shatter the imagined connections. The above model would have to be replaced with something like this:

You have a body.	You may perform an identity.	You may have desires.

Note that in this model, not only have the words become very undeterministic – they assume very little – but also the arrows have gone, so your body does not determine your gender or identity, and this will not help us to predict your desires.

Butler argues that if 'sex' – the binary division of people into male or female – has a history, if people were not always divided in this way, if scientific discourses have formed our view of the duality of 'sex', then it is not a universally fixed term (1990: 7). Histories of science and sexuality have shown that this view of sex did not develop without discussion and contestation; and in particular the well-known fact that some people are born who cannot easily be categorised as either male or female – hermaphrodites – shows that there is at least a *third* category in this supposed binary world of sex. (Such cases may be a minority, but that is not relevant to the straightforward question of how many categories there are.)

Butler therefore goes on to argue that the binary nature of sex is seen as a given, but this itself is a construction – a way of viewing bodies. It is our view of gender (which everyone agrees to be culturally constructed) which leads to this view of sex. So, if we see sex as a questionable category which has no necessary link to any particular gender or personality or identity, and which in turn cannot dictate desire, then we come to a new conclusion:

> If a stable notion of gender no longer proves to be the foundational premise of feminist politics, perhaps a new sort of feminist politics is now desirable to contest the very reifications of gender and identity, one that will take the variable construction of identity as both a methodological and normative prerequisite, if not a political goal.
>
> (Butler, 1990: 5)

In other words, feminism cannot assume that people will have certain kinds of identity just because they are 'female' or 'male', and indeed it should perhaps campaign *for* this proliferation of identities. Furthermore, Butler specifically warns that feminists should avoid making generalisations about sex: 'Feminist critique ought to explore the totalizing claims of a masculine signifying economy, but also remain self-critical with respect to the totalizing gestures of feminism' (ibid.: 13). She suggests that feminists are right to criticise generalisations about 'men' and 'women' made by those they identify as patriarchs and sexists – and so should avoid making such generalisations themselves. None of us should make universal assumptions. Butler soon follows this with a similar warning: 'The insistence [by some feminists] upon the coherence and unity of the category of women has effectively refused the multiplicity of cultural, social, and political intersections in which the concrete array of "women" are constructed' (ibid.: 14). The assertion that women make up one united, oppressed group, then, has not enabled a realistic understanding of women (or others) in society. (In her 1993 interview, Butler reasserts her connection with feminism, and says that she is concerned that queer theory has come to mean something quite anti-feminist. Nevertheless, whilst we can understand that she might not want to be seen to be *attacking* feminism as such, it is difficult to see how 'feminism' could have been very meaningful to Butler, around that time at least, since she had undermined its one universally defining feature – an emphasis on women.)

GENDER AS A PERFORMANCE

The ways that we think and talk about gender and sex, Butler notes, tend to 'presuppose and preempt the possibilities of imaginable and realizable gender configurations within culture' (1990: 9). We are constrained by existing discourses. Most humanist views of the person see gender as an *attribute*, which – once installed by culture, at least – becomes fixed, a permanent part of that person's self. But Butler prefers 'those historical and anthropological positions that understand gender as a *relation* among socially constituted subjects in specifiable contexts' (ibid.: 10). In other words, rather than being a fixed attribute in a person, gender should be seen as a fluid variable which can shift and change in different contexts and at different times.

Gender, then, is a *performance* – and nothing more. 'There is no gender identity behind the expressions of gender; ... identity is performatively constituted by the very "expressions" that are said to be its results' (ibid.: 25). Butler is here saying that we do not have a gender identity which informs our behaviour; on the contrary, that behaviour is all that our gender is. Gender, then, is what you *do* at particular times, rather than a universal *who you are*. (Ten years later, Madonna sung of love in the same terms – 'Tell me love isn't true, it's just something that we do' (*Don't Tell Me*, 2000) –

wishing it to be more of a cultural construction rather than an inescapable 'given'.) We already recognise gender as something of an achievement. If a woman puts on a new dress and make-up, she might declare 'I feel like a *woman* tonight'; similarly, a man who has put on overalls and picked up a power drill might see himself in the mirror and say 'What a *man!*' (In such cases, irony is common, but optional.) The fact that these expressions are not wholly meaningless shows that mostly people are at least partly aware that gender is some kind of performance (ibid.: 22).

It follows from this that no kind of identity is more 'true' or 'real' than any other. Thus, for example, where gay relationships seem similar in style and structure to heterosexual partnerships, this only reveals to Butler the 'utterly constructed status' of both types.

> Thus, gay is to straight *not* as copy is to original, but, rather, as copy is to copy. The parodic repetition of 'the original' ... reveals the original to be nothing other than a parody of the *idea* of the natural and the original.
>
> (Ibid.: 31)

Similarly, of course, there can be no 'real' or 'authentic' male or female performance. There are identity patterns that we have become familiar with, through their frequent repetition, but, Butler suggests, there is nothing fixed or predetermined about them.

Of course, the mass media conspicuously circulates certain kinds of male and female performance as preferable, thereby making the gender categories more 'real'. At the same time, though, the changes in gender representations in the past three or four decades (see Chapters 3 and 4) show that the recommended expressions of gender are eminently flexible. Within particular moments, then, the media might make gendered behaviours seem more 'natural', but when considered over time, the broad changes reveal the very constructedness of gender performances.

SUBVERSION

If gender is a performance, then, it can be turned on its head – or turned into *anything*. We do not have to wait for a feminist revolution, or for society to become more liberal or different before gender roles can be transformed, Butler suggests (ibid.: 30):

> If sexuality is culturally constructed within existing power relations, then the postulation of a normative sexuality that is

"before," "outside," or "beyond" power is a cultural impossibil-
ity and a politically impracticable dream, one that postpones the
concrete and contemporary task of rethinking subversive possibilities for sexuality and identity within the terms of power itself.

Gender and sexuality can be reinvented in the here and now, in other
words. Some commentators have focused on Butler's suggestion that existing gender forms could be undermined through *parody* – as can be done by
the drag performer who parodies the stereotypical routine of the other
gender. But Butler is also aware that drag artists can easily be incorporated
by traditional and even conservative humour, where sex roles are recognised
with laughter, but not challenged. In fact Butler's ideas for undermining
traditional understandings of gender go well beyond obvious parodies in
any case; she welcomes any alternative performances of identity. As she
explains in typically verbose style at the end of her introductory chapter:

This text continues, then, as an effort to think through the possibility of subverting and displacing those naturalized and reified
notions of gender that support masculine hegemony and hetero-
sexist power, to make *gender trouble*, not through the strategies
that figure a utopian beyond, but through the mobilization, subversive confusion, and proliferation of precisely those constitu-
tive categories that seek to keep gender in its place by posturing
as the foundational illusions of identity.

(Ibid.: 33–34, my emphasis)

So Butler is proposing that if society were to witness unpredictable, seemingly 'random' performances of identity, which challenge our expectations
about gender – that's the proliferation of 'subversive confusion' that she's
talking about – then our taken-for-granted gender categories would be
shaken and, if subjected to enough challenges, might eventually fall apart
altogether. This manifesto for radical change, almost buried in the heart of
her unexpectedly popular book, is the call for 'gender trouble' of its title.

Butler reminds us that we do not face a choice of *whether* to give a
performance, because identity is a performance already – it's *always* a
performance. The self is always being made and re-made in daily interactions, so the decision to steer it in a different direction might not be such a
big deal. Or, in Butler's prose:

To enter into the repetitive practices of this terrain of significa-
tion is not a choice, for the "I" that might enter is always already

inside: there is no possibility of agency or reality outside of the discursive practices that give those terms the intelligibility that they have. The task is not whether to repeat, but how to repeat or, indeed, to repeat and, through a radical proliferation of gender, *to displace* the very gender norms that enable the repetition itself.

(Ibid.: 148, her emphasis)

This is, in effect, Judith Butler's mission statement. By giving a different form to our daily performances of identity, we might work to change gender norms and the binary understanding of masculinity and femininity. Everyday life, then, is a political project, and one which everyone can work on and potentially transform.

DID BUTLER *REALLY* SAY THAT?

After *Gender Trouble* was published, some people interpreted it as saying that sex and gender were just social constructs that we could 'wish away'. Indeed, my preferred reading of the book, given above, is quite close to that optimistically flexible view. As we have seen, Butler *does* suggest, at the very least, that current understandings of gender can be challenged and subverted through alternative performances of identity. However, this argument also got Butler into trouble with people who thought that this was a very idealistic view of how sexual politics in modern societies could be transformed. The entrenched forces of patriarchy, it was suggested, would not vanish just because a few queer theory fans made fun of them. This point seems, in part, to have been accepted by Butler. Interviewed in 1993, she said:

> One of the interpretations that has been made of *Gender Trouble* is that there is no sex, there is only gender, and gender is performative. People then go on to think that if gender is performative it must be radically free. And it has seemed to many that the materiality of the body is vacated or ignored or negated here – disavowed, even. [...] So what became important to me in writing *Bodies that Matter* [1993] was to go back to the category of sex, and to the problem of materiality, and to ask how it is that sex itself might be construed as a norm. [...] I wanted to work out how a norm actually materialises a body, how we might understand the materiality of the body to be not only invested with a norm, but in some sense animated by a norm, or contoured by a norm. So I have shifted. I think that I overrode

the category of sex too quickly in *Gender Trouble*. I try to recon-
sider it in *Bodies That Matter*, and to emphasise the place of constraint in the very production of sex.

(Osborne and Segal, 1994)

So Butler started thinking that, although there are possibilities for subversion, we still need to attend to why it is that being male or female, defined
by biology, feels like a specific reality to many people. This doesn't contradict her previous work, although it was clearly more (depressingly, perhaps)
focused on 'realism' rather than liberation.

Furthermore, we do not have to worry too much about this: every
thinker puts forward tools which we can choose to use, or modify, or reject.
I feel that the tools in *Gender Trouble* are more useful, relevant and exciting
than some of the more cautious ideas in Butler's later works, and would
argue that it's not necessarily important to worry about what Butler has
thought about her own previous ideas since. We can also note that in some
subsequent pieces, such as Butler (1999), she has written again about the
excitement generated by the idea that sexuality could be seen in terms of
'bodies and pleasures' (as Foucault had put it), with no necessary connection to existing categories of gender or sexuality. In any case, Butler has not
disowned the *Gender Trouble* thesis; she has simply added some sensible
notes of caution, acknowledging the complexity of social life.

USING BUTLER

An obvious criticism of Butler is that she doesn't really spell out how people
should resist genders, or cause 'gender trouble', beyond the broad assertions quoted above. Monique Deveaux (1994) has complained that it's not
clear how Butler's idea of everyday resistance would work in practical terms,
for example, and in a review of *Gender Trouble*, E. Ann Kaplan (1992)
noted that she would have liked 'more concreteness, particularly in relation
to Butler's proposed politics of repetitive parodic gender performance'. On
the other hand, it's not hard to *imagine* what these forms of resistance
would involve, even though Butler doesn't provide illustrations. Feminists
and gender theorists were quick to spot, rightly, that in the early 1990s, the
pop icon Madonna seemed to be the living embodiment of Butler's manifesto. The *Sex* book (1992), the videos for *Express Yourself* (1989), *Justify
My Love* (1990) and *Erotica* (1992), and the whole *Erotica* album, did it all
– the blurring and confusion of genders, fluidity of sexuality, transgression
of masculine and feminine stereotypes, were all what Butler appeared to be
calling for (see Schwichtenberg, 1993; Lloyd, 1993; Frank and Smith,

1993; Faith, 1997; Brooks, 1997). Madonna's communications were on a global media canvas, of course – on a different level to the everyday interactions we mentioned above. (In her everyday life, most interviews and articles suggest, Madonna was usually more conventional.) Nevertheless, Butler's proposed gender challenges would gain much strength if a lead was taken by popular media figures – and the idea of a 'proliferation' of identities makes much more sense if we can assume that the mass media would play a key role in spreading these images. To destabilise the taken-for-granted assumptions about the supposedly binary divide between female and male, masculinity and femininity, gay and straight, what could be more powerful than a two-pronged attack, on the levels of both everyday life and popular media?

For examples of this in practice, we can probably think of certain 'challenging' representations in arthouse movies or socially-concerned TV programmes. But we can see it happening in the mainstream as well. For instance, the 'reality' TV show *Big Brother* – in its numerous international variations, which have been annual events since the first Dutch show in 1999 – is typically a showcase for a range of different straight and gay, male and female, and sometimes transgendered characters. The similarities and alliances between individuals on the show routinely cut across traditional dividing lines. Meanwhile the hit movies discussed in Chapter 4 also offer gentle challenges to conventional groupings. The *Fantastic Four* (2005, 2007) and *X-Men* (2000, 2003, 2006) series celebrate the 'freaks', both male and female, who are different but special; and both *Fantastic Four: Rise of the Silver Surfer* (2007) and *Spider-Man 3* (2007) remind us not to judge bad guys on first appearances. Even the sometimes-laddish comedy *Knocked Up* (2007) offers a sweet alternative vision of unstereo-typed parental partnership. Hollywood films are often *mostly* conventional, but success does not necessarily follow the most traditional representations.

THE ANTI-BUTLER: MARTHA NUSSBAUM

To help us think more about Butler it may be useful to consider a much-discussed review article by Martha Nussbaum, published in the American current affairs magazine *The New Republic* in February 1999. The article is a sustained attack on Butler's work. It contrasts the goals of activist feminists, who have sought to make life better for women in the real world, with Butler's stance, which Nussbaum seems to think involves fighting against nothing, merely playing with parodies of gender in the margins of society. She asserts:

The new feminism [led by Butler] ... instructs its members that there is little room for large-scale social change, and maybe no room at all. We are all, more or less, prisoners of the structure of power that have defined our identity as women; we can never change those structures in a large-scale way, and we can never escape from them. All that we can hope to do is to find spaces within the structures of power in which to parody them, to poke fun at them, to transgress them in speech.

(Nussbaum, 1999)

This seems to be a serious misunderstanding of Butler, however. The call for 'gender trouble', as we have seen, is one which seeks to shatter the whole idea of gender throughout society – 'large-scale social change', in other words. Gender parody, and subversive performances, are not just a way of playing in the margins of social oppression to cheer oneself up; they are the tools by which, Butler suggests, we might overthrow the oppressive constraints of sex and gender roles altogether. Nussbaum, though, repeatedly reads Butler's ideas of subversion as quiet play rather than radical protest. She suggests that Butler is saying that 'We are doomed to repetition of the power structures into which we are born, but we can at least make fun of them' (Nussbaum, 1999), but this hardly tallies with Butler's assertion at the end of *Gender Trouble* that:

If identities were no longer fixed as the premises of a political syllogism, and politics no longer understood as a set of ready-made subjects, a new configuration of politics would surely emerge from the ruins of the old. Cultural configurations of sex and gender might then proliferate or, rather, their present proliferation might then become articulable within the discourses that establish intelligible cultural life, confounding the very binarism of sex, and exposing its fundamental unnaturalness.

(Butler, 1990: 149)

In her typically wordy way, Butler is clearly saying the *opposite* of what Nussbaum claims she says – we are *not* 'doomed to repetition of the power structures into which we are born', and these must be actively *challenged* and *transformed*.

Nussbaum is enthusiastic about feminist social changes brought by laws and other political action on the 'macro' level; maybe this is why she is unable to see Butler's ideas as a real challenge working on a different level, from the grass roots 'micro' level of everyday life. Nussbaum wants the state to force people to change, whereas Butler (in my interpretation) wants the popular culture of everyday people to be transformed from *within*. There isn't really any reason why, if she understood it more sympathetically, Nussbaum should object to Butler's contribution.

This is similar to the difference of opinion between Giddens and Meštrović, discussed in Chapter 5. Butler, like Giddens, would like to assume that people have the power to transform their own lives and make the world a better place. Nussbaum, like Meštrović, takes the more authoritarian view that the world isn't going to get any better unless a critical elite forces the population in a particular direction.

Nussbaum does have one democratic card to play though – her critique of Butler's writing style. In addition to the standard criticisms of its lack of charm ('ponderous and obscure ... exasperating'), Nussbaum argues that if Butler really wanted to encourage people to challenge the prevailing norms then she wouldn't write in such a frustrating and inaccessible style. She has a point there. She is also right to point out that Butler's failure to clarify how she is using complex terms makes her books difficult to interpret, even for the most scholarly of readers:

> A further problem lies in Butler's casual mode of allusion. The ideas of these thinkers are never described in enough detail to include the uninitiated (if you are not familiar with the Althusserian concept of 'interpellation,' you are lost for chapters) or to explain to the initiated how, precisely, the difficult ideas are being understood. Of course, much academic writing is allusive in some way: it presupposes prior knowledge of certain doctrines and positions. But in both the continental and the Anglo-American philosophical traditions, academic writers for a specialist audience standardly acknowledge that the figures they mention are complicated, and the object of many different interpretations. They therefore typically assume the responsibility of advancing a definite interpretation among the contested ones, and of showing by argument why they have interpreted the figure as they have, and why their own interpretation is better than others.
>
> (Nussbaum, 1999)

Nussbaum concludes that Butler is addressing an uncritical audience of 'young feminist theorists' who are so much in awe of Butler's dense prose that they cannot see that there's not much there.

> The ideas in these books are thin. When Butler's notions are stated clearly and succinctly, one sees that, without a lot more

distinctions and arguments, they don't go far, and they are not especially new. Thus obscurity fills the void left by an absence of a real complexity of thought and argument.

(Ibid.)

I would not agree that Butler has failed to give us new and interesting things to think about. The arguments I outlined above are genuinely innovative, challenging and useful. (We have also seen that Nussbaum didn't really seem to understand what Butler was calling for anyway, which weakens her critical position.) Nevertheless, Nussbaum may be right to suggest that Butler's good ideas are thinly spread through some pretty horrendous and pretentious texts. And in the years since *Gender Trouble* was published, Butler hasn't really got any better. *The Psychic Life of Power* (1997), for example, is record-breakingly dense. More recently, Butler may have sought to counter this 'difficult' reputation with *Undoing Gender* (2004), seen by some reviewers as a more accessible book. Nevertheless, 'accessible' Butler means that you only need to re-read each sentence twice.

Overall, though, I think that Nussbaum's attack on Butler is wrong and fails to appreciate the radical challenge to social life, to be fought on the everyday fields of interaction and communication (and, potentially, the media), which Butler puts forward. Her comments on the elitism and arrogance of Butler's style, however, are probably spot-on. Nevertheless, Butler has provided tools which others can take up and popularise, and has therefore made a valuable contribution.

ANOTHER ATTACK ON QUEER THEORY

In an article published in the journal *Sexualities*, Tim Edwards provided what he called 'a strong critique of queer theory and politics' (1998: 471). Considering this article may also help to clarify what queer theory stands for, and illuminate possible misunderstandings of it. For clarity, I have broken Edwards's argument into a set of numbered points.

1 Identities are usually stable

Edwards notes that the definition of queer theory is not clear-cut, but rightly observes that 'queer theory is primarily defined as an attempt to undermine an overall discourse of sexual categorisation and, more particularly, the limitations of the heterosexual–homosexual divide as an identity' (ibid.: 472). The author is unhappy with this 'utopian' orientation, however. 'The reality for many people much of the time is that their sexualities remain remarkably constant and stable over time even when lived experience may contradict this' (ibid.). This may be true – although Edwards doesn't actually provide any evidence for his assertion – but nevertheless, sociologists and cultural critics are left with a choice which philosophers have faced for centuries: do we look at the world optimistically, assuming that people and conventions can change, or pessimistically, assuming that the world will stay as we already think it is? Edwards takes the supposedly 'realistic', pessimistic view, as is his right, but this seems to be a matter of personal choice rather than the necessarily 'correct' view that he seems to think it is.

2 Queer theory cheats, by focusing on fancy theories and cultural texts rather than real life

Edwards notes that some versions of queer theory make use of poststructuralist and psychoanalytic theories which are not founded on conventional kinds of empirical study. This is true, but it doesn't make the theories wrong. Indeed, the arguments may not rely on these elements anyway – for example, although Butler draws on psychoanalytic theories a lot, I outlined her approach above without feeling the need to mention them, as the basic argument works without them (and there's no point making the theory more speculative than it needs to be). Queer theory makes sense with or without psychoanalytic elements.

Edwards also complains that many queer theorists are from a literary background and that their gender-bending arguments are supported by examples from literary texts, rather than real life. This is a fair point: illustrating an argument by reference to a few novels does not equate with decent research in the real world. So Edwards is right to suggest that this is a weakness within queer theory's claim to broad social relevance at this time, but again it does not actually show that queer theory is *wrong* about anything in particular. Furthermore, if the pioneers of queer theory happen to come from a background in literary studies, it's not really a surprise if they focus, in part, on literature. If queer theory has no sociological relevance, it will wither on the sociological vine anyway.

3 Queer theorists gaze optimistically at popular culture

Edwards notes that some of the followers of queer theory have found comfort in their analysis of certain texts carefully selected from the worlds of popular culture and art:

What is perhaps most striking concerning such works is the comparative lack of attention paid to the oppression of sexual and even racial minorities in favour of a form of cultural optimism focused primarily upon issues of representation from Rock Hudson's movies to Della Grace's photography.

(1998: 477)

Clearly Edwards is on safe ground arguing that an academic study of some 'transgressive' art photos is not going to change the world. But it's a cheap shot. The implications of the queer studies of cultural representations – films, pop stars, art, advertising – are that a proliferation of alternative views of gender and sexuality in popular culture will eventually lead to some changes. They are emphasising the importance of *culture* alongside more heavy-handed ways of changing society through legislation and regulation.

I would agree with Edwards that very detailed academic studies of challenging texts do not, in themselves, get us very far, and are possibly even a waste of time, but such studies are not at the heart of queer theory in any case. You wouldn't dismiss Marxism *as a body of thought*, for example, just because some English Literature professors had published any number of rather pointless Marxist analyses of some classic novels.

4 Seeing gender as a discourse ignores its real-world significance

Edwards says that Butler's argument that gender exists at the level of discourse ignores its significance as 'an institutionalised social practice'. This sounds like a legitimate concern, but it doesn't really stand up, because Butler is *well aware* that gender and sexuality are firmly established as seemingly 'real' and robust social phenomena. It is the discourses of gender and sexuality which make them real. And Butler's argument is precisely aimed at *collapsing* the institutionalised power which Edward is concerned about.

5 The celebration of diversity may lead to individualism and fragmentation

Edwards seems to think that marginalised groups should 'stick together' rather than focusing on differences. This makes sense. However, it's also what white feminists used to say to black women to keep them quiet – race had to be ignored as an issue so as not to split the women's movement.

Queer theory certainly does question the idea of clear-cut identities, and the idea that 'women' or 'gay people' *necessarily* have something in common. This is liberating and powerful in some ways, but also, as Edwards warns, seems to take away the case for getting equality for women (as a group) or gay people (as a group), even if society is discriminating against them *as a group*. On the other hand, queer theorists might assert that they would like to see an end to all discriminations *and* all groupings.

6 By celebrating difference, queer politics reinforces the idea of gays and lesbians as marginal and 'alternative'

This is an odd criticism, based on some misunderstandings that we have to pick apart. Edwards argues that several difficulties emerge if activists empha- sise *difference* as a political strategy, and play up the significance of altern- ative lifestyles:

> The first and more theoretical [problem] centres on the ambigu- ous sense of gays and lesbians as intrinsically different, which seems to play straight into the essentialist trap of seeing the gay man or lesbian as a specific type of person.
>
> (1998: 479)

This point is easily dispensed with, as queer theory emphatically *rejects* the idea of gay people as 'intrinsically different'. The point of the celebration of diversity and difference is that *everybody* is a little different from everybody else (and that we are happy about that). So this is quite contrary to the kind of 'heterosexuals versus homosexuals' ideology that Edwards is trying to link with it. He goes on:

> A secondary and more empirical factor is that while for some gay men and lesbians their sexuality is about a way of life and a central part of their identity, for others it amounts to little more than preferring tea or coffee. Neither is intrinsically right or wrong, yet there is a clear emphasis in queer politics upon the former approach.
>
> (1998: 479–480)

Having previously worried that queer theory might lead to apolitical fragmentation, then, Edwards is here concerned that the approach might be *too* political in relation to individual identities. This criticism is thin, at best, and since queer theorists support a proliferation of different identities – which do not all have to be 'radical' ones – it holds little sway. It is reminis- cent of when the excellent gay drama series *Queer as Folk* was first shown on

British television in 1999: a gay man complained on the viewer feedback programme *Right to Reply* that the characters were not 'normal' enough. 'I don't know anyone like that', he protested, as though the three (very different) central characters in the drama should be compelled to represent an average, blanded-out spirit of uncontroversial gayness.

7 Queer theory celebrates pleasure, sex, the visual, the young and trendy

In his final set of points, Edwards argues that queer theory should place less emphasis on *pleasure* and the *visual*. He acknowledges that there is a place for pleasure to be emphasised as an uplifting alternative to the stigmas of AIDS, homophobia and purely 'political' identities, but worries that this places too much emphasis on sex. This is a pointless, miserable complaint – what can be wrong with aspirations to pleasure? – and even Edwards keeps this bit quite short. His concern about the visual is similar: we see quite a lot of images of sexy gay people these days, he notes unhappily, but this seems to be a general complaint about the uniformity of media images of attractiveness in general. Surely if gay people are portrayed as being as sexually attractive as straight people, that's not really a problem?

These jibes tie into a more general problem for Edwards:

> Contemporary gay and lesbian politics are, in their entirety, centred upon the needs and activities of a minority: namely, those who are usually young, often affluent and frequently living in major cities where they adopt a gay (or queer) identity as a way of life. This quite clearly either excludes and/or underrepresents the interests of those who are older, poorer, live outside of major cities, and who do not run their lives around their sexual orientations.
>
> (1998: 480–481)

It is clear that this would be a problem, but again I think that Edwards has either accidentally confused himself, or is misleading his readers. The criticism quoted above might work as an attack on some of the glossy gay lifestyle magazines, but it has nothing at all to do with *queer theory*. Queer theory celebrates diversity and variety. No theory could be happier with asexual, elderly blind people. All in all, I hope I have shown that Edwards's critique of queer theory – based on an inventive variety of misrepresentations and misunderstandings – carries little weight; and hopefully this has illuminated what is good, rather than bad, about the approach.

SUMMARY

Queer theory is a radical remix of social construction theory, and a call to action: since identities are not fixed – neither to the body nor to the 'self' – we can perform 'gender' in whatever way we like. Although certain masculine and feminine formations may have been learned, these patterns can be broken. By spreading a variety of non-traditional images and ideas about how people can appear and act, the mass media can serve a valuable role in shattering the unhelpful moulds of 'male' and 'female' roles which continue to apply constraints upon people's ability to be expressive and emotionally literate beings.

FURTHER READING

Butler's *Gender Trouble* (1990) is a good next step, although not an easy read. *Undoing Gender* (2004) discusses her more recent thoughts in this area, in a slightly more accessible style. Short introductions to Butler's key work appear in Segal (1997) and Bristow (1997). Helpful book-length introductions include Salih (2002), Kirby (2006) and Lloyd (2007). More advanced readers might try some of the essays in Sönser Breen and Blumenfeld (2005) and Carver and Chambers (2007). *Sex Acts: Practices of Femininity and Masculinity* by Jennifer Harding (1998) provides a useful discussion, and links Butler's ideas to other related theories and areas. Diane Richardson's *Rethinking Sexuality* (2000) discusses queer theory and mounts a defence of radical feminism. See also *Performativity and Belonging* edited by Vikki Bell (1999) and *Revisioning Gender* edited by Ferree *et al.* (1999).

Chapter 8

MEN'S MAGAZINES AND MODERN MASCULINITIES

ALTHOUGH THEY ARE now an everyday and taken-for-granted sight in shops and on news stands, lifestyle magazines for men are a relatively new phenomenon. In this chapter we will consider the ideas about manhood conveyed by the magazines, and see whether they are simply mainstream vehicles for old-fashioned attitudes and 'soft porn' pleasures, or whether they are offering new models of male identity to modern men – or perhaps a bit of both.

In her book *OverLoaded: Popular Culture and the Future of Feminism* (2000), Imelda Whelehan argued that magazines like *Loaded*, *FHM* and *Maxim* are an attempt to override the message of feminism, promoting a laddish world where women are sex objects, and changes in gender roles can be dismissed with an ironic joke. Whelehan recognises that these magazines may not have straightforward effects – she notes that 'to assume that these readers internalise the lad credo in its entirety is to underestimate the uses to which popular culture is put by individual consumers' (p. 6). Neverthless, she says, 'it is impossible to ignore the growth of this image and its depiction of masculinity ... its prevalence offers a timely warning to any woman who felt that gender relations were now freely negotiable' (ibid.). It's a persuasive and worrying argument, especially when illustrated with some unpleasant sexist quotes from *Loaded*. However, whilst I would not want to defend the dumb excesses of many of the men's titles, this remains a rather superficial analysis, based on a caricature of what modern men's magazines are about. Their 'depiction of masculinity' can be regressive and cringe-worthy on some pages, but overall is not quite as one-dimensional as

Figure 8.1   Men's magazines: seeking masculinities for the modern world

Whelehan suggests. Furthermore, Whelehan's assumptions of how the magazines will have an impact on men's identities is too casually damning and pessimistic.

I would say that many of the academic commentaries on men's magazines – such as those by Whelehan, Rosalind Gill (2007), and others that we will look at – suffer from a *failure to explain*, in terms of the key questions: What do these magazines mean to their audience? Why do many men buy them and what do they get out of them? It is extremely easy to argue that the magazines include sexist material – whether 'humorous' and ironic or not – since they clearly do. You don't need a PhD to make that observation. Picking on instances of sexism in the magazines is simple, but it doesn't explain why men want to read these things. Close analyses of particular bits of a magazine often also come unstuck because *overall* the magazines are contradictory and do not convey one single message. Rosalind Gill (2007: 213–215), for instance, spends a couple of pages picking apart one article from *FHM* entitled 'Help! My woman is broken!'. She is critical of the stereotype in one part of the article 'that women will be coy, embarrassed and passive in the bedroom'. However, many *FHM* articles get excited about the idea of women as sexual tornadoes, and *love* the idea that the women included in their photo shoots would be sexually assertive and enthusiastic. We can predict that this would probably not make Gill much happier either, though. Indeed, even within the one article she has selected, Gill herself finds contradictions between apparently sensitive and callous solutions offered to the same 'problem'. We can endlessly criticise the foolish, coarse and sometimes nasty content of the magazines, then, but this does not help us to really understand what's going on.

Some critics seem to think that what-needs-to-be-explained is the set of devices which are used to generate ironic distance or knowingness, so that sexism can be both ridiculed and enjoyed within the same moment. That's certainly an interesting aspect of the 'lad's mags' – and may even partly explain their success, since they found a way to combine traditional male pleasures (such as looking at women without many clothes on) with a post-feminist discourse which simultaneously accepts and dispenses with the feminist critique. Nevertheless, it again doesn't really explain the appeal of the magazines (unless we accept that men are simply idiots, which may be a fun critical stance but, realistically speaking, can't be quite right). The critics are well-meaning: we don't want to see men pushed into a laddish stereo-type, or see sexism reinforced – of course not. But we really need a better understanding of the types of masculinities projected by the various maga-zines before we can even begin to try to assess their potential impact.

In Chapter 6, we saw that Foucault argued that identities were formed from the materials available to people in popular discourses. Tony Schi-rato and Susan Yell, in their discussion of men's lifestyle magazines in Australia, assert that magazines are a central point for discourses of male identity:

> It is interesting to consider how this change in the profile of men's magazines impacts on discourses of masculine subjectivity. Magazines certainly constitute a significant site within the culture for the discursive production of subjectivity – to para-phrase Janice Winship (1987: 162; writing on women's maga-zines), they operate within a nexus of 'identity – consumption – desire'. Consequently, changes in the market and profile of mag-azines indicate shifts in the 'available discourses' ... for con-structing identities.
>
> (1999: 84)

Of course, not all men read these magazines, and every person who *does* look at them will make a selective, active reading. Nevertheless, the maga-

ABOUT THE INTERVIEWS WITH READERS

In this chapter and the next, I will be referring to some qualitative interviews which I conducted by e-mail with various magazine readers in February and March 2001. Twenty women and 20 men, predominantly from the USA and the UK, were interviewed. These respondents were found by sending out requests to various (non-academic) e-mail mailing lists, asking for readers of women's or men's lifestyle magazines to contact me. Comments from these interviews are used here to illustrate and flesh out my arguments, and to show certain reactions to the magazines. The interview data does not reflect a scientific sample of magazine readers – at best, we have responses from a reasonably random bunch of self-selected people who are readers of lifestyle magazines, who are e-mail users, and who (as in all studies) are people who were willing to convey their responses to a researcher. The interviewees were encouraged to give their honest views and opinions, and discouraged from trying to make deliberately 'analytical' points just to look intellectual. (See also 'A note on methodology' in Chapter 1.)

zines are indeed a 'significant site' for discourses of masculinity, which are reflected, reproduced and perhaps manipulated on their pages. We should therefore begin with a quite detailed look at where the magazines came from, and what they're about.

THE EMERGENCE OF MEN'S LIFESTYLE MAGAZINES

The men's magazine market is relatively new. It's not that men never bought magazines in the past, of course – they were the primary purchasers of *What Car*, *Hobby Electronics*, *Angling Times* and numerous other titles dedicated to a particular hobby or interest. There were also the 'top shelf' pornography magazines such as *Playboy*, *Penthouse* and *Men Only*. But there was not really a general 'men's interests' magazine to parallel the numerous titles for 'women'. Publishers were aware of the gap in the market but felt that men would not want to read general 'lifestyle' material – glossy magazines were seen as rather feminine products, and 'real men' didn't need a magazine to tell them how to live. For instance, Joke Hermes found that the whole idea of a problem page was generally 'loathsome' and laughable to men, when she interviewed women and men about women's magazines in the early 1990s (1995: 52).

Commentators such as Tim Edwards (1997) and Sean Nixon (1996) trace the emergence of men's lifestyle magazines in the UK back to the launch of *Arena* in 1986. *Arena* was an upmarket fashion and style magazine for the urban man, which built upon the success of style magazines such as *The Face*, *i-D* and *Blitz*. These three titles had all been launched in 1980, and covered fashion, design and music for an audience of trendy young men and women. As publishers Wagadon noted that *The Face* was selling to more men than women, they encouraged its creator, Nick Logan, to launch *Arena* for slightly older style-conscious men (Nixon, 1996). *GQ* (*Gentlemen's Quarterly*), also centred on expensively stylish living and fashion, followed in 1988. These magazines were profitable but did not really smash open the market for most men. The staff of *Arena* were pleased with their early circulation figure of 65,000 (Nixon, 1996: 141), but the magazine was not reaching a significant slice of the population – and, indeed, had never intended to. *Arena* and *GQ*, as well as *Esquire* (launched in 1991), were seen as 'fashion for posh blokes – advertising executives', as one of my e-mail interviewees put it, although all three had upmarket lifestyle and literary aspirations as well.

The men's market as we know it today *really* took off with the launch of *Loaded* in 1994. *Loaded* is widely recognised as the cornerstone of the modern British 'lad' culture, and for years UK journalists regularly used '*Loaded* reader' as a shorthand for a kind of twenty-something, beer-drinking, football-loving, sex-obsessed male stereotype. However, sales of the less macho *FHM* (*For Him Magazine*) overtook those of *Loaded* in 1996, and it now sells twice as many copies each month. (*FHM* had a former life as a relatively unsuccessful fashion publication, before being relaunched as a lifestyle magazine in 1994.) Further titles, *Maxim* and *Men's Health*, were launched in 1995, and both sold well. Since then, publishers have sought to make the men's market even bigger and broader, with varying degrees of success. Overall, though, the expansion of this area has been incredible – market research by Mintel reported that by 2000, the UK men's magazine market had grown to ten times its 1993 size. And unusually, these British inventions have crossed the Atlantic: *Maxim* broke open a significant market for young men's lifestyle magazines in the USA in 1997, and was soon followed by *FHM* (although the latter ceased publication as a magazine in February 2007, apparently due to a decline in advertising revenue, although it continued as a website). At the start of 2007 there were 31 international editions of *Maxim*, and 28 of *FHM*, in a diverse list of countries around the world (see www.maximonline.com/press_room and www.fhm-international.com).

MEN'S MAGAZINES: THE ONLINE ALTERNATIVE

Men's consumer magazines might be selling less well these days, but lifestyle content appears in new forms: *Mansized* (www.mansized.co.uk), for example, is an online magazine 'aimed at men who think with their minds', offering an alternative to the *Nuts* and *Zoo* genre. It was launched in March 2006, and by mid-2007 was getting 170,000 unique visitors a month. I asked the editor, Will Callaghan, what the idea behind this 'alternative' was. He replied:

> First there seemed to be a gap in the market. Men's mags are either laddish (*Nuts, Zoo, FHM, Loaded*) or for men with money (*GQ, Esquire, Arena*) with very little in between. Sure they're read by lots of men, but I didn't know anyone who read them. I wondered, what's out there for the ordinary guy who likes a bit of everything?
>
> Second, I'd seen the quality of health, fitness and sex advice given by these kinds of mags slump over the previous few years. Men obviously want to ask questions and swap notes, but the advice they were being given was, frankly, damaging. Our aim was to do a good job on this front and it's paying off.
>
> (interview, 3 August 2007)

Asked about the current men's market, Callaghan says:

> Today's men's mags are a sad reflection on all of us. Are babes, cars, sport and a few fancy man bags all we're interested in? It's not clear who is to blame for all this. Is it the publishers who are circulation chasing and are too afraid to take a risk on something a little less formulaic, or advertisers who won't back anything unless it sells more than 100,000 copies a month?
>
> (Ibid.)

By making use of the interactive features available to an online publication, *Mansized* aims to 'end up sounding like what real men really sound like, not what *Loaded* or *FHM* think we should be like'. Although online publications are inevitably less mainstream than print magazines – which potential readers might see in the supermarket – this internet alternative seems to be having some success.

Sales of men's magazines in the UK in the second half of 2006 looked like this:

Table 8.1 Circulation figures of UK men's lifestyle magazines, 1 July–31 December 2006 (abc.org.uk)

FHM	371,263
Nuts (weekly)	295,002
Men's Health	238,568
Zoo (weekly)	204,564
Loaded	162,554
Maxim	131,497
GQ	127,505

Titles with circulations below 100,000 include *Esquire* (52,468) and *Arena* (34,556)

For the monthly magazines, these numbers are significantly lower than a few years ago. When I was writing the first edition of this book, for example, *FHM* sold 700,000 a month (in the first half of 2001), and *Loaded* was at 300,000 a month in the same period (news which at the time was seen as a disaster: 'Circulation gloom descends on *Loaded*', reported the *Guardian*). Today these figures are almost halved. To some extent this is explained by the impact of the newly popular men's *weekly* magazines, *Nuts* and *Zoo*, both launched in 2004, offering male readers cheaper issues, four times as often. If we assume that readers are only going to buy a certain number of magazines per month, more or less, then it is not surprising that *Nuts* and *Zoo*, together selling 499,566 every week, have taken sales from the more established monthly titles. Nevertheless, overall, this 'market sector' is typically seen as less novel and vibrant, and rather more desperate, than in its heyday almost a decade ago.

WHAT'S IN THEM

All of the men's lifestyle magazines cover aspects of men's lives today, which previous literature for men (the hobby and special-interest magazines) did not discuss. And they all include reviews of films, music, video games and books (except *Men's Health*). But the magazines otherwise differ quite a lot: *Loaded* celebrates watching football with a few beers, for example, but the *Men's Health* reader would forego the drink, and play the game himself. *FHM* encourages quality sex, but *Nuts* and *Zoo* might be more interested in quantity.

In the previous edition of this book, I discussed several leading magazines from both the UK and the US, with descriptions of typical content, and accounts of some of the editorial decisions that had been made in the development of each title. One of the key reasons for doing that was to show that the magazines were *not all the same*. All too often critics made sweeping statements about men's magazines – and sometimes men themselves – following an unfortunate encounter with something offensive in *Loaded*. I felt it was important to point out that, for instance, *FHM* was twice as popular, and was not exactly the same, containing more sensitive relationship advice and a less mechanical approach to sex.

In this edition, I will give less detail on separate magazine titles (which you can study for yourself easily enough), and will instead discuss some of their most prominent themes. Meanwhile, the more detailed discussion of men's magazines from 2001 can be found, if you want it, at www.theoryhead.com.

CORE NARRATIVES IN MEN'S MAGAZINES

Rather than going through magazines one-by-one, I will simply highlight some of the main 'stories of masculinity' which are most commonly presented in these texts. Although they show that the magazines are not *just* soft-porn photo sessions, these themes will not come as much of a surprise to readers of these publications.

Men like (to look at) women

Numerous photo-shoots of semi-clothed and topless women appear in the UK magazines such as *FHM*, *Loaded*, *Maxim*, *Nuts* and *Zoo*, and in US titles *Maxim* and *Stuff* – although the US magazines are somewhat more coy about nudity than their UK counterparts. The more 'upmarket' titles such as *GQ* (several international editions) also find excuses to photograph actresses and models in little clothing, including, for instance, Jessica Biel in a swimsuit (US edition, August 2007), or 16 pages on Victoria's Secret lingerie models (UK edition, June 2007).

... But don't know too much about them

Readers of men's magazines seem to need instruction in how to get along with women. Every issue of *FHM* and *Maxim* includes advice on how to be better in bed – to satisfy your female partner. Other articles of this type, for instance, cover seven reasons why a woman might not want to sleep with you (*Men's Health*, June 2007), a guide to the sexual preferences of women 'from 17 to 70' (*FHM* UK, June 2007), Gemma from TV soap *Hollyoaks* solving 'your sex and relationship dilemmas' (*Zoo*, 12 January 2007), how to catch a woman's eye (*Men's Health*, June 2007), and 'Ladies confess' in *Nuts*, which supposedly offers insights into women's racy lives for sex-starved readers.

Men like cars, gadgets and sport

A fascination with fast vehicles and electronic gadgets is reflected in almost all of the magazines. Sport features heavily in the UK men's weeklies in terms of spectatorship, and US monthlies as both spectatorship and participation. The fascination with hardware and masculine products brings a consumerist dimension to the publications. *GQ* man, in particular, buys his way to a sense of male specialness with expensive cars, meals, hotels, shoes, grooming products, suits and property. The UK magazine *Stuff* is focused on consumer electronics, whilst the US magazine of the same name broadens the theme to include movies, games, vehicles, and anything else that might be purchased (alongside more common men's magazine articles such as interviews with female celebrities). Men are therefore addressed as consumers – traditionally the role of women – although here it seems that ultimately it is a sense of masculine *pride* which is to be bought.

Men need help

The magazines are supportive of 'men's' activities in general, but they suggest that their readers need help along the way. Fashion and grooming advice appears in all of the magazines. Men are advised on relationships, as we have seen, but the advice does not stop there. Men are also helped with issues such as how to avoid alcoholism (*FHM* UK, June 2007), or addictions to food, sex, gambling and drugs (*Maxim* US, June 2007); how to get over a hangover (*Loaded*, June 2007); how to dress in hot weather (*FHM* UK, June 2007); how to become more intelligent (*Men's Health*, June 2007); how to succeed in job interviews, choose the ideal suit, massage a woman's foot and/or be a good father (*Esquire* US, June 2007); and how to be confidently romantic rather than macho and insecure (*FHM* UK, August 2007).

In the US, the more mature *Best Life* magazine offers advice on – for example – keeping romance alive in a long-term relationship, patching up a friendship damaged by an argument, how to switch off from work to focus on family, plus help with diet, exercise, health, even erectile dysfunction – and that's all in one issue (June 2007). Most of the magazines also like to teach 'skills', such as advice on ocean kayak fishing, riding a mechanical bull, playing foosball, cooking a meal and oral sex (all in *Maxim* US, June 2007).

Men are fascinated by bravery and danger

An obsession with heroism and jeopardy can be seen frequently, such as a feature on urban adventures including crane climbing and sewer surfing (*Loaded*, July 2007), an account of 'the world's biggest ever gold robbery' (*FHM* UK, August 2007), an interview with a man who was imprisoned and tortured in a Saudi Arabian jail (*FHM* UK, June 2007), and a feature on live bull riding (*Loaded*, June 2007). Toughness is also emphasised via negative features such as '15 most notorious nancies in sport' (*Maxim* US, June 2007).

Emphasis on these masculine pursuits is sometimes underlined by features such as 'The Truth about Women' in *Nuts*, where for instance model Lucy Pinder explains that 'women really, really love a man in uniform. I particularly like soldiers' uniforms – there's something quite testosteroney about them ... [they] just seem to offer masculinity and heroism' (18 May 2007: 28). On the other hand this appears alongside some somewhat less rugged questions-and-answers about relationships.

Here we have merely summarised the key narratives of masculinity that are presented by the magazines. They are not always predictable. For example *Maxim* (US edition, June 2007) included an informative analysis of the likelihood of a war between the US and Iran, whilst *Men's Health* (UK, June 2007) included a feature suggesting that you might want to take up wrestling. But the general themes (fighting, sport) are familiar, and the publications rarely turn their back on their standardised model of masculinity.

THE GLOBALISATION OF MASCULINITIES

Although models of masculinity have been circulated around the world in religion and literature for several centuries, and in film for over 100 years, the more specific outline of hegemonic masculinity presented by men's lifestyle magazines has become part of media globalisation. As noted above, different country- or region-specific editions of *FHM* and/or *Maxim* have been launched in Australia, Bulgaria, Croatia, Denmark, Estonia, France, Germany, Greece, Hungary, India, Indonesia, Latvia, Lithuania, Malaysia, Mexico, the Netherlands, New Zealand, Norway, the Philippines, Portugal, Romania, Russia, Serbia, Singapore, Slovenia, South Africa, Spain, Sweden, Taiwan, Thailand, Turkey, Venezuela and elsewhere. Apart from some variation in their level of rudeness, these magazines project fundamentally the same image of men, women, and men's interests and concerns – scantily-clad women, sport, drinking and the other themes listed above. Even the lust icons are frequently the same: the French *FHM* (May 2007), for instance, has features on American stars Kelly Carlson ('Le bombe de *Nip/Tuck*'), Avril Lavigne ('princesse punk') and Ali Larter from *Heroes*, plus UK pop star Sophie Ellis-Bextor; and French readers are introduced to Erin Jansen, recent winner of a 'Miss FHM' title in Australia. Men also get to pick their own favourites here ('FHM 100 stars les plus sexy election 2007') and in most other editions.

Sadly for the supposedly 'sophisticated' British, American magazines are generally a little less juvenile than their UK counterparts, with less nudity and sexual humour. Whilst almost all of the UK men's magazines are built around the broadly laddish themes of *FHM* and *Loaded*, in the US there is a clear alternative in publications such as *Men's Journal* and *Best Life*, which involve an appreciation of outdoor living, exercise and health, and tackle more 'responsible' concerns such as fatherhood and workplace issues. It would not be correct to say that these magazines are necessarily less macho, however. The reader of *Men's Journal* in the US, who is expected to be into whitewater rafting, mountain climbing, kiteboarding and fishing for sharks (all covered in the July 2007 issue), is more of a masculine archetype than the anticipated reader of *Nuts* and *Zoo* in the UK, who is merely expected to sit indoors gazing at pictures of 'boobs'. Both are constructions of masculinity, and both are distinct from femininity, but they are not quite the same.

Despite such differences, it is the *similarity* of these visions of men's interests that are the most striking. The point here, of course, is *not* that men are all the same around the world. Rather, ideas about manhood may vary from country to country, but the rather monolithic *Maxim/FHM* version is projected in numerous regions with little variation. Like many aspects of globalisation, it's not a conspiracy as such, but the repetition of ideas and images in diverse territories can seem rather one-dimensional and disappointing.

SO WHAT DOES THE POPULARITY OF THESE MAGAZINES *MEAN*?

The new men's magazines have been given predictably rough treatment by some cultural critics. Pro-feminist and left-wing writers often seem to see the provocative picture of a scantily-clad woman on the cover and assume that the meaning of the entire magazine can be 'read off' from that image alone – it's a sexist repositioning of soft porn, and that's all there is to be said. Even those who glance inside are quick to judge. For example, Andrew Sullivan (2000), writing in the liberal US current affairs magazine *New Republic*, dismissed contemporary men's magazines as plain 'dumb'. He had evidence from one issue of the US market leader, *Maxim*:

> The June issue features a primer on penis size ('How It's *Really* Hangin''), [and] a moronic guide to becoming a millionaire ('Rule #4: Ditch your loser friends').

Sullivan's smug rejection of these features ignores the humour and self-consciousness that riddle these magazines. Articles such as the one on becoming a millionaire are meant to be read as humourous, jokily aspirational but fundamentally silly; to sneer at the quality of their advice is to miss the point. Meanwhile, it would be wrong to see the penis article as a restatement of phallic dominance; on the contrary, surely a very un-macho cloud of *insecurity* hangs over the male audience for articles on penis size. It is difficult to imagine a masculine archetype like Arnold Schwarzenegger settling down to study *Maxim*'s guide to how he measures up in the trouser department.

The most perceptive and sensitive analysis of the 'new' men's magazines and their readers has been produced by the research team of Peter Jackson, Nick Stevenson and Kate Brooks, in work published 1999–2001 (Jackson *et al.*, 1999; Stevenson *et al.*, 2000; and most notably the book *Making Sense of Men's Magazines*, Jackson *et al.*, 2001). These researchers thankfully do not assume a moral superiority to the magazines or their readers, and do not try to 'prove' that the magazines are mere trash, enjoyed by a large audience of mindless fools. Instead, they take the huge growth of men's magazines to be a cultural phenomenon worthy of serious consideration, which should be able to tell us something about men and masculinity today. In the following sections I will discuss some of the points made by Jackson, Stevenson and Brooks, whilst also making my own argument that the magazines really show men to be quite *insecure* and *confused* in the modern world, and seeking help and *reassurance*, even if this is (slightly) suppressed by a veneer of irony and heterosexual lust.

ISN'T IT IRONIC

Jackson *et al.* rightly note that the men's magazines usually address the reader as a 'mate', of the same status as the magazine journalists themselves. The tone is generally 'friendly, ironic and laddish' (Jackson *et al.*, 2001: 77). The irony is used as a kind of defensive shield: the writers *anticipate* that many men may reject serious articles on relationships, or advice about sex, health or cooking, and so douse their pieces with humour, silliness and irony to 'sweeten the pill'. (I do not mean 'silliness' to be a criticism: the way in which *FHM* combines serious advice with funny and 'inappropriate' humour can be quite clever.) This use of irony is no secret. As publishers EMAP launched *FHM* in South Africa – just one part of the global expansion of the title – their internal marketing blurb proudly explained:

> Before *FHM*, conventional wisdom had it that women read magazines from an introspective point of view, seeking help and advice for, and about, themselves. Men on the other hand, read magazines about things like sport, travel, science, business and cars. *FHM* realises that men will read magazines about themselves if you give them the information in the right context: irreverent, humorous and *never* taking itself too seriously. The articles in *FHM*, although highly informative, are written tongue-in-cheek. The fashion is accessible, the advice humorous and empathetic.
>
> (www.natmags.com, 1999)

Jackson *et al.* note that the magazines 'are careful to avoid talking down to their readers' (2001: 76), and their focus group interviews confirm that men like to feel that they are flicking through the magazines and not taking them too seriously, which they believe is in contrast to women who read magazine advice 'religiously' (2001: 126). In fact, research on female magazine readers indicates that they too like to treat their magazines lightly and with little commitment (Hermes, 1995), but the fact remains that male readers seem to be extremely wary of being told what to do – they like to feel they know best already – which is why humour and irony has to be deployed. Jackson *et al.* note that the exception is *Men's Health*, where the magazine takes the role of a trusted health advisor, and (perhaps inevitably) has to use a more 'expert' tone. At the same time, *Men's Health* became increasingly successful as it started to mimic, in some parts but not others, the anti-serious tone of *FHM* – for example, a mental health quiz in the December 2001 issue was promoted with the cheerful cover line 'Will You Lose Your Marbles?'; and a September 2007 article on relationship psychology was sold to readers on the cover as: 'Jedi Sex Tricks: How To Read Her Dirty Mind'.

The fact that humour and irony is required in the magazines does not, of course, show that today's men do not 'really' want to read articles and advice about relationships, sex, health or other 'personal' matters. After all, the magazines could easily forget about these areas altogether, and focus on cars and guns and whitewater rafting. So we have to conclude that many men *want* articles like this, but do not want other people – or even perhaps themselves – to think that they *need* them. The humour of the lifestyle articles means that they can be read 'for a laugh' although, I would argue, men are at the same time quietly curious to pick up information about relationships and sex, and what is considered good or bad practice in these areas. It's difficult to prove this assertion, by definition, because men are not eager to admit to this curiosity – and indeed, in the focus groups conducted by Jackson *et al.*, many of the men said dismissive things about the magazines, but at the same time appeared to be familiar with their contents.

Irony provides a 'protective layer', then, between lifestyle information and the readers, so that men don't have to feel patronised or inadequate. But irony has other functions too. Jackson *et al.* assert that one of these is 'to subvert political critique' (2001: 78) – in other words, feminists or others who criticise the content of the magazines can be said to be 'missing the joke', making their complaints redundant. This is true, but I would say that irony is not used in order to provide a 'get-out clause' against critics. Although the sexism of some of the less popular magazines (such as *Front* or *Loaded*) can sometimes appear genuine, in *FHM* and its imitators I would say that it is the *irony* which is genuine. The *FHM* writer, and their projected reader, *do actually know* that women are as good as men, or better; the put-downs of women – such as jokey comments about their supposed incompetence with technology – are knowingly ridiculous, based on the assumptions that it's silly to be sexist (and therefore is funny, in a silly way), and that men are usually just as rubbish as women. In an analysis of an Australian 'lad's' magazine, *Ralph* – similar to *Loaded* – Schirato and Yell concur with this kind of diagnosis, writing that '*Ralph*'s performances of "stereotypical" masculinity are self-conscious "over-performances" of a set of discourses and subjectivities which it recognises are already in a sense obsolete' (1999: 81).

The idea that the underlying assumptions of these magazines are more anti-sexist than sexist may not always be true, of course, and is optimistic; and it is always possible for readers to read the sexist jokiness literally. But I would say that this 'sexist jokiness' of *FHM* is based on thoroughly non-sexist assumptions – the *intended* laugh, more often than not, is about the silliness of being sexist, rather than actual sexism, because in the world of *FHM* men are aware, however quietly or embarrassedly, that it's only fair to treat women and men as equals in the modern world, and that sexism is idiotic.

Having said that, it has to be admitted that many *FHM* readers may be sexist, in one way or another, and their reading of *FHM* may not challenge their sexism, and might indeed support it. That's sadly true. At the same time, though, *FHM* consistently teaches men to treat their girlfriends nicely, to try to be considerate and to give satisfaction, both sexually and in more general terms. It also teaches men various domestic skills – even if the justification is that it will 'impress your lady'. You could even say that *FHM*'s general project is to create a man who is competent in the home and kitchen, skilled in the bedroom, not overly dependent on his partner, healthy, interested in travel, able to buy his own fashionable clothes, a good laugh and a pleasure to live with. Based on this list, we have the kind of man that feminists would surely prefer to have around. The pictures of beautiful members of the opposite sex wearing little clothing, and the emphasis on sex rather than relationships, don't fit within this thesis, of course, although we can at least point out that several *women's* magazines today contain the same kind of material too.

WHY IRONY?

Jackson *et al.* do recognise that men's magazines are complex and contradictory (and indeed this view is emphasised most in their book (2001) compared to their earlier, slightly more antagonistic articles). Nevertheless, they generally tend to play down the nuances and conflicting elements, preferring to treat the magazines as more-or-less relentlessly laddish and 'masculine'. This leads them to get some things, in my view, exactly right, and other things wrong. For example, they provide a definition of irony, by Richard Rorty, which suggests that a person using irony does so to indicate an awareness that they are using terms which are uncertain, not necessarily 'true', and open to challenge. Jackson *et al.* ruminate that this would mean that men's magazines are not really being ironic at all, but are using a discourse of 'common sense' – although they find this account unsatisfactory too (2001: 104):

> It is precisely the lack of awareness of the constructed nature of masculine identity that seems so pervasive. Yet to argue that the magazines reflect the return of a form of masculine common sense is to treat the texts as less problematic than we believe them to be. Our argument is rather that irony is used as an ideological defence against external attack (only the most humourless do not get the joke) and an internal defence against more ambivalent feelings that render masculine experience less omnipotent and less certain than it is represented here.

Here, I would agree that irony is indeed used for both of the reasons given. The problem is that Jackson *et al.* seem to assume that the irony is *successful* as an 'internal defence' – in other words, that the use of irony really does 'protect' masculinity, and keeps those 'ambivalent feelings' hidden from view. This is also reflected in the authors' assertion, at the start of the quotation above, that there is a 'pervasive' 'lack of awareness of the constructed nature of masculine identity' in the men's magazines. I would argue that this is quite wrong – on the contrary, today's magazines for men are *all about* the social construction of masculinity. That is, if you like, their subject-matter.

In the past, men didn't need lifestyle magazines because it was obvious what a man was, and what a man should do, anyway. It is only in the modern climate, in which we are all aware of the many choices available to us, and are also aware of the feminist critique of traditional masculinity, and the fact that gender roles can and do change, that men have started to need magazines about how to be a man today. Jackson *et al.* suggest that the magazines foster a 'constructed certitude' built around the laddish values of responsibility-free sex, drinking and messing about (2001: 86) – where this 'constructed certitude' means a sense that 'this is the reliable essence of being a young man today'. But I would say that just as they do this on some pages, the magazines undermine it on others, raising questions about the different ways in which men can present an acceptable face today. (See Chapter 5, on the work of Anthony Giddens, for more on how people in 'late modernity' are increasingly required to choose a lifestyle, and construct a 'narrative of the self')'. Funnily enough, Jackson *et al.* seem to recognise this elsewhere in their book – noting, for example, that 'the magazines have encouraged men to "open up" previously repressed aspects of their masculinity (including attitudes to health, fashion and relationships)' (p. 22), and that 'the magazines signify the *potential* for new forms of masculinity to emerge even as the magazines are simultaneously reinscribing older and more repressive forms of masculinity' (p. 23, their emphasis).

There is little sign that people buy magazines just to reinforce ideas and assumptions that they are already familiar with. One of the key themes of lifestyle magazines, I would say, is that nothing in life is totally given and fixed. This is a message we welcome. Surveys show that a majority of people in society feel unsatisfied and would welcome change in their lives; having a well-paid job doesn't make respondents any more satisfied, and although many people today spend money in a bid to make themselves happier, this doesn't work (Layard, 2006). We read magazines partly for the pleasure of the glossy surfaces and attractive photographs, and partly to answer the question 'What can I do next?'.

Of course, talking about men's magazines is made more complicated by the fact that the content of different titles varies considerably. Jackson *et al.*'s view that the magazines are trying to re-assert a stable kind of more-or-less old-school masculinity makes much more sense when applied to UK *Loaded* than when applied to UK *FHM* or US *Maxim*. But the latter titles remain the market leaders. It's also curious to note that Jackson *et al.* quote former *Loaded* editor Tim Southwell describing the magazine as 'a weird mixture of lusting after women, failing to get off with women, thinking about heroes, thinking about childhood experiences' (Stevenson *et al.*, 2000: 374). This doesn't sound like a super-confident masculinity; frustrated desires and nostalgia are quite the opposite of a thrusting agenda. Of course, *Loaded* often *was* quite pig-headedly macho, but this seam of disappointments and memories was always there too.

Finally, on the debatable importance of irony, it is worth quoting one of the men I interviewed by e-mail about their consumption of men's magazines; I asked specifically about whether irony was a dominant theme:

> I've seen articles in the *Guardian* or whatever where they talk about the ironic tone of men's magazines. But everybody knows that, so it's not clever to point that out in the *Guardian* because all of the readers of *FHM* and *Loaded* know that anyway ... Many if not all of the articles [in the magazines] are written in that jokey tone, where nothing seems to be taken seriously. It's not heartless though because it's like having a laugh with your friends in the pub, so it's quite warm. The interesting thing about men's magazines is not the fact that they have this ironic style, but all the nervous concerns going on underneath. Men

don't read the magazines because they are fans of irony! They read them for other reasons.

(26-year-old male from Edinburgh, Scotland)

The 'nervous concerns' would be the questions which *FHM* and *Maxim*, and to a lesser extent *Loaded*, address all the time (within their jokey discourse, of course) – questions which can all be summarised as 'Am I doing this right?': Is my relationship OK? Is my sexual technique good? These things I do – am I odd or am I normal? Is everyday life always like this? And – how *do* you put up shelves?

FEAR OF INTIMACY?

Another theme in the arguments of Jackson *et al.* is the idea that men's magazines reflect a 'fear' of intimacy or commitment. They say that the magazines which emerged in the 1990s were focused – amongst other things – on 'obsessive forms of independence (read: fear of commitment and connection)' (2001: 78); and are a 'celebration of autonomy and a fear of dependence' (p. 81). Later we are again told that they are 'a desperate defence of masculine independence' (p. 82).

This all makes being independent sound like a psychotic tendency, and some kind of macho neurosis. But women's magazines have filled hundreds of pages, over *years*, telling women how to be independent, and it's a message they still carry. And that's fine: the message that you shouldn't depend on a partner for your happiness is widely seen as being a very good one. Being a 'dependent' person is not ideal, and if we think that's true for women, it's true for men too. Calling it a 'fear of dependence' is Jackson *et al.*'s sneaky way of making it sound like a product of dumb macho psychology, but the received wisdom from women's magazines and self-help books is that being wary of becoming dependent is eminently sensible. We can also note that feminism used to criticise men for being too dependent on their female partners, sapping women's energies by selfishly expecting women to tend to their emotional, sexual and domestic needs. That was a good criticism. But now if we criticise men for being maddeningly independent – as if men are selfishly *refusing* to rely on women for emotional support – it starts to get a bit silly.

To be fair, though, although Jackson *et al.* don't exactly explain *why* they view the promotion of independence as a bad thing in men's magazines, we can infer that they are concerned that the magazines encourage men to be *too* self-contained – the kind of man who couldn't express himself fully within a relationship, perhaps, and who was unable to give love and share his life with someone (like the 'Tin Man' syndrome discussed in Chapter 10). And we can agree that that would not be good. But do the magazines really encourage men to be excessively insular and unexpressive? Not really. As we saw in the 'Core narratives in men's magazines' section above, a significant feature of most of the leading men's magazines is that they are full of relationship tips, focused in particular on how to be a decent boyfriend in sexual, romantic and practical ways. Communication and fairness are consistenly emphasised, even if often put in reluctant or jokey-selfish terms.

The enormously successful US version of *Maxim* does sometimes seem to embrace the idea that women are eager to 'trap' men into a long-term relationship or marriage, and this, of course, is an irritating slice of sexism. The view that a person should not be tied too hastily into an imperfect relationship, however, especially when young, is a perfectly reasonable one. Without wanting to defend the dim sexism of some articles in the US *Maxim*, the advice itself isn't terrible. And we can note that after feminists went to such lengths to argue that marriage was a patriarchal system which trapped women into an unhappy life of exploitation and lack of freedom, it seems (again) a bit odd for us to start complaining that men's magazines are not in favour of marriage or similar tight commitments.

In general, there does not seem to be evidence for a 'fear of intimacy' in men's magazines; there is a *fear of anything that might stop you enjoying yourself*, which includes boring mates, the police, illnesses and partners that do things that prevent you from having a good time. Positive relationships are not to be feared, though, and the best-selling magazines are full of advice about how to keep your girlfriend happy.

REINSCRIBING SEXISM

As already mentioned in the sections on 'irony' above, men's magazines are often accused of trying to re-assert sexism and male dominance, and are said to be part of a 'backlash' against feminism. The view that they are sexist is often based on the observation that the magazines usually contain several pictures of women wearing clothes which are small, or not there at all, and in seductive poses (but without quite 'showing everything' in the style of pornography). One reply to this is that some magazines for women do the same thing back to men these days – in the UK, the celebrity magazine *Heat* delights in showing pictures of semi-naked hunks, and sells more copies than *Nuts* and *Zoo* combined – so this can't be a case of sexism as such, since both men and women are shown in these ways. A counter-argument to this might be that women are sometimes shown in 'fuck me' poses, whilst men are usually not. But we only need to use slightly different words to correctly point out that both men and women are shown in 'I'd like to have sex with you' poses.

Alluring pictures of semi-naked women could specifically be said to be sexist because this feeds into the objectification of women, which is a long-standing form of oppression. Since there is not a comparable historical tradition of the offensive 'objectification of men', pictures of semi-naked men do not have the same impact. This used to be a really good argument, but as time goes by we start to think that since magazines for women *and* those for men celebrate super-attractive people, both women and men, it probably doesn't matter in sexism terms. At the same time we might be annoyed that the same ideas of beauty are being regurgitated over and over again.

As for the idea that 'male dominance' can be resurrected by the magazines, we can quote an interviewee who made this pertinent point:

> Even if a guy, say, read *Front* and took it literally and 'learned sexism' from it, I don't see why feminists would find that threatening or worrying because what is this guy? He's nothing, he's a loser. You don't get on in the world today by being sexist. People will just think he's a stupid twat.
>
> (30-year-old male from York, England)

Another respondent made a similar point:

> Male readers drooling over these women [in the magazines] … It's not really an assertion of power is it. Women who can make men go weak at the knees, and make them do stupid things, that's power. Which is fine.
>
> (28-year-old male from Brighton, England)

We can infer from their ages that these respondents are men who have heard the feminist arguments of the late 1980s and early 1990s, when looking at scantily-clad women was clearly quite wrong for any right-thinking man, but have started to change their views as time has moved on and gender relations have changed again (including the development of the new language in popular culture where women can treat men as disposable eye-candy too). As another man commented:

> I used to agree, and I mean I really did agree, with women who said that naked women in magazines was a bad thing. But nowadays I can hardly even remember what the argument was.

> Women can look at handsome men in films and magazines, and
> men can look at attractive women ... it seems fair. What were
> we complaining about again? Is it because we were afraid of sex?
>
> (29-year-old male from New York, USA)

To move on to the remaining question, can all this be seen as a backlash
against feminism? Sometimes it might be: the cruder sexism found in some
of the magazines can seem to be fuelled by anti-feminist feeling, and the
sexism in itself is clearly unhelpful. I would argue that *FHM* and its imitators are not part of a backlash, though: *FHM* and *Maxim* are for men who
accept the changes that feminism has brought, and are working out how to
fit into that world. The magazines may not be doing terribly well at this –
hence the unfortunate bursts of unbridled sexism and not-funny homophobia. Nevertheless, the nuances of modern identity-seeking are being played
out subtly in their contradictory and imperfect pages.

MEN AND WOMEN AS CLEAR AND OPPOSITE IDENTITIES

Finally, Jackson *et al.* argue that in men's magazines, 'men and women are
[represented as] polar opposites in terms of their sexual identities and
desires' (2001: 84), and suggest that the magazines' model of 'new lad'
masculinity 'acts as a means of enforcing boundaries between men and
women' (2001: 86). They go on to say:

> The accompanying fear seems to be that, unless men and
> women are rigidly rendered apart, this would introduce a small
> grain of uncertainty within the representation of masculine iden-
> tity, thereby threatening to undermine it all together ... 'New
> laddism', as we have seen, leaves no room for doubt, question-
> ing, ambiguity or uncertainty.
>
> (2001: 86)

Again, this looks like quite a good argument on paper, but doesn't match
up with the actual content of the magazines – especially as these points are
made in relation to *FHM* in particular. As I have already argued, the magazines do *not* assume that their readers have a fixed and ready-to-wear masculine identity – if they did, they would not fill so many pages with advice
on how to achieve some basic competences in life. *FHM* in particular is
quietly brimming with the 'doubt, questioning, ambiguity [and] uncertainty' which Jackson *et al.* say is absent. In the late 1990s, when Jackson *et*

al. were looking at the magazines, even the *covers* of *FHM* were riddled with anxiety: 'Fat? Boring? Crap in bed? Does this sound familiar to anyone?' (February 1998), 'Look at the state of you!' (February 1998), 'Am I gay?' (February 1999), 'Is your love life just a hollow sham?' (April 1999), 'Are you going mental?' (April 1999) and 'Does your penis horrify women?' (July 1999) are typical examples.

As for the idea that women and men are shown to be 'polar opposites' sexually – Jackson *et al.* note an implication in a few articles that whilst men are perenially eager for sex, women 'would always prefer a candle-lit bath' (2001: 84) – this doesn't apply to most articles in most of the magazines, which generally assume that women will be eager and willing partners in sexual activities – especially if men deploy the pleasureable techniques suggested. Meanwhile, it's true that the magazines do often joke about general supposed 'differences' between women and men, although this can be at the expense of either sex. I would also repeat my suggestion that the magazines don't *really* think that the differences are fundamental, and that the 'sexist jokiness' is based on an understanding that men and women are not very different *really* – an idea underlined by the fact that men's and women's magazines are becoming increasingly similar in very obvious ways. Nevertheless, this discourse of difference can be a troubling aspect of the publications. One of my e-mail interviewees, a gay man who enjoyed *FHM*, said this:

> I think the fact that *FHM* – and *Loaded* maybe even more so – suggest men and women are fundamentally different is the thing that annoys me most about them. They generalise too much about the categories 'men' and 'women', and perpetuate the idea that there's a 'sex war' going on. (Having said that, the fact that I feel I can 'adapt' [the magazines] to my (different) lifestyle suggests there's some room for movement in the values they express...)
>
> (22-year-old male from Leeds, England)

In general it seems most appropriate to see men's magazines as reflecting a frequently imperfect attempt to find positions for the ideas of 'women' and 'men' in a world where it's pretty obvious that the sexes are much more the same than they are different. The magazines sometimes discuss men and women as if they were different species, but this is a way of making sense of reality, rather than reality itself, and readers (hopefully) understand this.

WHAT OTHER RESPONDENTS SAID

A few more comments from my e-mail interviewees are worth mentioning. One young man offered this interesting commentary on the unfulfilled promise at the heart of men's magazine consumption:

> I was thinking about this and there's a lot of disappointment involved in buying men's magazines. You get excited about buying a new copy of a magazine like *FHM*, it's so nice and glossy, and they have a style of photography that makes everything look so sparkly and desirable (especially, of course, the women). But then it's a bit disappointing because there's not really much in it, and it's disappointing to find that the women, when interviewed, don't sound that interesting really. And it's disappointing because you see these gorgeous women who wouldn't look twice at you, but then you remember that they probably look quite like people you know, really, and it's the very careful styling and makeup and photography that makes them so irresistible, but then that's quite disappointing too. Most of all, it's disappointing that you fell for it, and will continue to fall for it.
>
> (24-year-old male from Nottingham, England)

The troubling thing for this respondent seems to be his complicity in his own exploitation: the publishers know that he can be tricked into buying each issue with the promise of something 'sparkly and desirable'; the particularly galling thing is that he falls for it month after month, and that in spite of this there is still pleasure in the anticipation, and in the moment of purchase. This was echoed elsewhere too, such as in a London man's observation that he was drawn to the features on beautiful women which 'are tittilating, although contrived'. Another regular reader was troubled by the conflicting signals projected by the magazines:

> Every issue has some article on how to get women in bed. Men who require an article to be able to do this seem to be far from the marketed image of the self-confident, sophisticated male who reads these magazines.
>
> (22-year-old male from Nashville, Tennessee, USA)

There were interesting responses to my question, 'Do these magazines help you to think of yourself as a particular kind of person?' This man was a regular reader of *FHM*, *Loaded*, *Arena* and *GQ*, and liked the way in which they gave him a sense of fitting in with popular culture:

> [They help me think of myself] as an achiever or wannabe. Part of mainstream culture, doing the things mainstream culture requires ... They offer examples of 'success', and how to achieve this success.
>
> (23-year-old male from London, England)

Others were more reluctant to identify with the target audience, even where they probably *were* the target audience:

> I don't like to think of myself as the typical reader of these magazines [*FHM*], even though I secretly enjoy it. It makes me smile. I overlook the sexism. The whole magazine is undeniably attractive, I like the fact that it's like a glossy woman's magazine with a bit of everything, except it's for men.
>
> (26-year-old male from Bradford, England)

> I enjoy reading the problems and the advice [in *FHM*]. At school we always read the problem pages in the girls' copies of *Just Seventeen*, for a laugh, we would say, though actually we were curious about the sex advice too. It's good to have problem pages in a men's magazine – we obviously need it really!
>
> (27-year-old male from Cardiff, Wales)

These quotes confirm that men are aware of the changing social construction of masculinity and are willing to welcome the self-help aspect of women's magazines which were previously alien to men's reading culture. Respondents were often keen to show that they didn't take the magazines too seriously, but this gay subscriber to *Men's Health* embraced the publication wholeheartedly and with no sign of irony:

> This magazine definitely reaffirms my masculinity. I see what is going on in the straight man's world, and try to incorporate it into my life to be perceived as more desirable in the gay man's culture.... I try to become more like the men in the magazine – fitter, muscular, stylish, attractive. I am gay, and this is a straight man's magazine, but much of my style is directly influenced by this magazine. I have been a subscriber for almost five

years, and have used *Men's Health* for information on all sorts of topics revolving around what it means to be a man in the world today.

(24-year-old male from Chicago, USA)

He found particular *value* in *Men's Health*'s enthusiasm for physical improvement:

It gives men a self-conscious sense of style and appearance. It makes them more body conscious. This is not a negative trait, it brings men into the consumer culture of fashion [which] women have always been a part of. I think this is a positive thing, for both men and women. I don't think it will make the world a better place by making us all look beautiful – that is silly, but I do think that it provides men with images that would make them think twice about their appearance, and maybe begin to understand appearance like women do. Maybe it will bridge some kind of gap between the sexes. I don't know.

(as above)

The comments from female readers were also revealing. This woman felt that the magazines reflected a world where men were not coping well:

[Looking at the men's magazines] brings out the mothering in me, because it makes me feel that men are lost. Not that I particularly want to mother a man or a group of men, but it makes me sad and curious.

(34-year-old female from Melbourne, Australia)

This view seems to support my argument that the image of men which emerges from the magazines is not powerful and strong – rather the opposite, that men are seeking help. A younger woman read the magazines in more positive mode, because she found them preferable to the publications aimed at women:

It's annoying that these mags are aimed mostly at men, and I wish that some articles found in men's mags could also be like that in women's mags too! It defines the men as lads in the pub, real male bonding going on, and women as girlfriends and sexual partners, but I have a laugh too in the pub, laughing at men's crude jokes, playing pool (which I'm great at) and drinking pints. (But then sometimes they do have articles with successful and sassy women like [TV presenter] Denise van Outen for example).

(21-year-old female from Bristol, UK)

SUMMARY

In this discussion I have argued against the view that men's lifestyle magazines represent a reassertion of old-fashioned masculine values, or a 'backlash' against feminism. Whilst certain pieces in the magazines might support such an argument, this is not their primary purpose or selling point. Instead, I have suggested, their existence and popularity shows men rather insecurely trying to find their place in the modern world, seeking help regarding how to behave in relationships, and advice on how to earn the attention, love and respect of women, and the friendship of other men. To put this into the terms of the theories we discussed earlier in this book, in post-traditional cultures, where identities are not 'given' but need to be constructed and negotiated (see Chapter 5), and where an individual has to establish their personal ethics and mode of living (Chapter 6), the magazines offer some reassurance to men who are wondering 'Is this right?' and 'Am I doing this OK?', enabling a more confident management of the narrative of the self. At the same time, the magazines may raise some anxieties – about fitness of the body, say, or whether the reader is sufficiently 'one of the boys'. The discourses of masculinity which the magazines help to circulate can therefore, unsurprisingly, be both enabling and constraining. When considered in relation to queer theory's call for 'gender trouble' (Chapter 7), the magazines' conceptions of gender seem remarkably narrow. Nevertheless, the playfulness of the magazines and their (usually) cheerful, liberal attitude to most things – apart from the occasional nasty sting of homophobia – suggests that some fluidity of identities is invited. Furthermore, the humour and irony found throughout these publications doesn't hide a strong macho agenda, but conceals the nervousness of boys who might prefer life to be simpler, but are trying to do their best to face up to modern realities anyway.

Chapter 9

WOMEN'S MAGAZINES
AND FEMALE IDENTITIES

IN CHAPTER 3, WE traced the history of women's magazines
through the second half of the twentieth century, from the traditional
publications – with their emphasis on the home, beauty, finding a husband
and keeping him – through to the success of the 'independent and sexy'
Cosmopolitan in the 1980s and 1990s. But what messages do today's magazines convey? And what do readers make of them?

THE DEBATE ABOUT THE MAGAZINES' IMPACT

To establish the background to the debate about women's magazines, it is
worth looking at the way that the discussion of their impact on young women
has turned around in the past 25 years. The early work of Angela McRobbie,
in the late 1970s, is today seen as a case study in how *not* to approach such
research. McRobbie had examined various editions of *Jackie*, a magazine for
teenage girls, and her criticisms of their stereotypically feminine and romance-
obsessed content worked on the assumption that the ideology of the magazines would be absorbed in a direct way by its readers. Nowadays McRobbie
happily admits that this assumption was not tenable. For example, she reports:

> Frazer (1987) demonstrated (as did Beezer *et al.* 1986) that my
> own earlier work about *Jackie* magazine wrongly assumed that
> ideology actually worked in a mechanical, even automatic kind
> of way.
>
> (McRobbie, 1999: 50)

The study by Elizabeth Frazer (1987) involved group discussions with teenage girls about selected stories from *Jackie*. Frazer found that rather than absorbing the stories as if they were valuable lifestyle advice, these readers laughed at the tales, and criticised them as unrealistic fictions. This study (and others like it) are sometimes mistakenly taken to 'show' that people are not affected by the texts they read. In fact, that conclusion does not quite follow: just because the readers were able to criticise the text, and were aware that it was a constructed fiction, does not prove that they would never be influenced by its content. However, Frazer's study did successfully show that the effect of magazines could not be assumed or predicted.

A study by Joke Hermes, *Reading Women's Magazines* (1995), compli-cated matters further by suggesting that readers often didn't attach much meaning to their reading of magazines in any case. Hermes had conducted qualitative research in a bid to find the meaning of women's magazines in

Figure 9.1   Women's magazines: offering a range of contradictory suggestions about modern female identities

their lives; but this had turned out to be difficult because magazine consumption was often described as little more than a pleasurable way to fill moments of relaxation. Magazines were easy to pick up and easy to put down. Although readers did connect with *parts* of the magazines they read, Hermes warns that cultural studies often makes the mistake of assuming that 'texts are always significant' (1995: 148), when in fact the typical reader of any particular magazine article, say, may not be very bothered about it. Many studies of media reception, she suggests, are subject to the 'fallacy of meaningfulness' (ibid.) – the idea that when someone consumes a media text then 'meaning' is always produced. Although Hermes caught occasional 'glimpses' of the interests and fantasies that were related to reading women's magazines, she offers a valuable reminder to researchers that the 'relationships' they are investigating – between media products and consumers – are not always passionate ones.

Dawn Currie conducted another major study in 1993–94, which involved an analysis of teenage magazines in Canada and interviews with a sample of their readers. This was eventually published as *Girl Talk: Adolescent Magazines and their Readers* (Currie, 1999). The author found her interviewees (48 girls aged between 13 and 17) to be more enthusiastically engaged with the magazines than Hermes's older respondents had been. These teenagers were particularly attracted to the magazines' advice sections, for example, finding them to be both 'useful' and pleasurable. Currie herself is less happy about the magazine content, however, finding that quizzes and advice pages emphasised the value of pleasing others (in particular boys) – although they also highlighted the importance of 'being yourself'. She notes that these pieces typically encouraged their female readers to be selective about who they chose to go out with, but she criticises them for propagating the idea that one should be looking for the 'right guy'. Currie's discussion is interesting, complex and reflexive, but never really doubts its own assumption that the content of the magazines will be 'patriarchal', and although the author asserts, repeatedly and at some length, that researchers should not impose their own meanings on those of their subjects, she nevertheless seems to stamp her own broadly negative feeling about the magazines throughout the study.

More recently, Angela McRobbie has re-emerged as a sharp commentator on magazines for young women. In the late 1990s she was asking difficult questions about what kind of publication feminists would want, if they were unhappy with the feisty spirit of contemporary magazines; and then in the mid-2000s she seemed to become more critical of them again. We will return to McRobbie's arguments in more detail later in this chapter. First, we should examine the content of modern women's magazines.

THE MAGAZINES TODAY

The long-established women's market includes a lot of quite successful titles, which can be divided into distinct weekly and monthly categories. The monthlies tend to be the more glossy lifestyle magazines, which we are primarily concerned with here; whereas the weekly publications are usually colourful celebrity-and-entertainment magazines, or downmarket 'real life' weeklies peppered with true crime stories, life-threatening crises and holiday disasters.

Sales of women's monthly magazines in the UK in the second half of 2006 looked like this:

Table 9.1 Circulation figures of UK women's monthly lifestyle magazines, 1 July–31 December 2006 (abc.org.uk)

Glamour	588,539
Good Housekeeping	463,645
Cosmopolitan	455,649
Yours	383,577
Marie Claire	334,729
Woman & Home	316,034
Prima	315,149
Candis	301,309
More! (fortnightly)	271,629
Company	264,095
Slimming World Magazine	255,237
Weightwatchers Magazine	244,231
Healthy	229,769
Red	224,072
NW (New Woman)	222,076
Vogue	219,026
Elle	209,172
Easy Living	200,116
Instyle UK	181,909
Eve	172,419
She	151,713
Top Sante Health & Beauty	117,968
Psychologies Magazine	115,398
Harpers Bazaar	105,731

A number of other titles sell less than 100,000 per issue

The list of women's weekly magazines is also extensive:

Table 9.2 Circulation figures of UK women's weekly magazines, 1 July–31 December 2006 (abc.org.uk)

Take a Break	1,027,013
OK! Magazine	624,091
Closer	614,141
Heat	598,623
Now	540,132
Chat	537,464
That's Life	464,762
New!	456,987
Pick Me Up	424,410
Hello!	412,807
Love It!	407,914
Woman	388,998
Woman's Weekly	387,098
Best	362,417
Woman's Own	356,811
Reveal	345,508
Bella	316,281
Real People	311,075
Star	269,723
Grazia	210,200
My Weekly	195,809
Full House	181,555
First	100,439

Many of these titles are not just 'women's lifestyle' magazines in a straightforward way. *Heat*, for instance, is a popular celebrity gossip magazine which is bought and read by an audience of women and men (but mostly women). When first launched in 1999, it was not apparently 'gendered', but was not very successful either; its fortunes improved as it repositioned itself as more of a women's weekly, both physically in the newsagents, and in terms of how it addressed its readers. Nevertheless, messages from male readers still sometimes appear on its letters page.

Meanwhile, the market leader *Take A Break* portrays a world which is rather separate from the sexy professional reader assumed by *Cosmo* or *Marie Claire*, and has little to do with the celebrities featured in *Closer* and *Heat*. The website of its publisher, H. Bauer, happily admits that it is aimed squarely at 'C1C2 women [clerical or skilled manual workers] aged 25–55 with children', and of course it does very well, with a mix of 'real life stories', prize puzzles and competitions. The lifestyles portrayed are less aspirational, the narratives are about the challenges of everyday life, and – rather oddly – its 'real life stories' are typically rather horrifying and frequently involve rape. *That's Life*, from the same publisher, uses a similar formula for a slightly younger audience ('Young, mass market women with children'). *Chat* and *Pick Me Up* are similar, with the latter boasting cover lines such as 'My son lost his virginity in front of me', 'My mother-in-law hired a hit man to kill me' and 'Arrested on a sex charge – because of this stripper' (all 19 July 2007). In short, real life sex and violence are the leading themes in these popular weeklies.

We should also note that this broad market includes lifestyle magazines for teenage girls as well:

Table 9.3 Circulation figures of UK 'teenage lifestyle' magazines for young women, 1 July–31 December 2006 (abc.org.uk)

Sugar (monthly)	200,541
Bliss (monthly)	151,729
Cosmo Girl (monthly)	131,956
Shout (fortnightly)	80,910
Mizz (fortnightly)	59,934

These publications establish the magazine-reading habit in early-teenage readers – and mirror the themes of adult lifestyle magazines, but for more of a 'beginner' audience, with features such as '105 love tips: Where to meet him, when to text him, how to flirt with him', '250 new looks' and 'The rich girls' workout: Get it for free!' (all in US *Cosmo Girl*, August 2007); 'Summer snogs: Lip-locking secrets inside!', 'I've had five facelifts' and 'Supersize your popularity: Never feel out of your league again!' (all in UK *Bliss*, August 2007). These titles play on teenage insecurities quite unashamedly: for instance, the dominant coverline on *Bliss* is typically a question, and in 2007 these have included 'How normal is your body?', 'Should you be on a diet?', 'Could you be a model?', 'Are you a good kisser?' and 'How pretty are you?' – a veritable list of adolescent anxieties.

MAGAZINES INTERNATIONALLY

Every country has its own mix of women's magazines, of course – although they do all tend to cover similar themes. Although this book addresses Western media in a range of countries, there is not room here to list the circulations of magazines from lots of different places – the lists of top selling titles in just the UK are long enough! You can usually get figures for different countries online, from the relevant national auditing body, which can be found via the International Federation of Audit Bureau of Circulations (www.ifabc.org). In the US the ABC website is at www.accessabc.com. In Canada the relevant body is the Print Management Bureau (www.pmb.ca). Circulation data also may appear in newspaper stories about the magazine market, which you can find using Google.

KEY THEMES

Women's magazines are, of course, all about the social construction of womanhood today (just as men's lifestyle magazines, as we have seen, are all about the social construction of men). Some of their content is pretty self-evident – the 'fashion and beauty' material, which takes up many pages in all of the magazines mentioned above, contains very few surprises in terms of gender representation. Critics would say that these sections represent a not-very-subtle and relentless insistence that women of all ages must do their best, and go to considerable expense, to look as 'glamorous' as possible – and it is difficult to disagree (although we all know from everyday life that many people choose to disregard this message, to greater or lesser degrees). In the following sections we will consider some of the more non-traditional features of modern women's magazines.

Men as sex objects

Women were objectified for decades in men's media, advertising and pornography. But nowadays several women's magazines objectify men using the same kind of language and imagery as the men's magazines – and at times, even in ways which some of the men's magazines might be embarrassed about. For example, *Cosmopolitan* (UK edition, June 2007) features a sealed section of 'Cosmo naked centrefolds': readers of this 'ogle-fest' are invited to send a text message to vote for the 'fittest' man

---

DON'T JUDGE A BOOK BY ITS COVER?

The covers of magazines are extremely important to their public image and sales. Liz Jones, editor of the UK *Marie Claire* from 1999–2001, says: 'Nowadays, when the average time spent choosing a magazine and lifting it off the shelf is about three seconds, the covers make or break a magazine. You need lots of cover lines [– the phrases like 'Great sex today!' promoting articles in the magazine], and they all have to be compelling' (Jones, 2001a).

(but, to be fair, it's for charity). Mirroring men's magazines, the naked celebrities are objectified as 'TV totty' and 'the sexiest six packs in sport'. The magazine's US website includes a 'Guy Gallery' and boasts a monthly 'Guy Without His Shirt' ('Check out this month's half-naked hunk'), whilst the UK site offers a selection of 'centrefolds' ('Choose your favourite hottie from our gallery of gorgeous blokes and download him as a wallpaper or screensaver...'). Articles such as '21 sneaky tricks to get guys to do what you want' (US *Cosmo*, October 2006) would seem too unpleasantly cynical and controlling to be offered by most men's magazines. Most other monthly magazines include similar features, and even the titles for teenage readers include articles such as 'The Anti-Pub Pulling Guide' (*More*, 3 July 2007) and 'Hook a hottie!' (*Bliss*, August 2007). It is also notable that the sex tips in *Glamour*, *Company*, *Cosmo* and other titles, assume that men will do whatever the woman asks – unlike sex tips in men's magazines, where it is assumed that male readers will need to win the consent of a partner.

This approach to men, of course, is done with a smile, and *knowingly* treats men in the way that men have traditionally treated women. Some 'men's rights' groups have objected to this kind of objectification, but inevitably end up looking self-pitying and pompous. The magazines' assumption is that men can't really complain, because men (as a group) have been doing this kind of thing for decades.

Men are not, of course, always treated as just bodies or sex machines. Even *More*, perhaps the most sex-obsessed UK magazine, has regular features where ordinary men are asked for their answers to readers' personal problems, and these answers are usually thoughtful and sensitive; and the regular 'Men & Sex' section shows that men have to be dealt with as human beings. The approach of *More* and *Cosmo* is similar to that of *FHM* and *Maxim*, then: the opposite sex is great for sexual antics, but we are aware that they are also thoughtful, emotional beings that we will (probably) try to make some effort to understand.

Sex and sexuality

The magazines for young women like *Cosmo*, *Glamour* and *More* include numerous features on different sexual positions and techniques, 'sex tricks', 'driving your man wild', 'the best sex ever' and so on. (There are so many of these articles, in every imaginable permutation, that there's not much point giving particular examples here. Typical cover stories include 'Sex goddess secrets: Experts in seduction share their blow-his-mind mattress moves' (US *Cosmo*, April 2006), 'Sexposé: 10 Things Guys Crave in Bed' (US *Cosmo*, May 2007) and 'The Orgasm Diet' (UK *Glamour*, August 2007).) Unsurprisingly, this aspect of the magazines has its critics. On the one hand, the conservative US organisation Morality in Media has an ongoing campaign to stop the 'open display' of 'overly sexualised magazines, notably *Cosmopolitan* and *Glamour*, in [supermarket] checkout aisles', arguing that these 'pornographic' magazines should not be placed 'where even children old enough to read are exposed day after day' (MiM, 2000, 2006). Quoting cover lines such as '*Cosmo*'s Kama Sutra' and *Glamour*'s '30-Day Climax Class', they note that 'Naturally, those of us offended by such trash would prefer that it not be sold at all' (MiM, 1999). Furthermore, 'Some may call that "Adult Sex Ed," but we call it "pornography."' (MiM, 2006). This is the conservative objection: that the magazines are much too open about sex (and they even seem to go further, suggesting that material about sexual pleasure should not really be available to anyone).

There is also a feminist objection: that the magazines are too *limited* in their coverage of sex, because their articles are almost always heterosexual. Stevi Jackson (1996), in an article based on looking at a handful of magazines, asserts that they are 'relentlessly heterosexual' and observes that lesbian sexuality is not regularly and routinely celebrated in the way that heterosexuality is. This is true, of course, although the magazines are more positive about lesbianism and bisexuality than Jackson thinks. (The same cannot really be said of the men's magazines, which often contain casual, subtle homophobia.)

In her 1999 book *In the Culture Society*, Angela McRobbie was not impressed with Jackson's approach; she seemed to suggest that this was a monolithic, determinedly grumpy form of feminism crashing into a slice of popular youth culture and dismissing it out of hand. McRobbie agreed that lesbianism was not covered in great detail, or in every issue:

There is no explicit information about the finer details of lesbian sex, no position of the fortnight for lesbian lovers. This point then marks the limits of permissible sexualities within the field of the magazines ... But does this mean we turn away from the magazines, dismissing them entirely on these grounds? Surely this ... is an issue that has to be thought through more seriously.

(1999: 57)

McRobbie pointed out that the magazines are not only read, but also written and edited, by young women who want to have exciting and inter-esting lives, and who should have no desire to perpetuate patriarchy. Although it is regrettable that lesbian sexuality is not routinely included within the magazines' celebration of sexuality – which could cause misery and even psychological trauma to young women trying to come to terms with their excluded desires – McRobbie noted that the magazines show the clear impact of feminism in their coverage of (heterosexual) sex:

The idea that sexual pleasure is learnt, not automatically dis-covered with the right partner, the importance of being able to identify and articulate what you want sexually and what you do not want, the importance of learning about the body and being able to make the right decisions about abortion and contracep-tion, the different ways of getting pleasure and so on, each one of these figured high in the early feminist agenda. This was the sort of material found in books like *Our Bodies, Our Selves* (Boston Women's Health Collective 1973), the volume which started as a feminist handbook and went on to sell millions of copies across the world.

(Ibid.)

This leads McRobbie to pose interesting questions about how feminist critics might now develop a dialogue with the producers and consumers of women's magazines, which we will come back to at the end of this chapter.

Relationships

A common assumption about women's magazines is that they are all about 'How to get a man'. The magazines are accused of suggesting that a man is the route to happiness; the implication is therefore that the magazines are reproducing a smartened-up version of the old-fashioned idea that if

women manage to be sufficiently lovely and fragrant, then they will be fortunate enough to have a man come along and sweep them off their feet,
making their life 'complete'. For example, in a *Washington Monthly* article,
Alexandra Starr (1999) writes that, 'For the most part ... women's magazines are pushing the same message they were half a century ago: women's
existence revolves around landing the right guy' – although, she adds,
today's technique is great sex rather than great cooking. She goes on to say
that 'while these [sex] articles are packaged under the "liberated woman"
motif, they're really just another variation on the "snagging and keeping a
guy" theme'.

   But the woman of today's magazines is not waiting for any man to
come and pick her up; instead she is tracking down partner perfection like
a heat-seeking missile. We have already seen, in the 'Men as sex objects'
section, that the magazines like to rate men on their status as 'eye candy'.
Cover stories such as *Cosmo*'s 'Man overload! How to reel in bunches of
boys' and *Company*'s 'Will this be your summer of lust?' hardly suggest the
image of a woman waiting for a nice husband to come along; and the
advice for those in relationships – such as *B*'s 'Six love ultimatums and how
to use them', and *New Woman*'s 'Make him a slave to your rhythms' –
show that women should be in control. The advice pages of all of the magazines consistently argue that if a man is a serious disappointment, in any
sense, then he should be ditched. Any reader who had taken all of these
messages to heart would be the very *opposite* of the desperate-for-marriage
wallflower.

Transformation and empowerment

Another common criticism of women's magazines is that they make women
feel bad about themselves. Their repetitive celebration of a beauty 'ideal'
which most women will not be able to match, but which will eat up readers'
time and money – and perhaps good health – if they try, as well as the many
pages of advice on how readers can improve their looks, sex skills or personalities, are likely to make some readers feel somewhat inadequate. This argument is made, for example, in Alexandra Starr's article mentioned above,
which is entitled 'You've got a long way to go, baby: Women's magazines
continue to create – and exploit – women's anxiety' (1999). As well as
saying that magazines emphasise 'landing the right guy', Starr is also critical
of the emphasis on physical perfection. '[Most] importantly,' she asserts,
'there isn't an acknowledgment that a solid sense of self-worth is a prerequisite to being in a successful relationship – or, for that matter, leading a
healthy life.' Here Starr's argument wanders off the rails, because women's

DO WOMEN'S MAGAZINES AFFECT BODY IMAGE?

There is an ongoing debate about the influence of women's magazines and, in particular, images of skinny fashion models and celebrities, upon the body image of women. It is even an issue discussed in the pages of women's magazines themselves: in an article entitled 'Why models got so skinny', for example, *Cosmopolitan* (US edition, August 2001) found that designers, fashion editors and casting agents were picking ever-more waif-like models through the 1990s; already thin models were losing work to even skinnier women, and had to become even more willowy to keep working with top-rated designers. The increasingly close links between Hollywood and the fashion industry has led female movie stars in the same direction. Despite seeming unhappy about the unrealistic 'skinny trend', the *Cosmo* article offers little hope of a change, except from some quotes from men saying that they prefer a fuller figure. Elsewhere it has been suggested that the women's magazines – particularly at the 'high fashion' end of the market represented by *Vogue* and *Elle* – have no desire to change. Liz Jones, when editor of *Marie Claire* during the year 2000, tried to introduce initiatives to encourage magazine editors to feature a greater diversity of women – models of different sizes, and also more Black and Asian women. Her suggestions were pointedly and explicitly rejected by the industry. Jones resigned in April 2001 because, she said, 'I had simply had enough of working in an industry that pretends to support women while it bombards them with impossible images of perfection day after day, undermining their self-confidence, their health and hard-earned cash' (Jones, 2001b).

In scientific terms, the evidence for the negative impact of these images is mixed. A report by the British Medical Association, *Eating Disorders, Body Image and the Media* (BMA Board of Science and Education, 2000) noted that eating disorders such as anorexia and bulimia have one of the highest mortality rates of all psychiatric illnesses, and that 'the degree of thinness exhibited by [fashion models] is both unachievable and also biologically inappropriate, and provide unhelpful role models for young women' (p. 36). Media influences could not be said to directly *cause* eating disorders, however. 'Eating disorders are caused by a complex interplay between genetics, family history, and the cultural environment', the report notes. The point remains that, for those who are psychologically predisposed to anxiety about the body, or control of the self, media images can play an unhelp-ful role.

In her book *Body Image*, Sarah Grogan (1999) finds that body dis-satisfaction can affect both women and men, but is most common in women. Surveying the mass of literature in this area, she concludes that 'The factors that seem to predict body dissatisfaction most accurately are social experiences, self-esteem and perceptions of control over one's life (including perceived control over the body)' (p. 167). This percep-tion of control is particularly important, Grogan suggests – anorexia is an extreme way of demonstrating control over the body, of showing self-discipline and raising self-esteem in the short term by denying one's own needs (p. 173) – a finding which is 'well documented' (p. 181). Media images of slenderness – or, for men, the combination of a slender but muscular body – may prompt feelings of dissatisfaction, but at the same time 'interview work suggests that women in particular are cynical about media portrayal of the "ideal body", and want to see more realistic images of women in the media' (p. 189). Grogan also notes that, ironically, the empowering notion that individuals can change themselves, in modern society – which we discussed in Chapter 5 and elsewhere – can lead a person to feel a sense of failure if they cannot achieve the body of their dreams (p. 191).

Overall, then, we have a slightly contradictory set of findings:

- Media images are likely to have *some* impact on how people view their own bodies. It would obviously be better if unhealthily skinny models were not promoted as icons of beauty by fashion magazines.
- However, media images are *not* the main cause of extreme con-ditions such as anorexia or bulimia. These are potentially grave ill-nesses which should be taken seriously.
- Audiences view the culture of 'ideal bodies' critically, and say that they would like to see more diversity.
- However, the industry asserts that, regardless of what readers say, images of thin models are 'popular' and will sell magazines. ('If you stick a beautiful skinny girl on the cover of a magazine you sell more copies', as model agency Premier told reporters (BBC Online, 2000b).)

In 2006, 'size zero' models Luisel Ramos and Ana Carolina Reston died from the impact of their starvation-level diets, prompting the organisers of Madrid Fashion Week to ban models with a body mass index below

18. These incidents sparked an international debate about 'size zero' (which is UK size four). The fashion industry has made further moves to stop the use of ultra-skinny models and those aged under 16 (Campbell and Asthana, 2007), but it remains the case that fashion models tend to be extremely thin.

The fact that the 'size zero' debate was widely discussed in newspapers, magazines, TV shows and online, seems positive: at least people were critically discussing this problem. However, Laurie Penny (2007), writing on *The F Word*, a website for 'contemporary feminism', argues:

> The 'size zero' woman is a media fiction, spawned in the twisted brains of fashion editors and media scare-monkeys – and a dangerous fiction, at that ... It's a fiction that centres upon the degrading idea that women are stupid, frivolous and impressionable ... Anorexia is not a fashion statement, or a lifestyle choice, but a psychological breakdown that leads to physical collapse. The 'size zero' myth crucially undermines the illness, reducing it to a frivolous pique of silly little girls who aren't clever or mature enough to take proper care of themselves. In fact, most sufferers from eating disorder are perfectly aware of what they are doing to themselves, but have lost the ability to stop – a crucial part of the pathology of the eating disorder spectrum.

The statistics and arguments can help us to think about these issues, but the raw experience of young women is especially important here. In 2007, BBC Radio One, the music station aimed primarily at the 15–29 age group, conducted an online survey which was completed by 25,000 listeners. More than half of the female respondents said that they would consider plastic surgery, and a third of those who were UK size 12 [US size 10] said that they consider themselves to be overweight or fat. Almost half of the female respondents said that they had skipped a meal to try to lose a few pounds, and 'more than 50 per cent of younger teenage girls reckon their body image stops them getting a boyfriend' (BBC, 2007). The Radio One webpage reporting these findings quickly filled up with comments posted by teenagers – over 350 different posts – which make heartbreaking reading. To quote just a few:

RACHEL: 'I'm 19, 5'6" and size 8–10. I hate my body! It's horrible. I am VERY self concious. I get worried when people look at me in case they're thinking "eurgh, look at her, isn't she fat". It does my head in!'

SARAH: 'I am 16 and a size 12 in jeans and a 10 in tops, I never really used to mind until I noticed all my friends are size 8 and want to be thinner and they're my height so this made me think hmm maybe I need to lose weight. so I dont eat lunch at school any more and barely eat when I go home and this works well as the weight comes off but then when weekends come around I end up eating even more than I used to its like a viscious cycle – the less I eat during the week the more I eat on a weekend.'

SANAM: 'I'm 18 years old, 5'4" and I am size 8! Recently my friends have been nagging me about how fat I am, and I should consider losing some pounds.'

LEAH-JAYNE: 'I'm a 15 year old girl standing at 5ft 4, and weigh 9st 10. I would class myself as overweight. I am a size 10 and hate the way I look, I've been dieting since I was 12 years old … I've been with my 18 year old boyfriend for 6 months and we're really happy, but the fact I feel so fat is wrecking our relationship. We argue over my size and weight.'

CAROLYN: 'I'm 20 years old, 6 foot and a size 14/16 depending on the store. I have a really unhealthy relationship with food, some days I don't eat anything, some days I eat really healthy and some days I'll have a jacket potato with loads of cheese and a chocolate bar. I'm terrible, I know I am! I desperately want to lose weight, I don't want to be a 4, but I'd love to be a 10/12 still nice and healthy, but slimmer. I'm finding it so hard, and I've got to be honest this whole skinny thing [the debate in the media] really doesn't help. I don't want to get down to my size 10/12 and wish I was thinner.'

SAMANTHA: 'I'm 17 years old, and a size 10, I'm like 5'4" and weigh 9 and a half stone, loads of my friends weigh less than me but eat more than I do! I'm the only one with a hourglass figure and all my mum does it tell me how lucky I am with my figure, but I dont feel lucky I feel pressured to lose weight by everyone. I don't agree with size zero as it does have an effect on us and certainly makes me feel more pressured to lose weight. I spend most of my time on a diet and I wish I was strong enough to say I didn't care about how I look to others, but I do. I'm glad Radio 1 have addressed this issue, reading other peoples comments as I do not feel as alone in this.'

Another response to this issue has come from Dove, the soap and beauty products manufacturer (owned by multinational, Unilever), which has cleverly positioned itself on the side of 'real women'. The company established the Dove Self-Esteem Fund in 2006, which aims to be 'an agent of change to educate and inspire girls on a wider definition of beauty' (Dove, 2007). Their Campaign for Real Beauty website (www.campaignforrealbeauty.com) features the short video *Evolution* – also viewed by millions on YouTube – which shows the transformation of a model from 'normal' to 'supermodel' looks through physical and computer manipulation. Despite this raised awareness of the ways that the fashion and beauty industries operate, the impossibly 'high standards' set by the imagery that they produce continue to distress customers.

FURTHER READING: Wykes and Gunter (2005); Rumsey and Harcourt (2007); Pruzinsky and Cash (2004); Benson (1997); Davis (1995); Grogan (1999); Orbach (1993). (See also the 'Selling beauty' section in Chapter 4).

magazines contain an unavoidable stream of feel-good advice about having a positive self-image and being confident.

But the magazines are full of beauty ideals too, and this can certainly seem *contradictory*. Pamela Fraker (2001), in a similar article, is closer to the mark when she says: '*Elle* is going to share with their readers the criteria for emotional and physical health, and then encourage them to disregard it all in the name of beauty? Does this seem a little twisted to anybody else?' You could just as easily say it the other way round – that the magazines spell out the secrets of beauty, but then encourage readers to disregard it all in the name of emotional and physical health; but, in any case, it's true that these elements don't sit comfortably together. Nevertheless, you can't really miss the fact that women's magazines speak the language of 'popular feminism' – assertive, seeking success in work and relationships, demanding the right to both equality and pleasure.

WHAT THE READERS SAY

As in the previous chapter, e-mail interviews were conducted with readers of the magazines, mostly from across the USA and the UK, but also from

Australia, Hong Kong, Poland, Germany and India. Although this sample of readers – who were able and willing to e-mail their thoughts about women's magazines – will not be exactly representative of the average reader profile, they *are* all examples of magazine readers, talking about the magazines which they actually routinely read in their everyday lives. The interviewees were encouraged to say what they *really* thought, rather than to make 'clever' critical points just for the sake of it. The following sections represent an overview of what the readers said.

The 'pick and mix' reader

Analysis of the interviews suggests that female readers of women's maga-zines, from various developed countries, tend to share a feeling of ambiva-lent pleasure about these publications. They *enjoy* the magazines, and may at times learn bits and pieces – ideas for how to look or behave, as well as more straightforward information about health, popular culture or social issues. At the same time, these readers would not really argue that the mag-azines are 'perfect' or 'ideal' in terms of how they address women. This young German clearly articulates the 'pick and mix' approach to the maga-zines which many respondents shared:

> [The magazines] give an overview of what's 'hot' and celebrate consumption in every way, which is fun. *Elle*, and really all of the women's magazines I know, make it look so easy to become the sort of woman they idealise. That's not the point of reading these magazines. You get something to compare yourself with but you don't have to accept the ideal or follow it, that depends on the reader. They tell you how to dress, to do your make-up and how to behave in relationships. Still it's up to you, you can take up these things or leave them. What I regard as valuable is getting an idea of style and that can help you in the develop-ment of individual taste. So the influence of these magazines on me is mainly in the area of fashion. Still, I am not a fashion victim! The psychological tests and hints on solving problems with your significant other are pure fast food for me, fun for the moment but to take it seriously – no way.
>
> (24-year-old female from Berlin, Germany)

The magazines are not taken literally, then, even though they may suggest some good ideas; and some parts – such as the 'tests and hints' – are pure entertainment. This woman goes on to say:

I can't identify with the '*Elle* woman' because I don't have the money, the perfect figure of a supermodel and I don't belong to any hip young group of people (as *Elle* defines them). It is a bit easier to identify with the [German magazine] *Allegra* ideal reader because she is a bit more down to earth but still one of the in crowd. I think my problem identifying with any group or ideal is that I never believed in such things. So I always take the bits I like and discard the rest of the identity. I certainly don't care if I fit into the target group of a magazine or not, if I like it.

(as above)

Interestingly, those respondents who picked the more 'girly' interests – beauty and fashion – as high points of the magazines were also successful career women, who in their working lives might have to work *against* stereotypes of femininity, but nevertheless seemed to enjoy the fantasy-world of women's magazines when they had time to relax. For example, this reader was an information architect, specialising in website organization and management:

[I like the magazines because] I like fashion and beauty. I have a really stressful job and enjoy the alternative reality of 'fashion books.' In addition, I take fashion seriously as a minor art form. They are sensual as physical objects: glossy paper, heavy weight of the magazine, super-saturated colors, etc.

(38-year-old female from Chicago, USA)

This woman, a producer in the competitive world of television, has similar preferences:

[I like the magazines because] they offer the latest news on cosmetics and facial products. But at the end of the day, they are just easy to read magazines which help to kill time when one is at the hair-dresser's or waiting at restaurants for friends to show up. *Cosmo*: The presentation and style makes reading easy. It's an easy magazine to pick up and put down. *Her World*: Good articles on tried and tested beauty products, good tips on where to dine.

(26-year-old female from Hong Kong)

This woman works for a Polish government agency:

[I like the magazines because] I am interested in fashion. I like professional pictures of it. That is the main reason, I think. Also

I like to know what's new in the cosmetics market ... and some
other things (news, fitness, etc.). It is good for 'casual' relaxation.

> (25-year-old female from Gdansk, Poland)

And a graduate student in Hong Kong said:

They give me the most updated fashion news and what designers
are doing. Some designers that I used to like may be shifting to
things that I hate. And I can find out new favourites too. I can
also check out new make-up or skincare products. And as
fashion trends are like cycles, flipping through the magazines can
give me ideas or inspirations – how to make my old clothes
look fashionable by way of adding new accessories or new
coordination.

> (35-year-old female from Hong Kong)

Nevertheless, she didn't take the magazines' fashion advice too literally:

To be frank, I don't like to identify myself with the ideal reader.
I want to be more critical, otherwise I have to spend much more
money on those clothes and beauty things than I am doing now.

> (as above)

The respondents were well able to analyse their own enjoyment of the magazines. This woman, for example, gave an incisive and open account:

[The magazines] provide an imaginary space of self-indulgence
[where] I can play at being a different, more glamourous, shal-
lower, richer version of myself. I love the sensuality of them – the
heavy shiny pages, high production values, the scented sachets,
silly free gifts (I'm a real sucker for the free gift). I also enjoy the
polymorphous perversity of lots of images of gorgeous, naked or
half dressed or fantastically clad young women who present
themselves for a gaze that is somewhere between objectification
and identification but clearly can't be reduced to either. I enjoy
the engagement with consumerism – I love the fashion and
beauty product information – that Creme de la Mer is the face
cream of the moment, the Fendi Baguette the bag to have – even
though I've no intention of actually purchasing either.

> (36-year-old female from London, England)

Thinking through identity

When asked about whether, and how, the magazines helped them to think about their own identity, respondents gave a range of answers. Some were straightforwardly aspirational:

> You kind of look at the images in the mags of attractive, success-ful, well dressed and healthy women, and I like to think of myself as perhaps nearing this type of image – and hopefully in the future – be a successful person.
>
> (21-year-old female from Bristol, England)

> I think the magazine you buy or read can say a lot about you as a person in the sense that it can be what the person aspires to be. For example, when I was in my teens I always bought the maga-zine *More* which I bought because it is very open on sexual issues, although not always in a entirely factual way. And I used to use this information to share with my friends, to appear grown up and knowledgeable about sex although still a virgin.
>
> (21-year-old female from Lincoln, England)

> [Reading magazines like *Cosmopolitan*] usually makes me feel pretty good about myself. When I read about the features of some women and how they are trapped in 'office politics/ affairs', 'love affairs they can't get out of', 'addiction to alcohol/ violence/sex', I feel that I'm in control of my own life. It also helps to establish that I'm in the know with the latest modern (female) gadgets, beauty stuff, etc. Helps establish a [certain young, upwardly-mobile] lifestyle.
>
> (26-year-old female from Hong Kong)

Some used the magazines for negative identification – feeling pleased that they did *not* share the same approach to life as the magazines:

> When I say that I don't identify with this 'type of magazine' [*Elle* (Polish edition) and *Vogue*] it could mean that I define myself as a person who is not so superficial, who is more 'intel-lectual', or something like that.
>
> (25-year-old female from Gdansk, Poland)

And some said that the magazines had little to do with their sense of self:

I don't think either of these magazines [*Allure* and *Seventeen*] help me establish my identity. They are 2 hours of entertainment each month. I sometimes buy some of the make up they feature, but that's about it.

(28-year-old female from Brooklyn, New York, USA)

The analytical Londoner quoted previously had an interesting response to this – asserting that the pleasure of the magazines was to do with fantasy, but not in the straightforward sense of wanting to have the looks or lifestyles put forward by the magazines:

The pleasure (and perhaps sometimes a certain sadness) of consuming these publications is the gap between the fantasy of self indulgent vapid luxury [in the magazines], and the more complex, grittier reality of my life. Not only is the image on offer impractical and unattainable, but it's not even one I particularly desire – this might not make sense, but the fantasy [indulged in while reading the magazines] is not a straightforward relation of aspiration or of role models at all.

(36-year-old female from London, England)

THE IDEAL WOMAN

When asked about the nature of the 'ideal woman' promoted by the magazines, responses were quite consistent – centred around being *independent* in attitude, and *attractive* in looks. These are typical comments:

[These magazines suggest that a woman should be] an attractive, well dressed and independent woman, who most often than not is very career minded. Also intelligent, and likes all modern types of things, for example, modern interior house decor and furnishings, types of clothes, books etc.

(21-year-old female from Bristol, England)

Someone who is active and independent. I guess they also believe that taking pride in one's appearance is a good quality – one can only agree with this in the world we live in where appearance is very important for success.

(21-year-old female from Warwick, England)

Sexy, beautiful, intelligent, superwoman.

(18-year-old female from Mumbai, India)

Clear skin ... Good (thin) figure ... Attractiveness. However the magazines do provide tips and ideas which suggest that anyone can look this way if they try. Also they promote healthiness and regular exercise, but then these are not all bad qualities to promote to women. And they give the idea that if you are single then it is okay to flirt and that you should be looking for men – they often provide tips on how to attract men when you go out, implying that it is an important quality.

(20-year-old female from Bristol, England)

Independence, strength, competence, ability in many different realms, compassion, martyrdom, Hollywood 'knowledge', sexual appeal ... fashion sense, sexual confidence, intelligence, craftiness (like a fox, as well as the ability to sculpt in soap ends).

(34-year-old female from Melbourne, Australia)

The following interviewee had subscriptions to *Marie Claire*, *Jane*, *Vogue*, *In Style* and *Glamour*, and she would read all of these 'pretty much cover to cover while working out at the gym'. Identifying herself as a feminist, she felt that three of these magazines did a reasonable job politically:

I think the good magazines (*Marie Claire*, *Vogue*, parts of *Jane*) hit the political content within the genre of women's magazines pretty well. They're not [feminist magazine] *Ms.*, obviously, but they suggest a sort of 1970s liberal, sisterhood-is-powerful kind of feminism by focusing on women's issues around the globe and in the US. Their take on these issues is that these women, though different from 'me' (the ideal reader who wants make-up tips and has the money to spend on new fashion fads), are worthy of my attention, concern, letters to Congress and charitable donations. I think they promote a kind of informed, politically conscious perspective. All are explicitly pro-choice, and all have run articles about lesbians (two of my lightning rod issues for how much I like a magazine). Also, they suggest that while it's fine for women to want to look good, there are a variety of ways to look good (okay, [this doesn't apply to] *Vogue*) – and that looking good isn't the be-all and end-all. *Marie Claire* and *Jane* promote a kind of low key feminism that while it's not as 'radical' as I think of myself as being, is pretty solid within the genre. [On the other hand,] *In Style* and *Glamour* are embarassing.

I don't like *Glamour*. I'm cancelling my subscription when it comes up. The articles are too focused on sex tips for pleasing men, and the magazine seems aimed at young (early 20s) women who are insecure about their jobs, their sexuality, and their body. The tips are all about being 'better,' but I think the tips are either too dumb ... or too self-explanatory. *In Style* is all about celebrities ... very fluffy ... so I'm a little embarrassed by it.

(33-year-old female from Wisconsin-Madison, USA)

The downside

Few, if any, of the interviewees were entirely happy with the women's magazines that they read, but some were much more critical than others. This young woman, a manager at an IT training company, and a regular reader of *Elle* and *Marie Claire* ('I probably buy one of them every month, sometimes both') had interesting thoughts on the possible negative impact of women's magazines which are worth quoting at some length here:

The most harmful thing about [women's magazines] – and I do think that they can be harmful – is that they encourage you to question your life and your happiness and tell you what you ought to be doing and feeling. I realise that women are perfectly intelligent human beings but it's like being attacked from all sides sometimes. You ought to be doing this or that, you ought to look like this or that. I still think John Berger's *Ways of Seeing* [which I read at university] describes fashion magazines perfectly. Men watch women, and women watch men watching women. That's exactly how it feels. The thing is that you want to think that it's just the men in society that make us think we should all be blonde and thin with big breasts but in reality it isn't. We pretty much know that men like us whatever, and it's other women that the pressure originates from – which is mad, and we shouldn't accept it but we do, and it's fashion magazines where it's women telling other women all this harmful stuff, yet claiming that they are part of some kind of 'sisterhood'. Basically they say one thing and do another – you'll have an article at the front of the magazine about how wonderful [large comedian] Dawn French is – 'and so pretty!' – and then 'How to be as thin as Kate Moss'.

(23-year-old female from Leeds, England)

This woman is also frustrated by the way the magazines promote the idea that women and men are fundamentally different, which, she suggests, is a fiction invented for entertainment and 'self-help' purposes which even the journalists writing the articles are unlikely to believe in:

> In the magazines aimed at women in their twenties (*Cosmo*, *Elle*, *Marie Claire*, *More*), lots and lots of articles are about how different we are, how we communicate differently, how we see sex differently, how we want different things ... I personally notice this specifically because my view is so totally opposite ... In articles in magazines aimed at older women, e.g. *Red*, they're more obviously in line with my view – that we're fundamentally very similar. I think the disparity comes from the fact that men and women in their twenties in the twenty-first century are portrayed in certain ways – [the idea is that] men are immature and only concerned with pulling birds, and women are pretty much grown-up. Letting these hackneyed stereotypes inform their articles is just bloody lazy. I bet if you asked the women that write these articles about the men they actually know they'd be far nicer about them than they are about men in general in print.
>
> (as above)

It is worth noting that the same respondent saw the magazines for teenagers and younger women as being more responsible and less flippant about sex and society:

> I think the girl power thing has really helped young girls, and magazines can provide a sort of role model whether by showing them or tacitly expressing the sort of woman they think the reader should/could be. I was teaching at a secondary girls' school in London where 90 per cent of the pupils are black or Asian, and groups like Destiny's Child are fantastic role models and can be accessed through these magazines. 'Independent women, honeys making money.' I certainly learned a lot from magazines such as *Just 17*, when they are aiming at younger readers they can be more basic and honest – they're more responsible because they're thinking about the readership. It all gets more covert, complicated and hidden, and therefore sneaky, in magazines aimed at older teenagers and women.
>
> (as above)

Interviewees also made the point that the magazines could also be alienating to lesbian readers, or people wondering about their sexuality – as we noted above in the discussion of sex and sexuality in the magazines. The following lesbian respondent said that she occasionally 'felt the urge' or 'needed a fix' of 'glossy paper and seductive imagery' and so would purchase *Red*, *Nova*, *She* or *Elle* – or she would read those magazines when her partner had succumbed to the same impulse. Although she asserts that she doesn't look to the magazines for lifestyle guidance, she notes that they can nevertheless make her feel like an outsider at the (heterosexual) party. She explains that she doesn't want to be like the women in the magazines, but:

> [Despite] saying that, I am seduced by 'cool.' I think I used to be very influenced by [style magazines] *i-D* and *The Face* when I was in my 20's. Now I don't feel I have so much to prove. I feel more comfortable with who I am. I don't need a glossy mag to tell me I am on the right track anymore. [But on the other hand] I can feel so left out and marginalised. These women's mags can make me feel so depressed and isolated – accentuating my otherness. I don't like to admit to this as I feel that most of the time I don't feel this way, but sometimes the attraction of the 'normals' is very compelling.
>
> (40-year-old female from London, England)

Although the magazines would be positive and encouraging on the occasions when they addressed homosexuality, the continuous emphasis on heterosexuality in the vast majority of features – which is also the case in men's magazines – might make anyone considering their attraction to the same sex think twice before stepping outside the attractive and popular world of the 'normals' (as this interviewee put it).

The readers' conclusion – women win?

One respondent, when asked whether the magazines suggested that women and men are fundamentally similar or different, replied:

> Fundamentally different. I think these magazines often, for example, give the impression that women are secretly *better* than men, but feel strongly the need to protect [men] from this knowledge so that their delicate egos are not damaged. Women are also represented as more emotionally competent, more able to cope with life changes, better able, maybe even 'naturally'

adept at, child rearing, of higher endurance, possessing better fashion sense and – well, lots of other things – I could go on. Suffice to say I think that they pump women up to believe they are better than men, and must care for them in ways the men do not understand.

(34-year-old female from Melbourne, Australia)

She felt that the magazines for women, like those for men, were not really helping people (female or male) to get on with each other. At the same time, though, we can appreciate that the view of women as competent and powerful, projected by women's magazines, might be encouraging for female readers. However, others of course would point to the emphasis on conventional ideas of attractiveness, and in particular thin or skinny bodies, as a very negative aspect of the magazines.

A slightly uncertain but generally optimistic assessment of the ideas communicated by women's magazines is offered by the young German interviewee:

So, the way I understand [what the magazines say overall] is: stay who you are, don't let others get you down, and take risks. It's then good for a woman to be a 'bad girl', but from time to time it works as well for her to try out the traditional 'good girl' behaviour. Especially when it comes to getting what you want, everything seems to be appropriate. In a way [this message is] liberating...?

(24-year-old female from Berlin, Germany)

A less upbeat general feeling was that the magazines were good or enjoyable in some respects, but that the repetition of messages about 'looking great' was rather annoying – although readers could try to ignore or skip over those parts.

SUMMARY AND CONCLUSION

Women's magazines, then – like men's magazines, but for different reasons – offer a confusing and contradictory set of ideas. Many of their messages are positive – most readers agreed that the magazines communicated a picture of assertive, independent women – although the emphasis on looking beautiful, too, was generally inescapable. But the readers also agreed that they didn't take all of the magazines' messages seriously anyway – favouring a pick'n'mix attitude to the various ideas in the magazines – which might suggest that those who fear for the reader-victims of these publications are overemphasising the power of the texts, and under-estimating the ability of readers to be selective and critical. On the other hand, one could fear that even readers who think they read the magazines very unseriously are still absorbing lots of messages about what society (as seen through the magazines) thinks is important – such as beauty and sex – and what readers can be less bothered about – such as serious political issues.

In terms of the theories discussed in previous chapters, then, we find that women's magazines – like men's magazines – suggest ways of thinking about the self, and propose certain kinds of lifestyle, which are then actively processed by the readers as they establish their personal biography, sense of identity, and technologies of the self (see Chapters 5 and 6). The magazines for young women are clearly anti-traditional, emphatically rejecting older models of how women should behave, and encouraging women to embody *a certain kind of* 'liberated' identity instead. Femininity is exposed as artifice and performance in the magazines, which celebrate women's opportunities to play with different types of imagery, which is in line with queer theory's proposition that gender is always a performance (Chapter 7). *However* – and this is a big 'however' – although women's magazines encourage a degree of playfulness in terms of clothing and make-up, they would never encourage women to step outside their carefully imagined boundaries of the 'sexy', the 'stylish' and the 'fashionable'.

Criticisms of women's magazines often come from a 'feminist' perspective, but as Angela McRobbie has pointed out, the magazines themselves have incorporated – or at least respond to – many feminist ideas. Commenting on the publications for teenagers, she wrote:

> The place of feminism inside the magazines remains ambiguous. It has presence mostly in the advice columns and in the overall message to girls to be assertive, confident, and supportive of each other. It is also present in how girls are encouraged to insist on being treated as equals by men and boyfriends, and on being able to say no when they want to.
>
> (1999: 55)

We can add that in the magazines for older teenagers and young women, the encouragement of women to be sexual actors – even predators – rather than sexual objects or victims, reflects a 'feminist' turning of the tables. Feminists never really suggested that having sex with lots of men was a goal in itself, but the rejection of passive femininity, and the *freedom* to openly desire others, is feminist progress. McRobbie added:

For writers like Stevi Jackson the magazines only provide girls with the same old staples of heterosexual sex, body anxieties and 'the old idea that girls' sexuality is being attractive and alluring' (Jackson 1997: 57). So she is saying that there are no great advances here. What I would say in contrast is that feminism exists as a productive tension in these pages.

(Ibid.)

Since feminism 'has become both common sense and a sign of female adult authority', McRobbie suggested, the young female readers and writers have 'a desire to be provocative to feminism' – which we have to accept is fair enough – although, McRobbie noted, this tension between female genera-tions comes as rather a surprise to feminists. She observed, 'Young women want to prove that they can do without feminism as a political movement, while enjoying the rewards of its success in culture and in everyday life' (1999: 56).

McRobbie therefore put some new questions on the table. If we accept that women's magazines carry one kind of feminist argument – to be assertive, confident, sexual, 'true to yourself', demanding rights and plea-sures – then how can this view and the more 'traditional' feminist view (which is unhappy about the magazines for other reasons) talk to each other? Does the more critical, radical (and perhaps only 'academic') femin-ism know what it would like 'popular feminism' to say to young women today? McRobbie suggested that by merely criticising the existing popular magazines as 'not good enough', the critical feminists escape the respons-ibility of saying what they would really like to see in a magazine for young women that would actually be popular. In some ways it's obvious – a better magazine would be wholly accepting of bisexual and lesbian sexualities, treating them just the same as heterosexuality, and would use images of a broad range of women instead of just conventionally beautiful, thin models. McRobbie seemed to suspect – perhaps unfairly – that this simple formula still wouldn't satisfy the critics of the magazines. But she rightly suggested that since ' "ordinary women" are themselves set upon improving, often against the odds, their own lives and those of their daughters' (1999: 128), the critics of women's magazines would do well to escape the simplistic view that the women who write and edit the magazines are evil, and that their readers are victims. The debate needs to be more sophisticated, pro-ductive and sympathetic.

The debate doesn't end here, though. Eagle-eyed readers will have spotted that the account of McRobbie's argument, above, is written in the past tense. Perhaps realising that she had cut off critical voices – including her own – McRobbie has changed her tune (again), and in more recent publications (McRobbie, 2004, 2005, 2006) has sought to reclaim some critical distance from the optimistic voices of 'post-feminism'. In a piece from 2004 she finds that the new trend of 'porn chic' is perhaps taking things a bit far:

> Last summer, as I walked towards my local Tube station, a girl went past me wearing a tight T-shirt with the words 'Pay To Touch' across her breasts. Across from me on the Tube, another girl sat in a very short cropped top, tight Lycra trousers that barely skimmed the pubic bone, and in the space between breast and crotch she showed an enormous bare pregnant belly resplendent with a glittering belly piercing. Of course, we are used to provocative slogans on T-shirts such as that sported by the 15-year-old singer Charlotte Church ('Crack Whore') that attracted tabloid attention, and likewise the Porn Star fashion label provides similar logos for its range of accessories.

These things represent 'a forceful coming forward of girls in a zone of sexual excitement and also sexual danger'. McRobbie realises that we cannot read these things in a reductive way, assuming that women are somehow victims of a patriarchal message, of course:

> Following gender theorist Judith Butler, we could argue that what coexists here is a production of sexual identity that draws attention to its own construction and, in so doing, shows it to be fluid, unstable, changeable and thus open to redefinition.

Young women, then, are questioning dominant constructions of gender, and playfully critiquing male fantasies, but not really rejecting them either. This is a choice the female consumers have made – isn't it? McRobbie continues:

> Butler would surely argue that this capacity and activity is, however, also normatively required, with girls now called on by consumer culture to display these characteristics of freedom as post-feminist subjects. But the conditions of their success require them to reject the kind of feminism that argued for freedom and emancipation in the first place. In short, consumer culture usurps and displaces the idea that young women might be in need of politics to help them navigate the complex field of sexuality.

Suddenly this playful construction of gender is nothing of the sort: instead it has been 'required' by the system, which girls are somehow 'called on' to perpetuate. One can see that this more 'critical' stance is tempting for an academic audience, especially when seen in contrast with the more *laissez-faire* attitude suggested by McRobbie's work in the late 1990s. However it seems to suggest that young women, who wouldn't normally like this 'porno chic' ideology, have been somehow tricked into not only going along with it, but perpetuating it themselves. The mechanism by which this happens is not identified. Surely McRobbie's stance cannot simply have gone full circle, and ended up like the one in her *Jackie* study, with its 'mechanical' model of ideology? A subsequent piece made the argument even more straightforward (McRobbie, 2005):

> So enthralled are young women by the seductive power of the media that critical faculties have been blunted. Female students, the very group who should be challenging these assumptions, are silent. Celebrity-led magazines such as *Heat* and *Closer* are as eagerly consumed by girls from ABC backgrounds – the student body – as by their low-income peers. Such publications trap their readers into cycles of anxiety, self-loathing and misery that have become a standard mark of modern womanhood. 'Normative discontent' about body image, about never being beautiful enough, about success and fear of failure, about not finding a husband at just the right moment in the life cycle, about keeping to the rules of dating, about the dire costs of breaking the rules: such values become all encompassing, invading the space of other interests and other activities. The girl becomes a harshly self-judging person.

These are reasonable concerns about the bonkers world of celebrity magazines, which are regularly delighted or horrified (choose at random) by the latest pictures of stars who are too 'skinny' or 'fat' (again, choose at random). But McRobbie makes things too easy for herself, and us, by reverting to a model of evil media empires versus female victims. We really need to understand the real psychological realities of media consumption and identity construction, rather than having easy rants against weird media or supposedly critically incapacitated women. (We try to make some efforts in this more constructive direction in Chapter 11.)

MAGAZINES FOR LESBIANS AND GAY MEN

Whilst gathering data about responses to men's and women's magazines, I was also able to conduct several e-mail interviews with lesbians and gay men about the magazines aimed specifically at them. There are, of course, many of these publications around the world. Lesbian titles include *Curve* and *Velvetpark* in the US, and *Diva* in the UK. Gay men's magazines include *Out*, *XY*, *Instinct* and *Genre* in the US, and *Attitude*, *Gay Times*, *Axm* and *Boyz* in the UK. In the US there is also a current affairs magazine for both gay men and lesbians, *The Advocate*.

It was clear from these interviews that gay magazines can help a person feel comfortable about their sexuality, and feel part of a broader queer community or identity:

- 'They provide me with a sense of a large queer community. Many times it is hard to identify with the heterosexual world. My issues are reflected in these magazines [*The Advocate* and *Out*]. They help me understand what it means to be queer. I feel more in touch with the queer world when I read these magazines', commented a 24-year-old man from Chicago, USA.
- 'By just recognising and catering for a gay audience, [the magazines] help. There is, I think, an implied ideal reader in the shape of a 'cool, young, slightly outrageous, sexual person', but there's also something in it that celebrates difference and acceptance. So you *want* to identify with it, but it lets you bend the image to suit yourself', said a 22-year-old man from Leeds, UK.
- 'They help me feel a part of a queer community', said a 28-year-old woman from Northridge, California, USA.
- 'What the magazine [*Lesbians on the Loose*] does for me is reduce the "othering" — I feel like I actually belong — that my relationship with a woman is not an aberration and is not as uncommon as dominant ideologies would have me believe. So the magazines help me feel "included" ', commented a 33-year-old woman from Adelaide, Australia.
- 'I like looking at other dykes! That's why I read these mags. I blush as I write this but it's true. It's like an

"imagined community". I only have half a dozen lesbian friends so this creates a sense of community', said a 38-year-old woman from New York, USA.

A minority of respondents, however, did not identify with the kind of gay person shown in the magazines:

- '[The magazines] don't help me with my identity today – they once did, when I was a "gay girl" in the seventies looking for some idea about how to live. Then I read *Gay Sunshine* and loved Allen Ginsburg's words about being an artist, a faggot, what I could be – different and still alive', said a 43-year-old woman from Chicago, USA.
- 'I am not like any of the lesbians and gay men portrayed in many senses – my sex life, physicality, economic status, occupation, mentality. I define myself in opposition to what is depicted', said a 40-year-old woman from London, UK.
- '[The magazines give me a sense of identity] only in the sense that they give me something to react to. If people know who they are by what they're not, I often look at these mags and think to myself "not that, not that, not that"', commented a 38-year-old woman from New York, USA.

The magazines were not seen as being very flexible about the gay identity; several readers pointed out that rather than seeing sexuality as fluid, gay magazines seemed to see homosexuality as a fixed identity:

- 'There seems to be a tight line drawn around this area, actually. Your sexuality is changeable until you realise you are gay and then it is absolutely fixed. Going back to heterosexuality is a major sin. I can see that the reason for this is that so many people are hurt and defensive, but it's an interesting paradox. The magazines definitely push the idea that gay is good and if you are gay there's no getting out of it, buster. *But* if you are heteosexual, then your sexuality is a fluid thing that you haven't bothered to explore – (laughs)', said a 34-year-old woman from Melbourne, Australia.

- Another lesbian from Australia explained that, although she did not agree with the view, she could see why magazines should see gay identities as innate, for 'political' reasons, so that others could not suggest that this condition, if cultural, could be changed or 'cured'.

Asked whether the magazines reinforced stereotypes of gayness, one woman replied that the publications promoted an image of readers as 'Thin, fit, economically independent – rich even, white, sexually active, sociable, popular'; but a different female reader suggested the opposite of this narrow view, saying that the magazines promoted 'A sense of pride in one's sexuality, a sense of community, and a sense of open mindedness and inclusivity'. A 22-year-old British gay man responded that although certain stereotypes were evident, in the British magazine *Boyz*,

> There's something in the gay image they project that suggests it's very much a performance and you can do what you want with the identity-options available to you. It suggests that it's okay to be gay and you can do what you want with it. Which is good. It knows what the commercial gay world (i.e. of clubs and music and stuff) is like, and it both provides for and criticises it. It lets me, as a reader, be camp if I want to be, serious the next minute, sleazy ... anything. And I carry that over into real life.

Chapter 10

DIRECTIONS FOR LIVING
Role models and self-help discourses

THIS CHAPTER CONSIDERS further kinds of media messages which suggest 'ways of living'. Popular movies, music and other media present particular 'role models' whose lives supposedly offer an inspirational example. Even more direct personality and lifestyle advice is offered by the huge market in self-help books and personal training, ideas from which tend to 'trickle down' into popular culture more generally. Here we will consider what these resources tell women and men about constructing a comfortable identity and lifestyle, and what the popularity of these messages might tell us about changing cultural ideas of masculinity, womanhood and the acceptable modern sense of self.

WHO'S A ROLE MODEL?

The idea of 'role models' comes up often in public discourse, and in discussions of gender and the media, but it's not always clear what the term really means. A 'role model' seems to be popularly understood as 'someone to look up to', and someone to base your character, values or aspirations upon. For instance, although we haven't considered the concept directly, this book has already mentioned 'role models' in a number of places:

- In the very first paragraph of Chapter 1, we noted that gender role models have changed over the decades.
- In Chapter 2 we saw that a child's modelling of gender roles may be based on particular role models.

- In Chapter 4, Joss Whedon argued that Buffy from *Buffy the Vampire Slayer* (1997–2003) is 'a good role model for not just girls but for everybody'.
- America Ferrera, star of *Ugly Betty* (2006–), was said to be an 'inspiring' role model for women.
- And we even wondered if Jessica Alba in the *Fantastic Four* movies (2005, 2007) would count as a role model.
- In Chapter 9, we saw that the British Medical Association had warned that skinny fashion models 'provide unhelpful role models for young women'.
- In the same chapter, a female interviewee argued that, for her, reading glossy lifestyle magazines was a kind of indulgence in 'fantasy' and did not bear 'a straightforward relation [to] aspiration [or] role models at all'.
- Whereas a teacher stated that magazines could offer 'a sort of role model' to girls, in an empowering sense. For instance, she said, 'I was teaching at a secondary girls' school in London where 90 per cent of the pupils are black or Asian, and groups like Destiny's Child are fantastic role models and can be accessed through these magazines'.

I've gathered these bits from around the book together again here to illustrate the point that we tend to talk about 'role models' quite casually and routinely, and without necessarily understanding whether, or how, this 'role modelling' actually takes place. This happens in the public sphere as well. You can easily find examples yourself – just search the internet, or Google News in particular, for 'role model'. To give just three examples from newspapers, all during July 2007:

- The *New York Times* on 19 July 2007 reported poll findings showing that 'a broad majority of Americans – 68 percent of respondents – think Hillary Clinton is a good role model for women' (Sussman, 2007). The article provides a wealth of statistical detail – '66 percent of men and 70 percent of women who responded to the poll call Mrs Clinton a good role model for women. Single and younger women are more likely to call Mrs Clinton a good role model than married or older women are …' – and so on – but at no point is the notion of 'role model' defined, and the poll respondents will have had to use their own interpretation of the term to answer the question. Nevertheless, this topic catches the public imagination: within five days of the report being posted online, visitors had added over 300 comments discussing Clinton's 'role model' suitability.

- On 4 July 2007, as the *Nancy Drew* movie was approaching release, Laura Barton considered the character in the UK newspaper the *Guardian*: 'Created in 1930, Nancy Drew was the girl detective who showed she was far superior to those Hardy Boys by doing all her detecting work herself ... She made a marvellous role model for young women – independent, resourceful, and staunchly convinced of the prevailing power of womankind' (Barton, 2007).

- In the same paper, on the same day, Zoe Williams was reflecting on the contest for deputy leadership of the Labour party. She was disappointed that the female candidates were unwilling to make anything resembling feminist statements, instead merely asking for votes because they were women. Williams does not believe that 'a simple female presence, like a flash of fuscia on a grey background, will stimulate female engagement and emulation among the wider population. Women in politics only operate as role models when they say admirable things.' Indeed, she goes on to say:

> Look instead at the conditions keeping women out of politics, which are the same as those keeping women at the bottom of any heap. The pay gap, the carer gap, the maternity drain, all the ossified iniquities that fence women into hardship. That's what closes down opportunities. Scratch anyone who uses the word 'role model' and you'll find they're either avoiding solutions which are ultimately fiscal, or they've given no thought to gender politics at all.
>
> (Williams, 2007)

Williams raises an interesting point, suggesting that a focus on role models is an apolitical way to dodge serious issues whose solutions lie in the economy and government policy. This may be the case, and is part of the perennial tension between personality (who you are) and policy (what you do) in the world of politics. Nevertheless, it seems at least *possible* that impressive, confident, ethical public figures could have a useful positive influence on their audiences, inspiring them through their good example. So let's look at this more closely.

SO WHAT EXACTLY IS A ROLE MODEL?

In an article seeking to clarify the notion of 'role models', John Jung (1986) noted that psychologists who had asked subjects about their role models had made 'no attempt' to verify whether these figures actually influenced their respondents, or to show how this role modelling might actually work (p. 529). The prevailing definition at that time seemed to be that a role model would be 'someone who demonstrates the appropriate behavior for a specific role or relationship with another person' (p. 528). This seems obviously unsatisfactory because, say, David Beckham could be an inspiring figure to someone even if they had no interest in filling the particular role of 'football player'. Jung spots this and suggests that the value of role models is that they can *inspire* and *motivate*: 'Perhaps role models are important not because they teach observers how to behave but because they inspire observers to want to learn to behave in certain ways or to assume certain roles' (p. 533). Similarly, a study of young people's role model choices by Anderson and Cavallaro (2002), suggested that young people are drawn to certain characters not simply because they have particular skills or abilities, but because they 'may see *possibilities* in that person' (p. 161, emphasis in original).

In the previous edition of this book, I offered a longer list of examples of people talking about 'role models', which you don't need me to repeat here (you can find them on the website at www.theoryhead.com). From that we were able to divide 'role models' into six slightly different types:

1 **The 'straightforward success' role model**: People who have been successful in their chosen field, apparently through hard work or talent, such as many popular film stars or leaders.

2 **The 'triumph over difficult circumstances' role model**: People who have overcome adversity to achieve success, who often become the most popular role models.

3 **The 'challenging stereotypes' role model**: These might be successful black, female, gay or disabled people in the public eye, who counter traditional or prejudiced ideas about the limitations of certain groups. (This type of role model is sometimes inappropriately used to argue against those who complain about injustice: as in, 'You can't say that Hollywood is racist – look at the success of Will Smith'.)

4 **The 'wholesome' role model**: These are the 'role models' which older generations are comfortable showing to their children, such as 'clean-living' pop bands, the better-behaved sports stars and stars who say 'no' to sex before marriage. (Supporting such figures is 'risky' for conservatives because there is always the possibility that the icon will become a public disappointment – as the Religious Right found with Britney Spears, for instance.)

5 **The 'outsider' role model**: Rejected by mainstream culture, the outsider role model is a hero to those who reject conventional social

expectations. (However, these stars – like Marilyn Manson – are often good capitalists, making lots of very conventional money out of their 'unconventional' public face.)

6   **The family role model**: This category includes looking up to members of your own family, and other popular celebrity parents such as Victoria and David Beckham.

These categories broadly summarise the kinds of people, and positions they represent, that become talked about as 'role models'. It remains unclear, though, in a psychological sense, how 'role modelling' might actually work. Social psychology books usually have little to say about 'role models', although they do trot out the shallow 'social learning theory' which suggests that people learn behaviour by observing it in others – such as role models – and will repeat the behaviour if it is reinforced – in other words, if it seems to have a positive outcome, or other people appear to appreciate it (Brannon, 2007; Carver and Scheier, 2006; Huffman, 2006; Pennington *et al.*, 1999). This 'theory' offers little real detail or complexity, but it could, of course, still be correct, even though we currently lack an understanding of the processes involved.

In a discussion of the psychological literature on 'role models' specifically, Nauta and Kokaly concur that 'the defining characteristics of role models and exactly how they influence various aspects of the career [and, we might add, aspirational] development process remains somewhat unclear' (2001: 81). Although they find there are different definitions of 'role models', there is general agreement that:

> role models are other persons who, either by exerting some influence or simply by being admirable in one or more ways, have an impact on another.
>
> (2001: 82)

Nauta and Kokaly assess the few theoretical discussions of how 'role models' might have an impact, but social learning theory is as deep as it gets, although the idea of people learning behaviour through observation has been expanded, in the obvious way, to accommodate the loose modelling of whole lifestyles. In other words, watching *Aeon Flux, Tomb Raider* or *Ugly Betty* might encourage girls to become somewhat more independent and feisty, without them needing to directly *copy* an extensive fight sequence, embark on a perilous quest for ancient artefacts or go to work at a top fashion magazine wearing a poncho.

In their preliminary survey research, Nauta and Kokaly found that 81 per cent of respondents could name a famous person who was a 'role model' for them, and could describe some reasons or attributes to explain this (2001: 84–86). Since the respondents were responding to a *request* to name a famous role model, however, it would be inappropriate to infer that the majority of these people felt that famous role models were deeply important to them; and we can note that when asked to name their greatest overall role model, 63 per cent of respondents chose one of their own parents.

The study by Anderson and Cavallaro (2002), which surveyed 95 girls and 84 boys aged between eight and 13 from ethnically diverse backgrounds, found that their respondents tended – to a certain extent – to choose a greater number of role models from their own ethnic group, and that they typically chose same-sex role models – especially the boys. Again the media failed to crush the power of family life, as the most commonly chosen role model was one of their own parents; but the researchers still felt it was important to emphasise that:

> Parents and educators must take pains to expose children to a wider variety of potential role models than popular culture does ... A variety of potential heroes and role models allows children to appreciate themselves and the diversity in others.
>
> (p. 168)

This view would also be supported by Assibey-Mensah (1997), whose study of the role models of young African-American males found that the range of heroes who were looked up to was narrow, being almost exclusively athletes and sports stars, with a few film and television celebrities, and very few intellectuals, academics or educators.

A more recent study by Fatimah Awan (2007) took a more subtle route into the role models question by first asking young people aged 13–14, from schools in two different urban areas of England, to make collages representing 'How I see myself' and 'How I think other people see me'. These were then discussed in interviews with 111 individuals about the collages that they had made, exploring questions about self-identity, including role models. (I was Fatimah Awan's PhD research supervisor, and this research process is one of the creative research methods which will be discussed more in the following chapter.)

Awan found that particular media stars and celebrities offered 'resources' which her respondents used when thinking about their identities. In particular they provided young people with sources of 'identification, aspiration and inspiration'. Rather than wholly identifying with these figures, young people picked up on certain traits which they saw as especially meaningful. The values of *integrity* and *authenticity* were especially emphasised, and these virtues were considerably more important than celebrity status. Furthermore:

> [Participants] also employed the role models' authenticity as a vehicle through which their own personal values and experiences could be communicated and validated, as well as a strategy for exploring external realities. Therefore, role models enabled these participants to consider their own identities and social worlds by acting as a tool for self-reflection; however, this was dependent upon the participants understanding their role model as 'normal', that is, someone who shared a familiar reality on an experiential level.

Rather than finding that meaningful media figures offer clear-cut 'models' to learn from, Awan identified a complex relationship between self and role model, where neither is straightforward:

> These participants did not always view the diverse elements of their selves as functioning harmoniously with one another but acknowledged that diversity could at times give rise to conflict, made evident within discussions which highlighted an awareness of ambivalence in role models – and by association their own identities – manifested through the 'good/bad' dichotomy. Consequently by negotiating the 'good/bad' dichotomy in role models, these children were afforded a method that provided them with a means to mediate ambivalence they perceived within their selves as well as their social worlds. Moreover, in identifying ambivalence within role models, participants demonstrated they recognised both positive and negative aspects of these figures and were able to actively discriminate between such qualities.

Therefore Awan suggests that role models do not perform a simple positive or negative function, but rather offer a 'tool box' which enables individuals to make use of ideas about certain facets of these figures within the formations of their self-identities.

GIRL POWER: ROLE MODELS IN POP MUSIC

The first edition of this book featured a set of material on 'role models' in pop music which now appears on the book's website, www.theoryhead.com. This includes:

- A discussion of the emergence of the Spice Girls (who were most popular 1996–98), whose 'girl power' message seemed to have a real impact on girls and young women at the time.
- A section on Destiny's Child, whose message of female independence was also very successful around 1999–2001.
- A discussion of the place of popular music in the lives of young men.
- A quite lengthy discussion of Britney Spears, illustrated with quotes from interviews with her fans, in which they predominantly asserted that she was a role model for female independence and empowerment.

These examples may seem rather dated – which is why this material is now parked on the website – but the basic principles, about the role which music and pop stars can play in people's everyday lives, remain meaningful.

If we consider who the 'empowering' female pop icons are today, it is not so easy. Who has stepped into the shoes of the previous 'girl power' stars? We might consider The Pussycat Dolls, whose international hit single 'Don't Cha' (2005) – asking 'Don't cha wish your girlfriend was hot like me?' – could be seen as variously confident, seductive or bitchy. In interviews, the group have said that the band is about 'female power – it's having a sense of strength and confidence and self-expression of who you are' (Soghomonian, 2005). However, the ideal of being a 'doll' doesn't sound very empowering, and the way in which the relatively faceless 'Dolls' come and go from the 'cast' – as laid bare in the TV series *Pussycat Dolls Present: The Search for the Next Doll* (2007) – does not really suggest that any of them is especially crucial to the band's success, or artistic integrity.

Meanwhile, UK star Lily Allen has won success (2006–) with her individual and independent approach, positioning herself as an altern- ative to the 'fake' posers who perform – but do not write – the songs in bands like Girls Aloud or the Pussycat Dolls. Allen's opinionated MySpace blog makes it clear that she does not want to follow the pack. Elsewhere, although there are many talented female performers, the idea of inspiring girls with a positive and confident message seems to have become less central to pop music in recent years.

ROLE MODELS: SUMMARY

The idea of 'role models' remains a little vague, in academic terms, and psychologists don't seem to have found any very clever way of describing the process by which individuals may employ role models in their self-development. That's fine, though, as it leaves the way clear for a straightforward understanding of how role models might work: that as people grow up, and indeed advance into their twenties and later years, they look for inspiring or comforting figures who offer positive-looking examples of how life can be lived. These identities are not 'copied' in any big or direct sense, but they feed into our ongoing calculations about how we see life and where we would like to fit into society. As we construct our narratives of the self – see Chapter 5 – we are able to appropriate (borrow) the positive bits of other people's attitudes or lives that we fancy for ourselves. We can also position ourselves in relation to more negative characteristics. This means that media stars can be seen as an inspiration for one aspect of their character but not for another – Paris Hilton, for instance, may be admired for her extreme confidence and assertiveness, whilst other aspects of her persona, such as her vanity and inability to obey basic laws, might be ignored. Because of this selectivity, it is perhaps unnecessary for authority figures to feel that 'role models' should be flawless.

SELF-HELP BOOKS AND THE PURSUIT OF A HAPPY IDENTITY

In Chapters 5 to 7 above, on the ideas of Giddens, Foucault and queer theory, we saw the emergence of an approach to personal identities which suggests that in modern societies, individuals feel relatively unconstrained by traditional views of their place in the world, and carve out new roles for themselves instead. As a person grows and develops, they typically continue to work upon their sense of 'self' – their self-identity – and gradually modify their attitudes and self-expression to accommodate a mix of social expectations and also, importantly, *what they themselves are most comfortable with*. (It is during this thinking-through of self-identity that role models may be of significance.)

It is anticipated that this role freedom will become even greater in the future. The media, as we've said before, gives us ideas about gender, and relationships, and ways of living. These ideas come over in TV, movies, magazines and pop music, all of which we have discussed above. The most explicit carriers of advice about gender, lifestyle and relationships, though, are self-help books – also known as 'popular psychology' and in some cases 'recovery' texts – which we turn to now.

Figure 10.1   Self-help books: packed with identity advice for women and
men

It may not be obvious why we'd be looking at self-help books here: they
may be popular as non-fiction books go – even a 'publishing phenomenon'
– but a lot of people don't read them. If they count as 'popular mass media'
at all, they are on the margins. But there are two reasons for taking a look at
self-help texts:

1   The ideas in self-help books 'trickle down' into popular culture. Woody
    Allen brought 'therapy speak' into mainstream movies over 30 years
    ago, and it has regularly appeared in popular culture. When Bette
    Midler says in *What Women Want* (2000) that men are from Mars, the
    audience knows what she's talking about. Women's magazines, in
    particular, both dissipate and assume a working knowledge of today's
    self-help clichés. And Elayne Rapping (1996) observes that there are
    numerous successful TV shows, in the mould of *The Oprah Winfrey
    Show* in the US (1986–) and *Trisha* in the UK (1998–2004, *Trisha
    Goddard* since 2005), which have a very strong relationship with self-
    help publishing, using self-help authors as star experts, and directing
    viewers to their books for solutions.
2   As well as noting that ideas from self-help books go forth into everyday
    culture, we can assume that the approach of the books – and the most

successful ones in particular – is in itself a *reflection* of the changes in society and the needs of (some) readers. Giddens has described self-help books as 'a kind of on-the-ground literature of our reflexive engagement with our everyday lives' (Giddens and Pierson, 1998: 141), and whilst we should be cautious about reading them as accounts of a universal reality, these popular publications must tell us something about life today.

The books aimed specifically at either women or men are of additional interest because they describe aspirational but reasonably realistic (as opposed to utopian) models of how we might expect women and men to present themselves in today's society. Where academic texts on feminism or masculinities fail to actually assert how women and men should act in modern society, these books step in and spell it out – a role which they share, incidentally, with lifestyle magazines (see Chapters 8–9).

EXTENDED ANALYSIS AVAILABLE

A somewhat longer version of this section on self-help books appears on this book's website at www.theoryhead.com (Gauntlett, 2008).

PERSONAL NARRATIVES AND LIFESTYLES

As we saw in Chapter 5, Giddens (1991, 1992) argues that in modern societies, individuals have to construct a 'narrative of the self' – a personal biography and understanding of one's own identity. Self-help books typically incorporate the same kind of idea, and I would argue that they typically suggest one of three challenges to the readers' own narrative:

1   Many self-help books suggest ways in which readers can make their narrative of self more strong, coherent and resilient, so that they can acquire a greater sense of personal power, confidence and self-direction. These are books for people who lack self-belief, and many of them are marketed at women.

2   Other self-help books are about *transforming* the self – rewriting the previous narrative, or ditching it altogether, in order to become a new, strong, positive person. These are books for people who want to overcome character flaws which prevent them from feeling fulfilled, and most of the titles for men fall into this category, as do many more for women.

3   A different kind of self-help book encourages the reader to amend their narrative of themselves and their view of others, so that the world 'as it is' can be accepted more happily. This approach is less common, but includes the super-successful *Men Are from Mars, Women Are from Venus*, which (as we will see) argues that men and women can get along really well as long as they accept that they are from totally different planets.

As we saw in Chapter 6, Michel Foucault became interested in 'techniques of the self' and 'the care of the self' – questions of lifestyle which today are tackled by self-help books. In the introduction to *The History of Sexuality, Volume Two: The Use of Pleasure*, Foucault helpfully proposes a methodology for this kind of study:

> A history of the way individuals are urged to constitute themselves as subjects of moral conduct would be concerned with the models proposed for setting up and developing relationships with the self, for self-reflection, self-knowledge, self-examination, for the decipherment of the self by oneself, for the transformations that one seeks to accomplish with oneself as object. This last is what might be called a history of 'ethics' and 'ascetics,' understood as a history of the forms of moral subjectivation and of the practices of the self that are meant to ensure it.
>
> (1992: 29)

Foucault, then, lends support to the idea that we can learn about our culture by looking at its self-help books; he was interested in the ways in which a society enabled or encouraged individuals to perceive or modify their self-identity.

SOLUTIONS TO EVERY PROBLEM

Self-help books cannot easily be pigeon-holed or stereotyped with any accuracy. Literally thousands of new self-help titles are published every year. In the US, $693 million was spent on self-help books during 2005, with self-help audiobooks taking an additional US$354 million (Marketdata, 2006). One out of every three Americans reports that they have purchased at least one self-help book (McGee, 2005a). Personal coaching, which mirrors the themes of these books, is also a huge industry. A Marketdata report (2006) states that an estimated 40,000 people in the US work as life or work coaches, and this US$2.4 billion market is growing 18 per cent per year. In the UK and Europe, the market for self-help literature is perhaps more modest, but still huge. Red Pepper (2005) reported that the UK publishing industry sells more than 6.8 million self-help books each year, accounting for approximately 33 per cent of the total consumer market for books. (This includes diet, fitness and beauty, as well as popular psychology books.)

The shelves of any major bookstore will offer many titles on being confident, being positive, being successful, and loving yourself. There are also numerous titles on relationships, covering issues such as how to find a partner, how to keep a partner, how to communicate with your partner, how to have better sex, how to escape your abusive partner and how to begin a new life afterwards. There are subdivisions of each category – books on each of the above areas aimed at larger people, older people and black people, for example. Many self-help books are explicitly aimed at women, many others are not gender-specific, and a smaller number are for men in particular. When asked about the relative numbers of women and men reading self-help books, some booksellers specialising in this genre indicated that a growing number of men were joining women in seeking advice from these texts on how to improve and transform their lives (see Gauntlett (2008), on website). Adam Khan, author of the book *Self-Help Stuff That Works* (1999), told me:

> I think more women read self-help books than men, but I think it's pretty even for my book. I'm basing that on who writes to me. I get a lot of email from readers of my book, and it is approximately the same amount of women as men.
>
> (E-mail, 20 August 2001)

On the popularity of self-help books, he says:

> For most of us today, there are far more things we think we can change than there was even a hundred years ago. We are less likely to feel we are helpless pawns than we once were. All by itself, that would explain the rise in self-help books' popularity. It's not that people are more interested in changing now, it's that in the past we didn't think it was possible. And if you don't think becoming happier is possible, you're not likely to expend any time or money trying to make it happen.
>
> (Ibid.)

An increasing number of men appear to be moving away from the traditional idea that men 'just deal with it', and are taking a more direct, psychology-oriented approach to their problems – as we also saw in the chapter on men's magazines. Furthermore, it seems that people in general feel a greater ability to transform the conditions of their everyday lives, and are turning to self-help books for advice.

SELF-HELP FOR MEN

To understand self-help books better, we should look at a few particular case studies. As noted above, the range of self-help books is broad and diverse, and individual titles cannot be expected to represent the whole market, but the examples here are popular publications which are more-or-less typical of the genre (although, of course, every book is unique and it's not quite right to generalise like that). First we will look at three books aimed at men – beginning with men simply because the idea of masculinity as *problematic* is the more unusual and new narrative. We can then contrast that material with the advice given to women.

Men's case study #1: the tin man

Understanding the Tin Man: Why So Many Men Avoid Intimacy by William July II (2001) is for men who avoid committed intimate relationships, preferring superficial sexual encounters, and emotionally uncommunicative men in general. Like many of the books about men, the cover says that the book is also 'for women who want to help their men' – sensibly enough, because the very definition of a Tin Man is one who wouldn't dream of touching a self-help book.

The author begins the introduction by saying: 'Whenever the subject of relationships comes up, many women ask why so many men can connect physically or on the surface, but avoid deep levels of genuine intimacy' (2001: 1). He quickly dispels the idea that men cannot help but be that way. 'We're human beings with spirits first, then men. We are not only capable of achieving intimacy, we're equipped and designed for it' (ibid.). Although the author feels that Tin Men are common, his view is not one of biological determinism – indeed, it's clearly social constructionist:

> Our society has long supported the view that being a man means that we have to conquer and control; make lots of money; have lots of women. Men must also learn to ignore physical or psychological pain; we pretend we don't have emotions. We men are groomed to only experience half of ourselves. But just

because we've been trained that way doesn't mean that it's right
or the best pattern by which to conduct our lives.

(Ibid.)

Men can change, then; and change is needed:

> We need a new paradigm for manhood. A new model of
> manhood for a new millennium. A manhood shaped by whole-
> ness, balancing masculine with sensitivity and connection. A
> replacement for the obsolete idea of manhood that has left us
> out of balance, disconnected, incomplete, and in many cases,
> utterly self-destructive.

(2001: 2)

But July is careful not to scare off his readers, quickly adding:

> While this is a major shift I'm talking about, I do want to
> emphasize an important fact: *This book is not a formula for the
> feminization of manhood.* I love being a man. I love being mas-
> culine. And I don't think women want men to be more feminine
> either. Just more human!

(Ibid., emphasis in original)

Quite a lot of the book is spent describing 'Tin Man' symptoms and
explaining why they do not lead to a fulfilled and happy life. Tin Men are
not necessarily the most obvious, strutting macho men, July sensibly notes;
they might just be ordinary men who work too much, at the expense of
their relationships, or men who avoid taking care of their health, for
example. Rather than being a distanced critic, July describes himself as a
'recovering Tin Man', having lived a former life of over-work, casual sex
and a false sense of invincibility which led to serious illness. Unlike other
self-help writers who may have spent their lives as middle-class professional
therapists, July is a black man who worked as a police patrol officer in
Houston, alongside other jobs, with lots of stress and a messy personal life,
before turning the corner and becoming the self-assured 'bestselling author
and motivational speaker' pictured on the book cover.

Part of Tin Man's problem is communication. But July doesn't just claim
that men speak macho rubbish: his thesis is that the macho rubbish usually
includes very clear messages which women can decode. Tin Man doesn't
keep his lack of interest in commitment a big secret, but typically flags it up
in clichéd phrases like 'I'm not ready for a relationship' and 'Let's not get

too serious'. So, unlike some other self-help books, the diagnosis is not that men are bad at communicating *per se*; the point is that their lives are screwed up in a much deeper way, which needs to be fundamentally sorted out. (In a pleasing spirit of sexual equality, July devotes a chapter to 'Tin Women', who have more-or-less the same symptoms.)

July talks tough with his male readers, reprimanding them for thinking that sex with several people will make them happy, for example, or for continuing 'the new and improved wife syndrome' where a newly successful man gets a new partner to match his new, higher status, whilst ditching the woman who supported him on the way up. For three-quarters of *Understanding the Tin Man*, though, we are told a lot about why tin-headed behaviour is unsatisfactory and destructive, but not so much about how to change it, or even what its causes are. Towards the end, though, some solutions and explanations emerge:

> The Tin Man's avoidance of intimacy is really about fear. He's afraid his feelings will make him vulnerable and leave him open to getting hurt. He's afraid that expressing his feelings may not look masculine.... For example, fear causes us to take jobs we hate (or remain in), and causes us to get into relationships for the wrong reasons (or to stay in bad relationships that are not working).... Overcoming fear of his feelings is a tall order for the Tin Man. To do this he needs to replace the fear that imprisons him with the motivating power of love.... Letting go of fear and living by love is the way the Tin Man can build his bridge to intimacy.
>
> (2001: 160–161)

At points like this, it is a good job that the author is a former 'Tin Man' himself, as this would not seem to be a message likely to be readily embraced by current tinheads. July offers both 'ten steps to start focusing on more intimacy' and then '28 ways to change your life right now', so he's not exactly short of suggestions, but the *willpower* and *motivation* to carry through the changes would need to come from the readers themselves, and the author doesn't really explain how these can be developed – apart from a general feeling that change will be its own reward.

Some of July's values seem quite traditional, but are advocated here not because of an attachment to the past, but because they respect human feelings and seem to work. If modernity (in the Giddens sense) can be characterised – albeit rather simplistically – as being about fluidity of relationships and the breakdown of traditional ties, then we can see writers like July serving a helpful function, stepping onto the contemporary pitch and saying 'This is all very well – I like sex as much as the next man – but isn't this leaving us feeling a bit empty?', and then offering advice on how we can combine modernity with long-term happiness. Whilst theorists such as Giddens discuss 'the democratisation of the emotions in everyday life' and the 'pure relationship' in relatively abstract terms, self-help writers like July take up the same ideas and spell out how they can be achieved, in the language of accessible, mainstream lifestyle advice. It could be said that late modernity, with its democratisation of relationships, may be a good idea, but the average male human isn't up to the job: he needs training – hence the market for men's self-help books like this.

Men's case study #2: the ordinary man

Ordinary Heroes: A Future for Men by Michael Hardiman (2000) is a rather more gentle discussion. The author's life as a psychologist in the rural west of Ireland is a far cry from William July's former fast-living lifestyle in a US metropolis. Nevertheless, their ideas about men have much in common, although Hardiman doesn't make big promises or offer programmatic solutions. The book's general approach is summarised on the back cover thus:

> Most personal development books are written by women, bought by women and read by women. Men are more reluctant to engage in efforts at self-discovery: they see it as a sign of weakness. But this can have serious consequences for men's health as well as for the functioning of society as a whole. *Ordinary Heroes* finally fills this gap: it is a personal development book written by a man for men and for the women who love them.

Hardiman's approach, like July's, is that men are formed much more by culture and society than by biology, and we can see that he would agree with the 'Tin Man' thesis:

> In general, men have been encouraged and rewarded for developing and using their minds and their bodies ... What they have lost, or never been allowed to develop, is what is often mistakenly called their feminine side. Sensitivity, affection, nurturing and feelings are not feminine qualities. They are human qualities that are often seen as feminine because they are less apparent in men. The inhibition of these aspects of development has created

a serious imbalance in the way men experience their lives and in
the way they live and behave.

(2000: x)

Hardiman notes how men inherit the traditional expectation that they will
be self-sacrificing providers, and the idea that their value as people, and as
men, is closely related to their work – notions which persist today, despite
other changes in society. His experience of working with a group of unemployed men is of moving relevance here: the men felt great despair and use-
lessness, because they were not employed – even though the jobs they had
lost 'were menial and often very boring and sometimes dangerous. They
could not be missing the work itself, what they were missing was the value
that society had placed in having a job, any job' (p. 33).

As the book goes on we get another depressing picture of men –
detached from their feelings, always having to show a tough exterior, isolated from having deep communication in their friendships with other men,
not good at having genuinely intimate relationships with women, and fool-
ishly repeating their father's emotional distance in their relationships with
their own children. As with *Tin Man*, we are well over half way through the
book before description of these problems gives way to some solutions; and
it's not clear that the solutions – all nice things about spending quality time
cultivating proper relationships with partner, friends and children – would
be readily taken to by the kind of over-programmed masculine robots who
need this help the most. (Nevertheless, this may be the Catch-22 problem
for all self-help books, rather than this one in particular.) The other disappointment is that the title *Ordinary Heroes: A Future for Men* suggests that
the book will present an exciting new way of thinking, by which, perhaps,
men can see themselves as the heroes of their own lives whilst interacting
with the world in a bright, full, new way, instead of the impoverished old
way. The text doesn't really follow through on this promise.

Men's case study #3: inside men's heads

If Men Could Talk, This is What They Would Say by psychologist Alon
Gratch (2001) claims to explain 'male behaviour', again for both men and
the women who want to understand them. On the book's cover, the blurb
signs up to the discourse, very common on self-help book covers, that men
and woman are fundamentally different:

> Dr Gratch's groundbreaking book acknowledges what women
> have known for centuries: men don't speak the same language as

them when it comes to talking about emotional issues – if they speak at all. The deep psychological differences that polarise men and women are decoded in *If Men Could Talk*.

But in fact this thoughtful book, based on Gratch's long experience as a therapist of men, argues that men and women aren't really that different inside (a theme developed further in *If Love Could Think* (Gratch, 2006)). Men, here, are not fundamentally bad, but may act in ways that look bad because of their deep emotional traumas, often – but not necessarily – stemming back to early experiences. As if fighting a battle with the claims on its own cover, the book tells us at an early stage:

> Obviously, men are different from women. But could it be that under their dull, cement-like exterior there's a world of riveting, warring emotions? Ultimately what I've learned from my male patients is that given a certain emotional environment, men can talk, and that, furthermore, what they have to say is nothing less than inspiring. This, in a word, is both the message and the content of this book.
>
> (2001: 7)

Just as in the books discussed above, *If Men Could Talk* is eager to tell men that a happy balance between 'masculinity' and 'femininity' can be achieved without them having to wipe out their proud male identity:

> Differences [between men and women] cannot only be bridged, they can be integrated. That is, men can learn to accept their own femininity despite the threat it poses for their own masculinity. And they can do so without becoming 'wimps'.
>
> (2001: 14)

Gratch is gentle and sympathetic in his discussion of men, who, he suggests, may act 'masculine' on the surface, but are hiding levels of insecurity, vulnerability and fear underneath. He discusses, in turn, men's shame; emotional absense; insecurity; self-involvement; aggression; self-destructiveness; and sexual needs and dysfunctions. The approach is both considered and challenging, recognising that change may not come easily, but that if a man can arrive at a deep appreciation of his problems and their roots, he will be able to begin the journey towards overcoming these flaws and become a 'fuller' human being.

SELF-HELP FOR MEN SUMMARY

Although they differ in style and approach, it's not hard to pull out some common themes in these texts. (The longer discussion online (Gauntlett, 2008) considers also *Ten Stupid Things Men Do To Mess Up Their Lives* by Laura Schlessinger (1998), and *Success for Dummies* by Zig Ziglar (1998).) The self-help books for men shared these messages:

- Men are not monolithic and unchangeable. Men can change for the better.
- Men are not good at intimacy, expressing their more vulnerable or loving feelings, connecting with others or admitting pain or failure. They can and should improve in all of these respects.
- Men generally place too much emphasis on work, and fail to develop a fulfilling personal and home life. Nobody on their deathbed regrets that they spent too little time at the office.
- You may be able to 'do what you like' in modern society, but you won't be happy without a mixture of love and responsibility.
- Men cultivate a tough outer appearance, distinguishing themselves from women, but inside they have a complex emotional life and needs that are remarkably similar to women's.

The books are generally built on the same assumptions that underlie theories of late modernity (or postmodernity, as some would call it), such as we saw in the work of Giddens: relationships have become more fluid; traditional ties have broken down; identities are flexible; and there are increasingly loose and 'free' choices of lifestyle and sexual activity available. The self-help authors do not want to be academic observers or theorists, though – their approach is, of course, much more proactive: they tell readers how they can lay a stable path through the quagmire of modern living, making firm (and usually very *responsible*) choices in order to gain happiness and fulfilment.

SELF-HELP FOR WOMEN

There are not many general self-help books for women, but rather an enormous range of titles for women with specific problems or in particular situations – women seeking confidence and assertiveness, overcoming divorce or wanting to succeed at work, for instance. Indeed, the more popular feminist books such as Natasha Walter's *The New Feminism* (1998), Germaine Greer's *The Whole Woman* (1999) and Jessica Valenti's *Full*

Frontal Feminism: A Young Woman's Guide to Why Feminism Matters (2007), fall partly into the self-help market, offering a mix of critical social analysis alongside an inspirational 'women can do it' message. Here, though, we'll focus on books aimed squarely at the 'self-help' audience.

Of the books I examined (discussion online, Gauntlett (2008)) – including *The Go-Girl Guide: Surviving your 20s with Savvy, Soul and Style* by Julia Bourland (2000), Laura Schlessinger's *Ten Stupid Things Women Do To Mess Up Their Lives* (1995) and others mentioned below – the most distinctive was *Sisters of the Yam: Black Women and Self-Recovery*, an excursion into self-help territory by renowned black feminist and cultural critic bell hooks (2005, first published 1993), which we'll look at more closely here.

Case study: bell hooks' self-help for black women

Sisters of the Yam is aimed specifically at black women because, hooks asserts, black women continue to face unique challenges at 'the bottom of everything' in 'white-supremacist capitalist patriarchy', even though they have made advances and positive 'interventions' in the mass media 'to offer radically different images of ourselves' (2005: 1–2). Although hooks is known for her academic writings, this book is not meant to be an 'academic' text but an authentic mainstream self-help book. Commenting on her desire to address a wide and diverse audience, hooks says:

> It was the success of the self-help book *Women Who Love Too Much* [by Robin Norwood, 1985] that convinced me that women of all races, classes, and sexual preferences would read work that addressed their concerns and most importantly their pain and their longing to transform their lives. This book, however, like many other self-help books for women, disturbed me because it denied that patriarchy is institutionalised. It made it seem that women could change everything in our lives by sheer acts of personal will. It did not even suggest that we would need to organise politically to change society in conjunction with our efforts to transform ourselves.
>
> (2005: 4)

hooks wants to challenge the political naivety of self-help discourses, then, but admits that she has found self-help literature helpful herself, and although many of her concerns are to do with broad social inequalities, she notes the need for 'self-actualisation' as part of the struggle – 'Toni Cade Bambara reminded us that "revolution begins in the self and with the self"' (p. 5).

Throughout *Sisters of the Yam*, hooks refers to several other self-help texts, including *Feel the Fear and Do It Anyway* by Susan Jeffers (which encouraged hooks to think positively, and gave her the courage to stop salaried university work and become a full-time writer), *The Road Less Travelled* by M. Scott Peck (on the importance of openness and honesty), *Do What You Love, The Money Will Follow* by Marsha Sinetar (on choosing rewarding work), *The Black Women's Health Book* by Evelyn White (on sharing painful experiences), and *You Can Heal Your Life* by Louise Hay (on care of the self). She also draws inspiration from a number of novels by black women, including those of Toni Morrison, Toni Cade Bambara, and Alice Walker – writers who address 'the deep, often unnamed psychic wounding that takes place in the daily lives of black folks in this society' (p. 11).

In spite of black people's advancement and successes, hooks argues, those working in the white-dominated world develop low self-esteem and 'become fundamentally estranged from life-affirming world views and life practices' and a sense of community (p. 10). hooks says that women have to heal the pain of past experiences, whether these have come from racist society, or from the harshly critical words of parents who did not want their daughters to risk failure or disappointment (pp. 33–35). She emphasises the importance of love, and emotional communication. She also stresses the need for black women to have a positive self-image, rejecting the 'internalised racism' spread by television (p. 81), and in spite of the mass media's failure to celebrate black people as beautiful (p. 84). She notes the lack of positive role models for women with natural hair – a sense which led her to later produce a children's picture book, *Happy to be Nappy* (with illustrator Chris Raschka, 1999).

Critics might say that, although the terrible histories of racism and slavery should never be forgotten, hooks dwells too much on the connections with history, repeatedly reminding young black women that their people were slaves, and emphasising the connections between black people and the land, nature and the earth (2005: 175–182). It could be said that we should look at the world anew: history should not be forgotten, but maybe should be parked at the back of one's mind as one tackles life with vigour, today – unburdened with thoughts of the past and excited about prospects for the future. Such an approach does not have to be 'apolitical', and can be uncompromisingly critical of today's problems and oppressions.

In any case, users of the book at Amazon.com find it to be excellent. Helena Romaine Henderson from Washington DC, for example, writes:

> This book has altered my thought process in ways I never thought possible. bell hooks has spoken with clear and simple

words about black women and our individual and collective need to self-recover – from racism, sexism, of course – but also from our own (often) self-imposed 'isms' carried from childhood. She's brutally honest in a book that sits unmoved from my bed-stand. A recommended read for black women. Period. Regardless of background and circumstance. A must read for those on the never-ending journey of self-introspection that eventually encourages self-recovery.

(19 December 2000)

Although *Sisters of the Yam* did not, ultimately, smash its way to the top of the self-help bestseller charts, it remains an interesting exercise which seems to have been of value and inspiration to many black women, and others.

SELF-HELP FOR WOMEN SUMMARY

Self-help books for women, as noted above, are diverse and often focused on particular issues. I have examined those mentioned above, plus a number of others including *How to Be an Irresistible Woman* by Lisa Helmanis (2006), *The Positive Woman: Simple Steps to Optimism and Creativity* by Gael Lindenfield (2000), and *Fabulosity: What It Is and How to Get It* by Kimora Lee Simmons (2006). Despite their varied approaches and emphases, the books seemed to agree on the following messages:

- Modern living can be difficult and stressful. The solutions include positive thinking and a planned approach, in which you tackle problems in an assertive but not reckless way. Thinking about your needs, with the help of a self-help book, is a good idea.
- You should absolutely *do what you want to do*. Doing things in life just because others expect you to, or because of habit or tradition, is a very bad idea.
- Self-esteem is very important. You have to feel good about yourself.
- Don't make excuses. Take control of your life.
- It can be noted that unlike the books for men, which focused on men's emotional tardiness, insecurity and screwed-up inner life, the successful books for women generally encourage readers to feel that they have no problems inside, as long as they can be confident; with self-assurance and a positive approach, they suggest, anything can be achieved.

MORE SELF-HELP FOR EVERYONE

There are, of course, many self-help books which are not aimed at either sex in particular, because their advice about life-planning, relationships or overcoming problems is intended to benefit everybody. Here we'll briefly look at four rather different examples.

General case study #1: intergalactic harmony

Men Are From Mars, Women Are From Venus by John Gray (1993) is one of the best-known self-help books ever published, often referenced (whether in admiring or mocking tones) in movies, TV shows and magazines. It has sold 'more than 14 million copies in the United States and millions more in 40 different languages around the world' (www.marsvenus.com). In fact the book has been turned into a publishing 'franchise', with the same basic ideas being reworked into many more books by the same author (including *Mars and Venus in the Bedroom, Mars and Venus in Love, Practical Miracles for Mars and Venus* and several others), plus cassettes, CDs, videos, computer software, courses, workshops, websites, a syndicated newspaper column, a radio show, a TV show, a musical stage play (!) and even a board game, all bearing the *Mars and Venus* brand.

Unlike most self-help books, which encourage readers to change their circumstances when they are not happy with them, *Men Are From Mars* is all about changing one's *perception* of reality so that it can be accepted more happily. 'When men and women are able to respect and accept their differences,' Gray explains, 'then love has a chance to blossom' (p. 14). The book is built on the explicit assumption that women and men are 'completely different' (p. 5), illustrated by the metaphor of the book's title, which suggests that the problem with (heterosexual) relationships today is that men and women have 'forgotten' that they originally came from different planets. This is, in short, a way of asserting that traditional sex stereotypes were right all along – men are rational and analytical, whilst women are emotional and talk a lot (p. 36). Gray says that when women and men don't get along perfectly in today's world, it is because they have made the modern mistake of assuming that men and women are fundamentally similar, which leads to misunderstandings, tension and frustration. The solution lies in appreciating these 'natural' differences, and taking the time to communicate more clearly based on these principles.

Although it is common to see the success of *Men Are From Mars* as a modern, liberal 'touchy-feely' phenomenon, then, this is quite inappropriate, as the book proposes a return to 1950s-style gender roles within relationships. The aim of *Men Are From Mars* is to foster relationships where a heterosexual couple are equally 'understanding' of each other – which sounds nice – but are not actually equals. The Mars–Venus programme may bring happiness and reconciliation to couples who were previously insufficiently sympathetic to each others' character traits – as many satisfied couples now apparently attest – but it remains problematic. If a Mars–Venus couple were to procreate, for example, they would seem to be destined to bring up children whose ridiculously outdated views of gender would cripple them in the modern world.

The main problem with *Men Are From Mars, Women Are From Venus*, though, is its failure to recommend real, root-and-branch change. Many of the men described in Gray's relationship anecdotes are emotionally retarded shells, unable to connect or communicate on any deep level. These cases could be read as a disturbing indictment of our culture which produces such men; but Gray's idea is that we should just accept it. He knows that change is difficult – and so he tells women to love and respect their male partners' strange behaviour. He tells men to change a little – by listening to their partners more, without responding with hurt or hostility – but it's not enough to break society's cycle of producing men and women who feel that they are from different planets (as the book's success shows). Whenever the book edges towards suggesting real change for its male or female users, it consistently shies away and seeks refuge in the idiotic mantra of its title. If a woman is frustrated that her man will not change, 'she is forgetting that men are from Mars!' (p. 104), Gray writes gleefully, but not all readers (one hopes) will find this glib explanation to be entirely helpful.

General case study #2: Dr Phil's strategies

An entirely different approach is proposed in *Life Strategies* by Phillip C. McGraw (2001). 'Dr Phil' rose to fame on TV's *Oprah*, and has hosted his own hit show, *Dr Phil*, since 2002. *Life Strategies* is another hit, having sold over one million copies within two years of its first publication in 1999. Unlike Gray, McGraw does not think that one should learn to accommodate unhappy situations. If something isn't working, says Dr Phil, change it. The words 'Stop Making Excuses!' are plastered across the book's front cover. The back summarises the content well:

> Whether it's a bad relationship, a dead-end career, or a harmful habit, Dr McGraw helps you wake up and get out of your rut. It is never too late to take charge of, and be responsible for, your life.

McGraw asserts that you have to be your own 'life manager', and make the same assertive demands of yourself that you would make if you had been hired to 'manage' someone else (p. 169, 226). McGraw asks his readers to consider whether they are doing what they *really* want in life, or if it is just the result of habit or compromise (p. 14). You have to be 'accountable for your own life' (p. 15), and accepting an unhappy deal is not recommended. You should work out exactly what you want, and then claim it. This is a process of introspection, tough decisions, but most of all careful strategising; it even involves making numerous lists and charts – so many that towards the end you are encouraged to make summary charts of your 'evaluation spreadsheets', which are then to be summarised in another chart, which itself is then analysed. Dr Phil's background in the legal system has perhaps made him over-reliant on paperwork. Nevertheless, no-one can accuse his process of being vague self-help optimism: if personal transformation is a battle worth fighting, Dr Phil suggests, then battle plans are needed, and by breaking down seemingly idealistic goals into attainable steps, activities and targets, then the process of change takes a concrete, do-able form. It's all about strategy:

> In contrast to the cruelty and harshness that are so much a part
> of the poorly managed or unmanaged life, if you have a clear-cut
> strategy, and the courage, commitment, and energy to execute
> that strategy at a project status level, you can flourish; you'll
> overcome the tough stuff. The world is not evil; it is just the
> world. It is not to be feared, just managed; and the key to man-
> aging it is having this consciously designed strategy.
>
> (2001: 176)

At Amazon.com, a few of the hundreds of people who have posted comments about this book are concerned that it may be overly 'blunt' or 'intimidating', but most are very positive. Readers seemed to appreciate the emphasis on personal accountability, the 'realism' and drive for solutions – as opposed to self-help books which would seek to persuade the reader that life is already good, or that they are a victim – and the author's 'straight talking' approach. On the other hand, one reader suggests that the advice is all common sense, and that Dr Phil fails to recognise that life is about the *journey*, not planning its conquest.

General case studies #3 and #4: easy living vs hard working

Our final pair of case studies are the more recent bestsellers, *Living the 80/20 Way* by Richard Koch (2004) and *The Rules of Life* by Richard Templar (2006). Both are sequels to earlier works in which their respective authors outlined principles to use in business; here, Koch and Templar have an eye on the lucrative self-help market and propose rules to apply in everyday life.

Richard Koch had previously written *The 80/20 Principle* (1997), primarily a book for business people, which is based around the principle that 80 per cent of results stem from just 20 per cent of causes or effort. Koch has a wide range of examples to support this claim. Although we might assume that more effort leads to more reward, on the contrary, 'the top 20 per cent of people, natural forces, economic inputs, or any other causes we can measure typically lead to about 80 per cent of results, outputs or effects' (2004: 11). Most people or businesses therefore spend far too much of their time on things which are ultimately – broadly speaking – pointless. As Koch puts it: 'Most people try too hard at the wrong things.' People therefore need to think intelligently about their priorities; but the author is not interested in 'time management' techniques designed to tinker with the way time is spent in the ever-roaring engine of business. Instead, he advocates a more radical approach where we should *only do* the small number of things that bring real benefits – and have the rest of the time off. Appealingly, this was a business book which said that readers should spend more time with their families, on the beach, or enjoying themselves generally, and would feel *more* fulfilled by doing *less* work. By doing what they loved, in a concentrated way – with the application of 'lazy intelligence' – they would also be more rich and successful, Koch argued.

This message appealed to people beyond the business market. In the follow-up book *Living the 80/20 Way*, Koch writes:

> *The 80/20 Principle* has been translated into 22 languages and has sold well over half a million copies ... Seven years later, I receive a steady and increasing stream of letters and emails from people everywhere around the world. Very few mention their business. They simply say what the Big Idea has done for their happiness and effectiveness: how it has helped them concentrate on the few relationships and issues that are really important to them, increased their sense of freedom, turbo-boosted their careers, and enabled them to escape the rat-race treadmill.
>
> (2004: 2–3)

Responding to this interest, this book goes on to apply the 80/20 principle to everyday life. Readers should stop spending hours and hours on things that make little or no difference, Koch argues, and should identify the *particular* things that make a genuine impact on their own happiness and that of the people who are important to them. This isn't necessarily easy to do: working out how to achieve more by doing less may involve some 'hard thinking', Koch says; but working out what *really matters*, and focusing only on those things, can bring great rewards. This approach therefore emphasises the choices we make – not only what to do, but also what *not* to do.

It's not very clear that this would work for everyone, of course, in practice; certain high-flying ideas producers might be able to make it work, but the economy would probably collapse if everyone decided to be a creative entrepreneur who would cause brilliant things to happen without actually doing the work themselves. Nevertheless, Koch is selling a dream to the particular audience of his readers, and the general idea – focusing on particular important and effective things instead of wasting time on mundane rubbish, and spending the time saved on having fun with family and friends – is bound to be a winner.

Or is it? Richard Templar, in *The Rules of Life*, suggests that life can be a bit like advertising: 'Someone once said that half of the money he spent on advertising was wasted but he didn't know which half' (2006: 58). With characteristic clunkiness the author spells out the meaning of this aphorism: 'Life is a bit like that ... you have to keep on doing the 100 per cent because you don't know which bits will pay off' (ibid.). This, of course, is the problem with Koch's 80/20 principle. It may be the case that 20 per cent of our actions will lead to 80 per cent of the results we desire, but how can we know, in advance, *which* 20 per cent? Koch suggests that we should be clever enough to work that out, and get more enjoyment out of life. Templar, on the other hand, isn't willing to risk it.

The Rules of Life (2006) followed its similarly-packaged predecessor *The Rules of Work* (2002) into the bestseller charts. As another successful manual for modern life it's worth noting briefly here, although unlike other titles we have considered, it lacks a 'high concept', or even much of an overarching theme. Drawing from a deep pool of cliché and common sense, Templar waffles his way through 100 rules including 'Be flexible in your thinking', 'Take an interest in the outside world', 'Aim to be the very best at everything you do' and 'Think for yourself'. The interesting thing here is not the plodding and obvious content of the text, but rather that people will pay good money for this kind of thing – in other words, the sociological point that people are increasingly seeking guidance about modern life and lifestyles. Meanwhile the success of Templar's book might demonstrate that life is as much about good luck, or good marketing, as anything else.

SELF-HELP: SUMMARY AND CONCLUSION

On the whole, the self-help literature proposes a quite consistent set of messages, centred around the acquisition of self-belief, self-esteem and the confidence to change things and seek a better life. All of them emphasise success in personal relationships above achievement at work, although several of them stress that *happiness* in one's work is important too.

With the exception of John Gray's compassionately worded but disturbingly stereotyped *Mars and Venus* thesis, self-help books typically assert that personal change is *necessary* and *essential*. They are usually very clear on this point – indeed, the tough-talking Laura Schlessinger would say that the failure to pursue fundamental change is 'pathetic'.

To summarise the most common self-help messages:

- Believe in yourself and you can achieve anything. Social 'barriers' can generally be disregarded if you have the will to overcome them.
- You can't let the world 'happen' to you; instead you must take control of your life.
- It may not be obvious what would make you happy in life, and what is available to you. These things have to be worked out; and then you can strive to get them. ('You have to name it to claim it', as McGraw says).
- Women and men are fundamentally similar on the 'inside', although men may have learned to be overly insular, emotionally withdrawn and bad at communicating, whilst women may not be confident or recognise the full range of their capabilities. But in any case, both women and men can adopt new ways of thinking and behaving so that they can become fully-functioning, balanced, self-assured, emotionally intelligent people.
- Change is always possible.

As I have noted already in this chapter, these approaches and ideas are very much in line with Anthony Giddens's view of modernity – a world of fluid relationships, where identities and personal connections have to be worked on and negotiated, and where we continually have to make choices about who we are, how we will present ourselves, and who we want to associate with. The book of tradition has been (more or less) ripped up, to be replaced with a bookstore bulging with new lifestyle manuals – some of which, like *Mars and Venus* and *The Surrendered Wife* (Doyle, 2000), offer a return to tradition for those who want it, whilst others, like *Life Strategies* and *Feel the Fear and Do It Anyway* (Jeffers, 2007) and thousands more, propose an assertive new approach where social forces are to be pummelled into submission by the independent, feisty individual.

In her book *Self-Help Inc.: Makeover Culture in American Life*, Micki McGee (2005b) argues that the rise of self-help discourses means that 'Americans have become belabored – urged to work continuously on improving themselves so as to remain ever-appealing in an increasingly competitive labor market' (McGee, 2005a). She suggests that the capitalist ideology from the world of work – 'an ends-driven, profit-motivated rationality' – is being applied to personal life, whilst 'values associated with the intimate sphere – for example, ideals of caring and camaraderie – have become part of management's human-resources tool kit' (ibid.). Whilst the latter part of this is true, I am not convinced that the self-help literature generally advocates cynical means-to-an-end rationality at the expense of niceness. Whilst much of the literature is about finding schemes or even 'tools' to achieve certain goals – such as greater self-esteem, success at work, or a more nurturing relationship with one's partner – these typically involve honesty, empathy with others and a critical awareness of oneself, but not manipulation or exploitation. Whilst the talk of 'strategies' and 'planning' can seem odd when applied to everyday life, the basic point is that *people should reflect carefully upon their lives, where they are going and how they deal with others*, and that's not a bad thing. Indeed, it's not new either, being a message found in The Bhagavad-Gita, The Bible, The Dhammapada and other ancient texts (which is why these three, and others, are included alongside more recent bestsellers in *50 Self-Help Classics* by Tom Butler-Bowdon (2003)).

Whilst commentators upon the self-help scene such as Elayne Rapping (1996) and Wendy Simonds (1996) are concerned that the desire for inner healing may have replaced the quest for bigger changes in society – which is a reasonable concern – I think the two are not mutually exclusive, but can go hand-in-hand. Rapping, to be fair, recognises that this might be a possibility, but she is further concerned about the tendency of self-help and the 'recovery' movement to lead people towards 'shelter from the storm of modern life', which she suggests is a weak ambition; 'staying dry, while important for survival, is not really our ultimate goal', she says (p. 185), meaning of course that modern life is something to be encountered and challenged, not hidden away from. This would be a good point, but I have found that most of today's self-help bestsellers promote a forceful engagement with the world, not a retirement from it. They are very individualistic, of course – they are about finding empowerment, success and happiness for yourself, not your community or social group – but they promote values of compassion and emotional sensitivity too, so we can hope that those individuals who reach a happy, self-actualised state will then go on to spread their good fortune, and try to help others. (That may be optimistic, but is not necessarily wrong.) Self-help books generally ignore social constraints – they do not tell readers that they will most likely not get on well in life because of sexism, racism or other forms of discrimination and oppression – which might make them weaker as social analyses; but they are not intended as sociological studies, they are meant to encourage and empower individuals to believe in themselves regardless of their social category or background, so it would not seem fair to criticise the books on this basis.

FEARLESS AND ASPIRATIONAL DISCOURSES

In this chapter, we have looked at the possible influence of 'role models' for inspiration and motivation, and the promotion of self-reliance and inner strength in popular self-help books. In each of these cases, as in the lifestyle magazines considered in the previous chapters, we see possible insecurities within modern self-identities being addressed through fearless, confident discourses, generally in a glamorous and aspirational form. In the following penultimate chapter, I will discuss some new research methods and approaches which might help us to understand how people actually fit this stuff into their everyday lives.

Chapter 11

EXPLORING IDENTITY STORIES

THIS CHAPTER WILL introduce a new approach to exploring identities, in which researchers have asked people to *make* things – such as videos, drawings, collages, or other visual items – as part of a process of reflection upon identity.[3] We will consider some of the advantages of this kind of research, and its philosophical underpinnings, before looking more closely at the results of my own recent study in which participants were asked to build metaphorical models of their identities using Lego, the colourful plastic construction toy. This chapter is all new to this edition of the book, and much of it is based on my other new book, *Creative Explorations: New Approaches to Identities and Audiences* (Gauntlett, 2007), which discusses the background to this approach, and the findings of the various studies, in much more detail.

WHY VISUAL METHODS?

As we have seen, identity is rather complex, diffuse and generally hard for people to talk about. We have considered the ideas that people use 'guerrilla tactics' to draw upon cultural resources which activate meanings in their everyday lives (Chapter 2), developing and re-editing a 'narrative of the self' (Chapter 5) which may be influenced by suggestions from popular media (Chapter 4), lifestyle advice in magazines (Chapters 8 and 9) or role models (Chapter 10). This may all seem more-or-less rational – as though making an identity is a deliberate set of actions, like putting together a photo album. Everyday experience, though, tells us that it's not like that, and researchers have certainly found that people don't have a simple 'identity printout' button which will somehow reveal their identity, on demand, as a simple linear explanation.

Because it is hard to interview people about their distinctive personal characteristics, some researchers have tried to devise processes for thinking about identities which employ more reflective and creative activities. Being asked to *make* something requires participants to take a roundabout route into the research topic. The 'data' that comes from such studies usually includes not only the things that have been made, but also observations and statements arising from the *process* of their production, and the participants' own *reflections* on the things they have created.

In comparison to the standard qualitative research techniques – such as interviews and focus groups – I believe that this approach offers a number of advantages, whether the research question is about identities or any other aspect of attitudes or experiences. These benefits should become clearer during the course of the chapter, but can be summarized as follows:

- Participants are given *time* to reflect on the research questions or issues, and to thoughtfully create a response.
- Therefore participants are *not* required to produce instant descriptions of their views, opinions or responses, in language (which is not easy for everyone).
- The process operates on the visual plane, to a substantial degree – like many aspects of social experience.
- Creative visual tasks get the human brain working in a different way, and, therefore, may 'unlock' different kinds of responses.
- Participants are able to present something as a whole, rather than in the linear sequence which language forces us into.
- Participants using certain methods (such as the Lego technique outlined below) can use metaphors to express abstract thoughts and feelings in a concrete way.

Of course, one would not want to assert that these visual and creative methods will be 'better' than language-based methods, in all cases. Nevertheless, they are certainly a useful addition to the researcher's toolkit, and have helped with our understanding of identities in particular, because identity is an abstract concept filled with abstract things (passions, experiences, memories, sensations, influences, repulsions and attractions) which may need to be mediated – given form – and expressed in ways that social scientists may not have traditionally accepted.

VIDEO-MAKING IDENTITIES

Giving people the opportunity to make videos about their lives or identities can be a fruitful research process. With the rise of less expensive video cameras, and popular video-sharing sites such as YouTube, video-making is not such an *unusual* activity these days, but still, *most* people actually don't spend time making videos about their lives. As I argued when I conducted a video-making project over ten years ago (in which young people were asked to make videos about the environment), the task of making a video requires participants to make particular decisions about what to include, how to represent it, and what level of importance or priority to assign to different elements (Gauntlett, 1997). As mentioned above, the valuable data that a researcher gets from such a project is not just the finished set of videos, but also the observations of the *process* through which they were made.

An interesting example is Ruth Holliday's project (1999, 2004) in which gay, lesbian or bisexual participants were given video cameras for up to three months and were asked to keep video diaries. The project aimed 'to examine the performative nature of queer identities' (2004: 49). Respondents were asked to consider different 'work, rest and play' aspects of their lives by dressing in the clothes which they would wear in different situations, and to speak about their 'self-presentation strategies'. This brought the often-ignored visual dimension of social life into the heart of the study, and as Holliday notes, the video diaries 'capture visual performances of identities and the fascinating ways in which identities are mapped onto the surfaces of bodies, homes and workspaces' (p. 54).

The video diary approach was clearly an invitation for respondents to produce a *representation* of themselves; they could 'stage', work on, re-record, or delete material before it was even seen by the researcher. Whilst some scholars might be concerned that this procedure would not produce sufficiently 'accurate' or 'authentic' results, Holliday argues that it is a positive feature, giving the participant 'greater "editorial control" over the material disclosed' (p. 51). Whilst 'staging' an identity for the camera might sound rather false, Holliday asserts that the video diary-making process is just an extension of the *reflections* of self which individuals necessarily already produce. Researchers obviously cannot actually 'capture' parts of a person's authentic self – whatever that would mean – so Holliday suggests that we should give participants visual tools and enable them to *share* instances of self-expression.

The process enabled Holliday to gain insights into 'the ways in which identities are performed in different times and spaces – which I call work, rest and play – and also how these performances become mediated by academic, political and "subcultural" discourses of sexuality' (1999: 475), and the idea of the body as a text which expresses identity. The performance of being out on the 'scene' was contrasted with that of being at home, typically seen as a place of greater comfort and authenticity (although not necessarily better for being less playful).

Video-making methods have some limitations, of course. One is that they are a pretty obvious *intervention*, where participants are being asked to specifically *do something* for the sake of the research. In that sense they have a somewhat artificial connection with 'normal events'. However, this also applies to the contrived setting of, say, a focus group; and because video production takes time to do, the feelings reflected tend to become more 'authentic' as time passes.

A more serious problem for video and photography projects is that in order to make pictures, participants must necessarily point their camera at things. Therefore, things close to hand – which it is easiest to point the camera at – are most likely to be filmed, and the process is given a rather literal orientation: the visual material is perhaps more likely to be concerned with the physical world that we live in rather than with the subjective life of the mind. (The *metaphorical* approach of the Lego study, discussed below, largely avoids this problem.)

DRAWING CELEBRITIES

In another study which attempted to engage with participants via a creative task, I sought to explore the connections between celebrities and personal identities, by asking young people to do a drawing of a celebrity. At the time (2003–04) there was a lot of discussion in the media about the relationship between young people and celebrities, and whether 'celebrity culture' was affecting young people's aspirations and their ideas about lifestyle and gender. The concept of 'celebrity' therefore also bounced onto the sociological radar, discussed in books such as Rojek (2001), Turner (2004), Cashmore (2006), and Holmes and Redmond (2006).

The participants were 100 young people, aged 14–15, at a number of schools in the south of England. I asked them to: 'Draw a star, celebrity or famous person who you would like to be. If there's nobody you'd like to be, at all, then choose someone who you think is good or cool'. They were also asked to 'put them in a particular setting and/or doing something', and were reassured that their drawing skills were of no concern.

Ideally each participant would have been interviewed in some detail about their drawing, individually. Because of the time constraints of doing the study in school time, however, the participants instead were asked to

Figure 11.1   Examples of drawings of celebrities produced by teenagers in the
study: clockwise from top left, Jennifer Aniston, Orlando Bloom,
Buffy the Vampire Slayer, Michael Jackson, Keira Knightley

complete an open questionnaire, which asked if they would like to be like
their chosen celebrity, and *why*, and to note common themes between how
the celebrity might be described and how they themselves might like to be
thought of.

The most striking finding of the study (Gauntlett, 2005) related to the
teenage boys. In spite of the relatively brutal culture of adolescent males
aged 14–15, the process – which required thinking and drawing rather than
instant reactions – seemed to enable a number of the male participants to
provide rather emotionally reflective responses, revealing a more sensitive
side than other studies of young masculinities have tended to attract (Buckingham, 1993; Frosh *et al.*, 2001; Barker, 2005). For example, David
Beckham was chosen by one male respondent not because of his sporting
prowess, but because he was seen as 'happy', and 'a family man' with 'lots
of friends'. Other male celebrities were chosen because they were 'warm',
'modest', 'mellow', 'funny' and 'sound', amongst other adjectives. Coming
from male teenagers, responses such as these – which are emotionally reflec-

tive rather than 'macho' – seemed quite refreshing. Discussing this finding (Gauntlett, 2005: 174), I noted that this suggests either that young masculinities are changing, or that the drawing process itself gives research participants more *time*, and a little less constraint, to develop nuanced thoughts about the subject-matter. It seems likely that there is some truth to both of these explanations.

BUILDING IDENTITIES IN LEGO

There are a number of other interesting studies which have used visual methods to explore people's lives and experiences, which are discussed in a number of books (for example, Prosser, 1998; Knowles and Sweetman, 2004; Gauntlett, 2007). Here, though, we turn our attention to the Lego identity study, which I have mentioned a few times already.

This project grew out of a wish to explore identities in a new way, using visual methods. I had noticed that in the kinds of methods discussed above, participants are led to create images of *existing things*. Photography or video methods necessarily require people to produce pictures of things which the camera can be pointed at, as we noted above, whilst the use of drawings is often constrained by participants' concerns about their lack of 'ability'. Studies using collage (such as the study by Awan (2007) discussed in the previous chapter) may also be limited by the range of collage materials available. Therefore, when I was contacted in 2004 by Per Kristiansen, who at that time was Director of Lego Serious Play, I saw an interesting opportunity.

Lego Serious Play is a form of consultancy for businesses and organisations, used as a problem-solving and team-building tool, in which groups build *metaphorical* models of their experiences. It is run as a kind of franchise by the Lego company, which trains facilitators (typically people from business consultancy companies) in the Lego Serious Play processes, licenses them to be official Lego Serious Play practitioners, and supplies them with Lego bricks and pieces. The different applications of Lego Serious Play have been carefully worked out with expert psychologists and business innovators. (Their website is at www.seriousplay.com.)

Because I was already doing studies in which people were asked to *make* things as part of the process of thinking-through an issue, Lego invited me to collaborate with them, and I developed a project which employed some of the Lego Serious Play techniques as a social research method for exploring identities. Because the process uses metaphors, participants can declare that any Lego shape, animal or construction represents whatever they like, and therefore this approach avoids the problem of having to point a camera

Figures 11.2–11.5 Participants building metaphorical models of their identities in the Lego identity study

at things, be good at drawing or have access to particular collage images. For full details and a much more comprehensive discussion, see the book *Creative Explorations* (Gauntlett, 2007).

In my study, ten groups of individuals took part in workshop sessions, each of which lasted for at least four hours. Groups were typically of seven or eight people; 79 people took part in total. Obviously, if a researcher was to begin a session by saying to participants, 'I want you to build a metaphorical model of your identity in Lego', this would probably be rather baffling, and would lead to some limited or confused responses. This is why the sessions were necessarily lengthy, as the participants were taken through exercises in which they became familiar with Lego building; then got used to metaphors, and building them in Lego; and then, eventually, built metaphorical models of their own identity, and influences upon that identity. Participants were from diverse backgrounds: three groups were unemployed or low-paid part-time workers; other groups included social workers, architects and charity managers. (Because it would be difficult to persuade most people to particip-ate in such a time-consuming session, most participants were paid or rewarded for their time: this is good research practice as it shows recognition and respect for the time that people have given up to take part.)

The use of metaphors meant that participants were able to build a representation of their identity and its elements – aspirations, influences and desires – which otherwise would be difficult to picture. Metaphors are also powerful because they suggest additional fruitful meanings, which is why we employ them so often in everyday speech (often without really thinking about it). Instead of saying, for example, 'I was really pleased', which is straightforward but bland, I might say 'I was over the moon', which conveys the idea that I was delighted whilst adding additional imagery: a kind of vertiginous leap for the stars, the unusualness of space travel, and the pleasing feeling of being 'up, up and away'. All metaphors offer images which communicate ideas more powerfully than their more literal, non-metaphorical counterparts. (To remind you of a few common examples: 'She devoured the book'; 'There was electricity between them'; 'He lives in an ivory tower'.)

To give an impression of the kinds of things built by participants, here are just a few examples of metaphors from the many hundreds which went into the 79 participants' models. Some were quite straightforward:

- A dinner table, representing family.
- A dish with bright shiny coins, representing friendship.
- A sequence of hurdles presided over by a 'witch figure', representing work.

- A man paddling along in a kayak, representing meditation.
- A bird on the ground, representing responsibilities ('because I feel like a bird that wants to fly away, but can't').

Others were more complex:

- People under a transparent plastic container, representing people from the past, who continue to have an influence but who cannot be accessed directly.
- Nine bodies with tubes going up into one big head, representing different sides of the personality.
- A tiger underneath the main representation of personality, representing an underlying pride and defensiveness.
- A see-saw with a crowned king figure opposite an 'evil' person, representing yin and yang, and the choices to be made in life between good and bad behaviour.
- A wobbly ambulance with only three wheels, representing health problems.

In addition to the individual metaphors that made up each model, we were also able to consider the metaphorical meaning of *the whole model*. Just as a poem may contain a number of different metaphors, but also have an overall metaphorical meaning, the Lego identity models could be viewed both as a set of individual meaningful parts, but also seen as a whole representation. Indeed, participants were typically struck by the way in which the thing they had made represented their identity *as a whole* even though, whilst building it, they had been focusing on it as a set of parts or areas. For example, one person's whole model might appear rather spacious and empty, suggesting loneliness, lack of fulfilment, or perhaps serenity; conversely, a model with many elements crammed into a limited space might suggest a sense of chaos, or a feeling of being 'swamped'.

In order to interpret the Lego identity model, its meanings and its metaphors, the project relied on the *participant's own* interpretations. This principle emerged partly from the history of the practice of art therapy: in the early to mid twentieth century, it was believed that the professional 'expert' should interpret the client's work, in some cases drawing on a standardised manual that would list likely interpretations of particular bits of imagery. More recently this approach has generally been replaced by the view that the interpretation should come from the client themselves, in a dialogue with the art therapist. (For more detail see Gauntlett, 2005: 162–163.) As art therapist Cathy Malchiodi writes (1998: 36):

In my own work with children's drawings from a phenomeno-
logical approach, the first step involves taking a stance of 'not
knowing.' This is similar to the philosophy described by social
constructivist theorists who see the therapist's role in work with
people as one of co-creator, rather than expert advisor. By seeing
the client as the expert on his or her own experiences, an openness to new information and discoveries naturally evolves for the
therapist. Although art expressions may share some commonali-
ties in form, content, and style, taking a stance of not knowing
allows the child's experiences of creating and making art
expressions to be respected as individual and to have a variety of
meanings.

In terms of social research, it similarly seems appropriate to value the knowledge and experience of participants, and to build explanations which begin
with their own interpretations. I do not believe that there is a justifiable
rationale for why the researcher should impose their own 'expert' interpretation, replacing that of the person whose identity is represented.

Of course, the act of explanation or interpretation brings the material
back into the world of *language*. The study doesn't, therefore, remain
'purely visual' – whatever that would mean. This is not surprising: talking or
writing about things in order to deal with them, especially in an academic
study, is almost inevitable. But what is important in these studies is the
visual and *creative* process, which takes *time*, and which involves thinking
and making with the *hands*, all of which importantly *precedes* the part where
the meanings are considered in language.

The study led to a set of 11 findings, which I will summarise here before
discussing three of them in more detail (summarised from Gauntlett, 2007:
182–195):

Three findings about method

Finding #1: Creative and visual research methods give people the opportunity to communicate different kinds of information –

> Whilst language leads people to give linear accounts (one thing
> after another thing, with ones mentioned earlier seeming to be
> more important than ones mentioned later), visual methods
> enable people to present information as a *whole*, as a landscape of
> interrelated parts. A creative task gives people *time* to think
> through and develop a meaningful response, and the process of

making with the hands prompts the brain to respond differently and fully to the challenge.

Finding #2: Metaphors can be powerful in social research –

As already mentioned, metaphors enable people to communicate about intangible concepts, experiences and feelings; and to encapsulate them in a meaningful image, which may suggest additional meaningful ideas. Building a whole metaphorical thing (such as a Lego identity model) means that both the *parts* and the *whole* can be seen as meaningful.

Finding #3: Research participants need reflective time to construct knowledge –

Giving people *time* to make something, and generate a response to the research question, as mentioned in Finding #1, allows people to assemble meaningful responses (rather than instant 'gut reactions') and can enable ideas to 'bubble up' from the subconscious and find expression within the creative activity.

Four findings about understanding social experience and identities

Finding #4: Recognition of 'identity' –

The notion of 'identity' is taken for granted, as a meaningful term, by researchers in this area, and probably by you as a reader of this book; but it seems possible that a sample of 'ordinary people' would actually find this confusing and not know what they were being asked to represent. But, no: the notion that 'I' have 'an identity', which could be represented in some way (such as in Lego), was already accepted by all participants. Indeed, the task of representing identity through visual items (which could often be seen, in some way, as metaphors) is often familiar to people who have put up posters and photos on their bedroom walls, or decorated their fridge with postcards, stickers, magnets and mementoes.

Finding #5: Identity theories are common currency –

Social theorists may like to think of their models of self and identity as specialist, privileged information, but the Lego study showed that certain notions about self-identity in everyday life are already known and understood, at some level, by most people already. Of course this takes the form of working knowledge, rather than academic discourse. For instance, the essence of Erving Goffman's classic sociological argument (1959) that people have to routinely generate a kind of social performance for different audiences, in order to appear competent and coherent in everyday life, was taken for granted by most participants. It was assumed to be unsurprising that their identity models would include, for example, 'back stage' areas where the more private aspects of identity were to be found, and a more 'public face' which looked out to and interacted with the external world. Similarly, Anthony Giddens's (1991) argument that individuals in contemporary western societies have to construct and maintain a personal biographical narrative of the self, in order to enjoy a coherent and stable existence, was recognised by the Lego study participants, who all took to the task of putting together their identity 'story' in a particular way, whilst acknowledging that there could be other ways of telling it.

Finding #6: Identities are typically unified, not fragmented –

Although postmodernists have propagated the idea that modern identities are 'fragmented', the Lego study found no evidence of this. On the contrary, every one of the participants built their identity as *one thing*. It may have been complex, but it was also a single, whole thing.
• This finding is discussed further below, in the section 'Fragmented identities?'.

Finding #7: Relationship between the individual and society –

Almost everyone likes to think that they are somewhat different to the general mass, and yet almost nobody wants to think that they have nothing in common with anyone else. This was the most common theme found across all of the identity models in the study: a tension between the desire to be a distinctive individual, and the need to be part of a broader social community.

- This finding is discussed further below, in the section 'The individuality paradox'.

Four findings about media audience studies

Finding #8: Media studies is often too much about the media –

All forms of media, from mainstream TV shows and movies to niche websites and fanzines, find their meaning within a social context, as people consume, discuss and interact with them, and embed them in their lives. Media studies, however, has a tendency to discuss 'the media' as an independently fascinating set of texts and technologies. We have to deal with the media as it occurs in the world, and in terms of the ways in which it finds a place in people's lifeworlds and identities. Therefore we cannot presume to know the meanings of media texts unless we have studied what people do with them in the real world.

Finding #9: Audiences are people, and people are complex –

Participants built a wide range of aspects of identity (even with my best efforts to group similar items together, there were 128 different themes represented), and influences upon their identity (again, even when grouped together, there were 100 different kinds of influences). Media audience studies tend to acknowledge at the beginning that they are dealing with a complex subject-matter – that audiences are varied and cross-pollinated and diverse – but then proceed anyway, as if talking about 'audiences' is fine as long as you mention this first. In fact, of course, it is the case that audiences are not only a diverse set of individuals, but that each individual is themselves complex, internally diverse and often somewhat contradictory in their attitudes, tastes and pleasures. Researchers need to accept this and incorporate a recognition of it into their studies, rather than trying to ignore it.

Finding #10: People generally do not think the media influences their identity much –

This study asked participants to consider influences upon their identity, but did not *ask* them to consider media influences in particular. Research projects which prompt people to talk about 'media influences' are usually able to elicit views on that topic; but, interestingly, when participants were given the chance to consider all influences in general, aspects of the media appeared very little. Of course, individuals are not necessarily aware of everything that influences them; and we like to think of ourselves as independent thinkers, so there is a kind of taboo against claiming to be heavily influenced by the media, of all things. As we noted at the start of this book, it seems highly likely that the media must influence how we see relationships, the purpose of life and how to spend one's time on the earth, in some way. We consume so many stories about these things; it doesn't seem far-fetched to suggest that they must have some impact on our consciousness. But this finding is that, in general, when asked to consider influences upon their identities, the participants in this study did not usually think of media products or technologies.

Finding #11: A role for media in thinking about identity –

Does this mean, then, that the media has nothing to do with the formation of identities? No, the Lego study did point strongly towards a way in which the media *do* influence our thinking about self-identity: by providing stories and narrative frames through which we understand our lives. As mentioned in Chapter 5, philosopher Paul Ricoeur argued that all the narratives in the world – of which thousands are circulated every day in the media – offer 'a vast laboratory for thought experiments' (1992: 148). We inevitably think through the implications of these stories and connect these with our own lives. We also draw upon particular frames and metaphors from these stories to help us understand our experiences.

- This finding is discussed further below, in the section 'Stories and identities'.

Those were the 11 findings of the Lego study. Now we will consider three of those in more depth, and then discuss the findings of the study in terms of gender.

FRAGMENTED IDENTITIES?

As we noted at Finding #6 above, over the past 25 years or so, postmodernists have circulated (and sometimes celebrated) the fashionable and cool-sounding notion that identities today are 'fragmented'. Jean Baudrillard (1988, 1994), for instance, claimed that identities in contemporary 'postmodern' society have become wholly fragmented, whilst Fredric Jameson (1991) suggested that identities had become discontinuous and 'schizophrenic'. However, the Lego identity study found no evidence of this. On the contrary, every one of the participants built their identity as *one thing* – even though it would have been perfectly possible to present identity as a shower of separate pieces, or as a set of different fragments arranged together. The identity models were often *complex*, but they were complicated *whole* things with a number of parts.

Rather than trying to find ways to express their fragmented consciousness, participants tended to seek unity and balance whilst building their models of identity. Participants showed no sign of believing that their identities were a fragmented mess. Indeed, even the most 'chaotic' of personalities presented their identity as a whole, even if it was somewhat messy and occasionally contradictory. Overall, with a remarkable degree of consistency, the participants in this study presented themselves as distinctive individuals, but whole identities, making their way on the journey of life. This may be a 'discourse' they have bought into, or a popular metaphor for experience which they have applied to themselves, but nevertheless we saw none of the painful 'fragmentation' which is supposed to be eating at (post)modern subjects (and which they are meant to be conscious of). There certainly was some uncertainty, but this was actively fought against by what we might call 'the will to coherence' – the desire to have solid stories about the self.

THE INDIVIDUALITY PARADOX

Right at the start of this book, we discussed Theodor Adorno's argument that mass media was increasingly leading the populations of developed societies to become a stereotyped, homogenous mass. We contrasted this approach with that of John Fiske, who believed that individuals were active producers of their own popular culture, using media merely as a resource which could be used to mark their own individuality. The Lego identity models reflect this tension between social sameness and individual difference, in a particular way. Certainly, the striking diversity of Lego identity models indicates that individuals typically take their individuality to be important, and offer little support for Adorno's fear that everyone under capitalism will become the same. On the other hand, people do not necessarily want to become as radically individualised as Fiske might seem to suggest.

In the Lego identity study, we see people carving out their individuality, but within a social sphere. (This is Finding #7, above.) Both dimensions are given weight – the distinctiveness of personal identity on the one hand, and the importance of social ties on the other. Thinking about the tensions between these elements, I found it useful to go back to the early German sociologist Georg Simmel (1858–1918). Simmel's reputation dwindled during much of the twentieth century, but enjoyed a resurgence in the 1990s, as theorists rediscovered his prescient work which engaged with contemporary topics in cultural theory such as the emotions, gender, fashion and the challenges of 'modern' life (Scaff, 2000).

Simmel saw social experience in terms of a continuous tension between the individual and society, which seems to mirror the way in which participants represented their identities in the Lego study (Simmel, 1971, 2004). This is not necessarily a difficult or destructive tension, but is something which everyone has to negotiate and come to terms with in some way. Simmel's work suggests that people are continuously trying to reconcile two things:

- On the one hand, there is the pull of society. Societies seek to incorporate individuals within their collective goals, and indeed individuals typically *want* to feel that they are part of a community of people who get along together and have some shared visions of social harmony and social good.
- On the other hand, there is the pull of individuality. Nobody would like to think that they are exactly the same as everybody else; most people would probably like to think they are special or distinctive in some way. Therefore their *difference* from the social collective is important too.

These two things are true, and attractive, simultaneously. This is the 'double relationship' that is a core theme of Simmel's work. As he wrote in *Introduction to the Moral Sciences* (1893): 'On the one hand the individual belongs to a whole and is a part of it, while on the other hand s/he is independent and stands opposed to it' (translated in Scaff, 2000: 255). Indeed, Simmel argued that the friction generated by the need to establish similarity with others, and difference from them, is the driving force in both individual and social development. He even stated that 'the cultural history of humanity can be interpreted as the history of the struggle and attempted conciliation between' these two forces (Simmel, 1890, translated in Frisby, 2002: 83).

Simmel suggested (1971: 218–223) that as social life becomes more complex, and different perspectives have to be taken into account, meaning

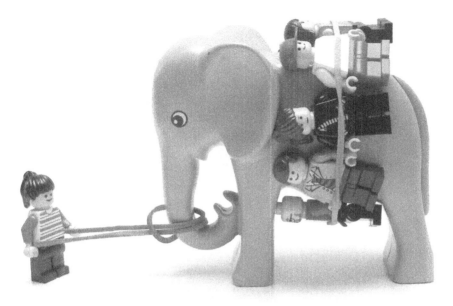

Figure 11.6   The individual and society: 'On the one hand the individual belongs to a whole and is a part of it, while on the other hand s/he is independent and stands opposed to it,' as Simmel remarked

does not come from external sources (such as art, media or other people) but needs to be achieved by the individual themselves, in relation to – but separately from – the social world of others. This process of establishing an individual self in a social context could be seen quite concretely in the process of constructing Lego identity models: individuals tended to set up a network of elements which gave them a kind of stand-alone strength, but accompanied by ties and interactions, of varying levels of intensity, with other human beings.

One of Simmel's concerns was that as the external world of technology and culture became so complex, and much too vast to be fully accessed by one individual, so the individual's own participation would come to seem relatively fragmentary and insignificant (see Chapter 6, 'The Style of Life', in Simmel, 2004). In the Lego identity models, we can see individuals engaging with this tension by asserting themselves against it, in this case literally building up a case for their own distinctiveness to shore up a defence against the powerful waves of consumer culture, information and fashion. The less 'walled in' models were often representations of a willingness to engage with this culture, whilst still retaining the crucial core of individuality.

We should also record, on a related note, that definite social constraints such as lack of money were included in a number of models. The participants' diverse constructions of self-identity were, of course, not able to release them from such practical constraints, although they produced a different set of relationships to them. The opportunities for free and pleasurable living were seen to be partly limited by lack of resources, or by the responsibility of having to go out to earn money to provide for a family. One participant summed up this dimension by building 'the stomper machine', a kind of robot which stomped around the edge of his model, representing these dismal everyday responsibilities and constraints, such as work and money.

STORIES AND IDENTITIES

As mentioned briefly at Finding #11 above, the Lego identity study led to the finding that the media can play a role in the shaping of self-identities as it suggests narratives and stories which we can use as frames when thinking-through our personal biographies, and giving order to our experiences. Paul Ricoeur's suggestion that all the millions of narratives offer 'a vast laboratory for thought experiments' becomes especially pertinent in the new media age, where so many stories are circulated in multi-channel TV, numerous online video sites, 24-hour news sources, as well as movies, magazines, radio and many other places.

These stories provide an opportunity for individuals to think about the kind of person that they want to be. As we saw in the discussion of story structures in Chapter 5, many dramatic narratives are about characters who, in one way or another, face failure in their journey towards potential happiness, but then learn – or are tragically unable to learn – from their mistakes. We can also relate to non-fiction stories in the news, such as when we hear of the heroic firefighter who confronts a would-be terrorist, and wonder what we would have done in the same situation; or read about the person appearing in court for a minor crime that we have committed ourselves.

All these different kinds of stories are resources which can be drawn upon as an individual constructs their own narrative identity. As Kenneth Burke said in Chapter 5, stories are 'equipment for living'. Stories which emphasise the importance of love, family and keeping one's word – themes which are at the heart of numerous popular movies, for example – help individuals to orient themselves towards these values, if you are inclined to share this cultural view; or more cynical entertainments are preferred by others as offering something more 'challenging' to reflect upon. In *Creative Explorations* I argue that since participants themselves recognised that they were assembling identity in the style of a narrative (Finding #5), and sought unifying themes (Finding #6), their identity-storytelling is bound to have been influenced in some ways by the media stories which are so prevalent in their social and cultural worlds, and which are the mainstream place (along with published novels and biographies) where 'the story of a life' is commonly presented.

LEGO IDENTITY MODELS: GENDER ANALYSIS

Dividing the Lego identity models in this study into those made by women and those made by men is potentially problematic. The sample is quite diverse but relatively small (40 women and 39 men) and it would not be reasonable to try to draw broad generalisations on this basis (which is why I didn't do a gender analysis in the *Creative Explorations* book[4]). However, we can perhaps learn something by observing similarities and differences between men's and women's models, whilst avoiding making grand or universal claims.

In terms of general building style, some aesthetic differences could be observed. Men's Lego models were sometimes rather more architectural, technically complicated, and/or built-up, whilst women's models were in some cases more beautiful and/or arranged more like a garden. Overall, though, the styles were diverse, but not very distinguishable along gender lines, and – unsurprisingly – some women built more architecturally complex structures and some men built more pretty, garden-like creations. Insofar as differences could be observed, I would of course argue that this is because of the different kinds of cultural learning that men and women experience (especially as Lego may remind people of the kinds of things they used to create as children), rather than any innate sex differences.

Both female and male participants tended to construct a model of identity which included elements of urban life and nature, responsibilities and escape, some down-to-earth realities and some future aspirations. Men and women equally included emotions, relationships and anxieties, demonstrating that today these aspects of life are not simply confined to the 'feminine' domain.

If we consider the participants' reflections on what they had built, we can note that the process reveals some facets of masculine and feminine identities. Some men suggested that, looking at their identity model as a whole, it showed a more confident and purposeful public face behind which there was a less certain and less organised internal world:

I think that people see me as:
Managing to juggle many things. Professionally confident. [...]

But in my Lego identity model, we can see me as:
Doing it with a certain sense of chaos. Needing to see and being surprised by what I achieve. [...]

(Male, 28, London architect)

I think that people see me as:
Remote/isolated. Responsible/dutiful. Ordered/safe.
But in my Lego identity model, we can see me as:
Engaged with people. Free. Carefree, random.

(Male, 35, London architect)

I think that people see me as:
Quite confident. Quite full of ideas. Chirpy most of the time. [...]
But in my Lego identity model, we can see me as:
Quite separated, almost anonymous. On a rather nebulous journey. Perhaps a bit torn between chirpy and quiet. [...]

(Male, over 50, Dorset art gallery manager)

I think that people see me as:
Calm.
But in my Lego identity model, we can see me as:
Somewhat fearful.

(Male, 29, Oslo student)

I think that people see me as:
Reliable and confident.
But in my Lego identity model, we can see me as:
Not totally secure, but able to face an audience.

(Male, 58, London unemployed)

In one case the difference between masculine exterior and a gentler self-identity was especially pronounced:

I think that people see me as:
Menacing looking. People see me as trouble.
But in my Lego identity model, we can see me as:
Peaceful person. I just wish to get on with my life.

(Male, 32, London unemployed)

However, others did not emphasise the masculine veneer at all:

I think that people see me as:
Caring, responsible, forward-looking, aware of the world, happy.
But in my Lego identity model, we can see me as:
The same – I hope.

(Male, 72, Dorset art gallery worker)

I think that people see me as:
Married, 51, steady, probably boring.
But in my Lego identity model, we can see me as:
Hopefully, within reason, the same, as I tried to be honest.

(Male, 51, Dorset unemployed)

I think that people see me as:
Unsure, soft, easy going, unstable and at times fun.
But in my Lego identity model, we can see me as:
Homely, protective, stable and sure footed.

(Male, 32, London unemployed)

If we turn to the female participants' reflections on what they had built, we find that the recognition of a gendered performance of competence, concealing a less confident personal identity, was just as common in women as in men:

I think that people see me as:
Organised, in control. There when they need me.
But in my Lego identity model, we can see me as:
Chaotic. Able to get there when I'm called.

(Female, 23, London architect)

I think that people see me as:
Confident. Organised.
But in my Lego identity model, we can see me as:
Insecure and too open. Disorganised.

(Female, 50, Dorset unemployed)

I think that people see me as:
Confident, clear, driven. Caring and supportive. Challenging/
creative.
But in my Lego identity model, we can see me as:
Busy and pulled in lots of different directions. Unsettled.
[Caring and supportive] but also slightly detached, looking to be
more settled and secure in my own right. Creative.

(Female, 38, Dorset charity manager)

I think that people see me as:
Warm, friendly, organised. Busy, many different hats. Younger.
But in my Lego identity model, we can see me as:
Frustrated but content. Homemaker. Older.

(Female, 57, Dorset art gallery worker)

I think that people see me as:
Carefree. [They] don't know that I'm religious. Confident.
But in my Lego identity model, we can see me as:
Slightly more stressed out. Religious. Worried about things.

(Female, 26, Winchester social care worker)

I think that people see me as:
Structured. Consistent.
But in my Lego identity model, we can see me as:
Unstructured. Struggling for consistency.

(Female, 43, Oslo academic)

I think that people see me as:
Very strong natured. Confident. Having a large family.
But in my Lego identity model, we can see me as:
Just a person with a family. Struggling to live better. Carrying a
great responsibility.

(Female, over 35, London unemployed)

I think that people see me as:
Very strong willed. Level headed. Good family provider. Wise.
But in my Lego identity model, we can see me as:
Someone who maybe has dealt with a lot in the past and maybe
tries to hide the fact that I'm not as strong as I might think. But
putting on a brave face.

(Female, 30, London unemployed)

The participants were asked to build the things which influenced their identities, and to add them to – or position them in relation to – their models. In total, participants built a very diverse set of influences (which I was able to group together into a total of 100 different kinds of influence, as mentioned above). Women and men most frequently chose *people* as influences upon their identities: family (including partner, parents and/or their children), friends and colleagues. Other influences formed a 'long tail' of varied items, including music, learning, the past, religion, travel, the workplace and many others.

Overall, the Lego identity study suggests that it would be wrong to overemphasise the differences between male and female identities. Similar numbers of female and male participants looked at their completed models and saw that they were having to produce a performance of gender and both the male and female performances were about appearing confident and competent even though they were actually feeling more insecure and less certain. Traditional versions of masculinity would have required this stoic performance, but traditional femininity would have encouraged a show of girlish incompetence. Today, however, we can see that this is not what women aspire to.

BUILDING UNDERSTANDINGS

In this chapter we have considered some visual and creative methods which can be used to explore identities, with a particular focus on the study in which I asked people to construct metaphorical models of their identities in Lego. We found that people today see themselves as complex but unified identities, seeking to be recognised both as interestingly distinctive and yet also part of the social community. Stories and narratives from the media offer individuals ways of framing and understanding experience, but do not prescribe or set limits on ways of living. The task of projecting an impression of being a competent, confident man or woman was found to be an everyday challenge for both sexes – one of the many ways in which female and male identities are really rather similar.

Chapter 12

CONCLUSIONS

A NUMBER OF themes have emerged in this book, which we will set out and briefly discuss in this final chapter. The themes are:

- Fluidity of identities and the decline of tradition;
- The knowing construction of identity;
- Generational differences;
- Role models;
- Masculinity in crisis?;
- Popular feminism, women and men;
- Diversity of sexualities;
- Gender trouble;
- Media power versus audience power;
- Contradictory elements;
- Change.

FLUIDITY OF IDENTITIES AND THE DECLINE OF TRADITION

We have seen various ways in which popular ideas about the self in society have changed, so that identity is today seen as more fluid and transformable than ever before. Twenty or 30 years ago, analysis of popular media often told researchers that mainstream culture was a backwards-looking force, resistant to social change and trying to push people back into traditional categories. Today, it seems more appropriate to emphasise that, *within limits*, the mass media can be a force for change. The traditional images of women as housewives or low-status workers were kick-boxed out of the picture by the feisty, successful 'girl power' icons of the late 1990s, and since then, images of confident, successful and assertive women have seemed entirely normal. Meanwhile the masculine ideals of absolute toughness, stubborn self-reliance and emotional silence have been shaken by a new emphasis on men's emotions, need for advice and the problems of masculinity. Traditional gender categories have not been shattered, of course: for instance, men's magazines in the first decade of the twenty-first century have become, if anything, *more* comfortable with gazing at semi-naked women in an old-fashioned, objectifying manner. Some things change and adapt at different rates, then, but if we look across the media landscape over the past couple of decades, things are clearly changing in a particular direction, and alternative ideas and images have created some space for a greater diversity of identities.

Since the events of 11 September 2001, the Iraq War (2003–), and subsequent terrorist attacks, the media has become somewhat more deferential to tradition. Religious faiths which tell people to behave in particular traditional ways, which previously would have been politely ignored as rather difficult and backward, are now accorded somewhat more respect by news and current affairs media; but subtly shunned in comedy and drama productions. In terms of sexual mores, though, contemporary media has little time or respect for tradition. The *Cosmo* or *FHM* reader still thinks: Why would we want to do the same as previous generations? What's so great about the past? In this way, popular media fosters the desire to create new modes of life – within the context of capitalism. Although one may not be happy with all aspects of the capitalist system, it creates media which – at least some of the time – encourages the overthrow of traditions which previously kept people within limiting compartments.

THE KNOWING CONSTRUCTION OF IDENTITY

Not only is there more *room* for a greater variety of identities to emerge; it is also the case that the construction of identity has become a *known requirement*. Modern Western societies do not leave individuals in any doubt that they need to make choices of identity and lifestyle – even if their preferred options are rather obvious and conventional ones, or are limited due to lack of financial (or cultural) resources. As the sociologist Ulrich Beck has noted, in late modern societies everyone wants to 'live their own life', but this is, at the same time, 'an experimental life' (2002: 26). Since the social world is no longer confident in its traditions, every approach to life, whether seemingly radical or conventional, is somewhat risky and needs to be worked upon – nurtured, considered and maintained, or amended. Because 'inherited recipes for living and role stereotypes fail to function' (ibid.), we have to make our own new patterns of being, and – although this is not one of Beck's emphases – it seems clear that the media plays an important role here.

Magazines, bought on one level for a quick fix of glossy entertainment, promote self-confidence (even if they partly undermine it, for some readers, at the same time) and provide information about sex, relationships and lifestyles which can be put to a variety of uses. Television programmes, pop songs, adverts, movies and the internet all also provide numerous kinds of 'guidance' – not necessarily in the obvious form of advice-giving, but in the myriad suggestions of ways of living which they imply. We lap up this material because the social construction of identity today is the *knowing* social construction of identity. This was clear in the Lego identity study, discussed in the previous chapter. Participants recognised that their life was a project to be worked on, and that this was gently but continually

Figure 12.1 The Lego study found that people were familiar with the task of constructing a meaningful story of self-identity

demanding. The media provides some of the tools which can be used in this identity work. Like many toolkits, however, it contains some good utensils and some useless ones; some that might give beauty to the project, and some that might spoil it. Everyone has different tastes, too, affected by their movement in different social groupings, so one person's 'bad' tool might be a treat for someone else.

GENERATIONAL DIFFERENCES

There are some generational differences which tend to cut across these discussions. Surveys have found that people born in the first half of the twentieth century are less tolerant of homosexuality, and less sympathetic to unmarried couples living together, than their younger counterparts, for example (see Chapters 1 and 4). Traditional attitudes may be scarce amongst the under-30s, but still thrive in the hearts of some over-65s (Pew Research Center, 2004b, 2007). We cannot help but notice, of course, that older people are also unlikely to be consumers of magazines like *Glamour*, *More* or *Maxim*, and are not a key audience for today's pop music sensations. In this book's discussions of popular media which appear to be eroding (some) traditions, I have focused on generally young audiences with the implicit assumption that anti-traditional (or liberal, or post-traditional) attitudes established in the young will be carried into later life. This may not be so, however: maybe conservative attitudes, rather than literally 'dying out' with the older generations, tend to develop throughout the population as we get older. There is evidence that people's attitudes become somewhat less liberal as they get older, but at the same time the 'generation gap' in attitudes is closing (Smith, 2000; Pew Research Center, 2007). We can note that those people who were twenty-something in the 'swinging' times of the late 1960s are now in their sixties. Nevertheless, as I have argued throughout this book, the mass media has become more liberal (in terms of sex and gender issues), and considerably more challenging to traditional standards since then, and this has been a *reflection* of changing attitudes, but also involves the media actively *disseminating* modern values. It therefore remains to be seen whether the post-traditional young women and men of today will grow up to be the narrow-minded traditionalists of the future.

ROLE MODELS

We have noted that the term 'role models' is bandied about in the public sphere with little regard for what the term might really mean, or how we might expect role models to have an impact on individuals. Nevertheless, in this book I have suggested that by thinking about their own identity, attitudes, behaviour and lifestyle in relation to those of media figures – some of whom may be potential 'role models', others just the opposite – individuals make decisions and judgements about their own way of living (and that of others). It is for this reason that the 'role model' remains an important concept. Although it should not be taken to mean someone that a person wants to *copy*, we saw that role models could embody values such as integrity and authenticity, and could have an impact which is less about 'modelling' behaviour per se, and more to do with being an *inspiration*. In this way, role models can serve as *navigation points* as individuals steer their own personal routes through life. (Their general direction, we should note, however, is more likely to be shaped by parents, friends, teachers, colleagues and other people encountered in everyday life.)

MASCULINITY IN CRISIS?

We saw in Chapter 1 that contemporary masculinity is often said to be 'in crisis'. As women become increasingly assertive and successful, apparently triumphing in all roles, men are said to be anxious and confused about what their role is today. However, the evidence for this is patchy at best. Headlines about male underachievement in education, and male suicide, may give some cause for concern in particular contexts, but overall men just don't seem to be in crisis. Certainly the Lego identity study, for instance (Chapter 11), found no signs of confusion about masculine purpose in the male participants, although like all men and women they felt varying degrees of confidence and personal achievement.

In the analysis of men's magazines (Chapter 8) we found a lot of signs that the magazines were about men finding a place for themselves in the modern world. Although the basic lusty photo-features featuring semi-naked models and actresses offered an obvious and usually very traditional narrative, we saw that these lifestyle publications were also perpetually concerned with how to treat women, have a good relationship, and live an enjoyable life. Rather than being a return to essentialism – i.e. the idea of a traditional 'real' man, as biology and destiny 'intended' – I argued that men's magazines have an almost obsessive relationship with the socially constructed nature of manhood. Gaps in a person's attempt to generate a masculine image are a source of humour in these magazines, because those breaches reveal what we all know – but some choose to hide – that masculinity is a socially constructed performance anyway. The continuous flow of lifestyle, health, relationship and sex advice, and the repetitive curiosity about what the featured females look for in a partner, point to a clear view that the performance of masculinity can and should be practiced and perfected. This may not appear ideal – it sounds as if men's magazines are geared to turning out a stream of rather similar men. But the masculinity put forward by the biggest-selling magazines we saw to be fundamentally kind and decent, even though the sarcastic humour sometimes threatened to smother this. Furthermore, we saw from the reader responses that the audience disregards messages that seem inappropriate or offensive. Although the magazines reflected a concern for men to find an enjoyable approach to modern living, then, there was no sign of a 'crisis' in either the magazines or their readers. Rather than tearing their hair out, everybody seemed to be coping with this 'crisis' perfectly well.

The self-help books for men (discussed in Chapter 10) also refuted the idea that changing gender roles had thrown men into crisis. The problem for men was not seen as being their *new* role – or lack of one; instead, men's troubles stemmed from their exaggerated and pointless commitment to men's *old* role, the traditional role of provider and strong, emotionless rock. Where men had a problem, then, it was not so much because society had changed, but because they as individual men had failed to modernise and keep up. Happily, the books took the view that people can change, and that troubled men would be able to create a satisfying and more relaxed life for themselves if they put in a bit of effort.

It's not all a world of transformed masculinities, though. Images of the conventionally rugged, super-independent, extra-strong macho man still circulate in popular culture. And as incitements for women to fulfil any role proliferate, conventional masculinity is increasingly exposed as tediously monolithic. In contrast with the popular 'you can be anything you want to be' message aimed at women, the identities promoted to men are relatively constrained.

POPULAR FEMINISM, WOMEN AND MEN

Although the rhetoric of 'girl power' now seems rather dated, it made a real impact on popular culture when circulated so enthusiastically by the Spice Girls and others in the late 1990s. That legacy generally endures: we see it in magazines for young women, which are emphatic in their determination that women must do their own thing, be themselves, and/or be as outrageously sassy and sexy as possible (see Chapter 9). Many recent movies have featured self-confident, tough, intelligent female characters (although it remains the case that a man is more likely to be the primary lead figure; see Chapter 4). Female pop stars sing about financial and emotional independence, inner strength, and how they don't need a man; and the popular mantra of self-help books is that women can become just as powerful as these icons, if they cultivate their confidence and self-belief, and draw up a plan of self-development (Chapter 10). This set of reasonably coherent messages from a range of sources – their clarity only disturbed by the idea that women can be extremely tough and independent whilst also maintaining perfect make-up and wearing impossible shoes – seems to have had some impact on the identities of young women, as well as being very successful within pop culture as an image/lifestyle idea.

These upbeat messages are today's most prominent expressions of what Angela McRobbie called 'popular feminism' – the mainstream interpretation of feminism which is a strong element of modern pop culture even though it might not actually answer to the 'feminist' label. Popular feminism is like a radio-friendly remix of a multi-layered song, with the most exciting bits sampled, and some of the denser stuff left out. As McRobbie noted almost a decade ago,

> To [many] young women official feminism is something that belongs to their mothers' generation. They have to develop their own language for dealing with sexual inequality, and if they do this through a raunchy language of 'shagging, snogging and having a good time', then perhaps the role this plays is not unlike the sexually explicit manifestoes found in the early writing of figures like [feminist pioneers] Germaine Greer and Sheila Rowbotham. The key difference is that this language is now found in the mainstream of commercial culture – not out there in the margins of the 'political underground'.
>
> (1999: 126)

McRobbie further argued that 'This dynamic of generational antagonism has been overlooked by professional feminists, particularly those in the academy, with the result that the political effectivity of young women is more or less ignored' (ibid.). Ironically, as she has got older, McRobbie herself has come to doubt young women's ability to think for themselves, and has become unhappy with their responses to popular culture (see discussion of McRobbie, 2004, 2005, 2006, in Chapter 9).

Meanwhile, in a book called *Future Girl*, Anita Harris (2004) has argued that twenty-first century Western societies invest in young women a particular aspirational ideology which is both an inspiration and a burden:

> Young women have taken on a special role in the production of the late modern social order and its values. They have become a

focus for the construction of an ideal late modern subject who is self-making, resilient, and flexible.

(2004: 6)

The celebration of female choice and independence means that stratification and disadvantage in the labour market appears only to be the result of individual failure, a lack of 'effort or vision, to be addressed through personal strategies alone' (p. 10). Capitalist societies are happy to celebrate the successes of young women, because they are also economically empowered consumers, Harris argues; and young women's voices are encouraged and 'heard everywhere', but this constitutes 'a kind of surveillance' and does not lead to real change, she says (p. 11). Young women are venerated 'as those most able to succeed' (p. 184), and yet this 'future girl' is generated by global capitalism to suit its own ends. In my experience, Harris's arguments are the kind of thing that makes younger women furious with feminism: surely today's pro-female messages and opportunities are just the kind of thing that feminists should be *pleased* about, they say. But Harris's thoroughly-argued and not entirely pessimistic book offers a valuable reminder that hearing *noise* about exciting social change is not the same as social change actually happening.

We can also note that the generational struggles within feminism have an interesting parallel in the scholarship on men and masculinity. The texts on masculinity are largely focused on the difficulties of middle-aged or older men who find it hard to shake off traditional masculine archetypes; and, perhaps predictably, these studies are apparently *written* by middle-aged or older men who also cannot help bringing in these older tropes of masculinity. Meanwhile there is a generation of younger men who have adapted to the modern world (in a range of ways), who have grown up with women as their apparent equals, and who do not feel threatened or emasculated by these social changes. These men and their cultures are largely ignored by the problem-centred discourse of masculinity studies.

DIVERSITY OF SEXUALITIES

Lesbian, gay, bisexual and transgendered people are still under-represented in much of the mainstream media, but things are slowly changing. In particular, television is offering prime-time audiences the chance to 'get to know' nice lesbian and gay characters in soap operas, drama series and sitcoms (see Chapter 4). But, to be honest, not *that* many of them. Tolerance of sexual diversity is slowly growing in society (Chapter 1), and by bringing into people's homes images of sexual identities which they might not be familiar with, the media can play a role in making the population more – or less – comfortable with these ways of living.

GENDER TROUBLE

In Chapter 7, we discussed Judith Butler's manifesto for 'gender trouble' – the idea that the existing notions of sex, gender and sexuality should be challenged by the 'subversive confusion and proliferation' of the categories which we use to understand them. The binary division of 'male' and 'female' identities should be shattered, Butler suggested, and replaced with multiple forms of identity – not a new range of restrictive categories, but an abundance of modes of self-expression. This joyful excess of liberated forms of identity would be a fundamental challenge to the traditional understandings of gender which we largely continue to hold onto today.

Butler, as we noted, did not make direct reference to the mass media, but it seems obvious that if there is to be a major proliferation of images in the public eye, then the media must play a central role. To date, there have only been a relatively small amount of media representations fitting the Butler bill. Some advertising – such as the sexually charged but androgynous imagery promoting the *CK One* fragrance 'for a man or a woman' – had reminded viewers of the similarity of genders, hinting that it wouldn't matter which of the attractive male or female models you chose to desire. Other ads (such as ones for *Impulse* deodorant and *Kronenbourg* lager) playfully teased heterosexual desires only to reveal that the lust object was more interested in their own sex, pointing audiences to the unpredictability of sexualities. In this book we have discussed further cases of films, TV shows and magazines which have also celebrated non-traditional visions of gender and sexuality. Nevertheless, there remains a great deal of scope for the mass media to be much more challenging in these areas.

MEDIA POWER VERSUS AUDIENCE POWER

In Chapter 2 we set out the background debate over whether the mass media has a powerful influence upon its audience, or if it is the audience of viewing and reading consumers who wield the most power, so we should return to that question here. During the discussions in this book we have found, unsurprisingly, that the power relationship between media and the audience involves 'a bit of both', or to be more precise, a *lot* of both. The media disseminates a huge number of messages about identity and acceptable forms of self-expression, gender, sexuality and lifestyle. At the same time, the public have their own even more robust set of diverse feelings on these issues. The media's suggestions may be seductive, but can never simply overpower contrary feelings in the audience. Fiske talked in terms of semiotic 'guerrilla warfare', with the audience metaphorically involved in 'smash and grab' raids on media meanings, but this imagery inaccurately sees change as a fast and noisy process. It seems more appropriate to speak of a slow but engaged dialogue between media and media consumers, or a rather plodding war of attrition against the forces of tradition and conservatism: the power of new ideas (which some parts of the media convey) versus the ground-in power of the old ways of doing things (which other parts of the media still like to foster).

CONTRADICTORY ELEMENTS

We cannot bring this discussion towards a close without noting the inescapable levels of *contradiction* within popular culture. Although we may occasionally find ourselves saying that 'the mass media suggests' a particular perspective or point of view, the truth is that not only is 'the mass media' wildly diverse, but that even quite specific parts of media culture put out a whole spectrum of messages which cannot be reconciled. It is impossible to say that women's magazines, for example, always carry a particular message, because the enormous range of titles target an equally diverse set of female audiences. Furthermore, even one magazine will contain an array of viewpoints. As we saw in Chapter 3 via the account of one *Cosmo* editor, magazine staff – like many other media producers – are far more interested in generating 'surprise' than in maintaining coherence and consistency. Contradictions are an inevitable by-product of the drive for multiple points of excitement, so they rarely bother today's media makers, or indeed their audiences.

The contradictions are important, however, because the multiple messages contribute to the perception of an open realm of possibilities. In contrast with the past – or the modern popular view of the past – we no longer get singular, straightforward messages about ideal types of male and female identities (although certain groups of characteristics are clearly promoted as more desirable than others). Instead, popular culture offers a range of stars, icons and characters from whom we can acceptably borrow ideas from bits of their public persona for use in our own. In addition, of course – and slightly contradictorily – individuals are encouraged to 'be yourself', and to be creative – within limits – about the presentation of self. This opens the possibilities for gender trouble, as discussed above. Today, nothing about identity is clear-cut, and the contradictory messages of popular culture make the 'ideal' model for the self even more indistinct – which is probably a good thing. For instance, in the Lego identity study (see previous chapter), participants often identified aspects of identity which could appear to be contradictory, but this was not seen as a problem; on the contrary, individuals were happy saying 'I know this doesn't seem to go with that, but they are all parts that make up "me"'.

CHANGE

As we have noted many times in this book, things change, and are changing. Media formats and contents change all the time. Audiences change too, albeit more slowly. Views of gender and sexuality, masculinity and femininity, identity and selfhood, are all in slow but steady processes of change and transformation. Even our views of change itself, and the possibilities for personal change and 'growth', have altered over the years. Although we should be careful not to overestimate the extent or speed of transformations in society and the media, it is worth reasserting the obvious fact that things do change, because some authorities within the disciplines of media studies and gender studies tend to act as though things do not really change over periods of ten, 20 or 30 years – filling textbooks with mixed-together studies from the 1970s, 1980s and 1990s as if they were providing accounts of fixed phenomena. These things are not stationary. To discuss gender and media is to aim arguments at moving targets – which, again, is just as well.

FINALLY . . .

In this book I have sought to argue, and demonstrate, that popular media has a significant but not straightforward relationship with people's sense of gender and identity. Media messages are diverse, diffuse and contradictory. Rather than being zapped straight into people's brains, ideas about lifestyle and identity that appear in the media are *resources* which individuals use to think through their sense of self and modes of expression. In addition to this conscious (or not particularly conscious) use of media, a wealth of other messages may breeze through the awareness of individuals every day. The media is a source of numerous stories, about lives lived happily or disastrously, with compassion or with cruelty. We use these narratives to frame our experiences and to bring order to the stream of 'stuff' that goes on in our lives.

Furthermore, people are changing, building new identities founded not on the certainties of the past, but organised around the new order of modern living, where the meanings of gender, sexuality and identity are increasingly open. Different aspects of popular media can aid or disturb these processes of contemporary reorientation. Some critics say that the media should offer traditional role models and reassuring certainties, but this view is unlikely to survive. Challenges, uncertainties and exciting contradictions are what contemporary media, like modern life, is all about.

NOTES

1 We should note that in the tough world of IMDB voting, 8.2 is a very positive score; and it's also worth pointing out that scores are usually closer between the sexes: for *The Matrix* (1999) and *Hannibal* (2001), for example, both popular films with interesting male and female lead characters, the average score from men and the average score from women was exactly the same (8.6 for *The Matrix* and 6.6 for *Hannibal*). (Ratings quoted are from November 2001.)

2 This is probably not quite right, especially for the late 1990s. In 2006 a beauty industry conference boasted that the UK market was worth £6.2 billion. This is still huge, of course: the same conference heard that 'Women in the UK spend on average £2,000 a year on beauty treatments and cosmetics' (Future Beauty & Body Visions, 2006).

3 This chapter includes some abridged bits and pieces from the book *Creative Explorations* (Gauntlett, 2007), but is only able to cover creative visual methods, and the Lego identity study, rather briefly here.

4 This gender analysis therefore appears here for the first time.

REFERENCES

ABC (2007), *Ugly Betty* website, http://abc.go.com/primetime/uglybetty

Adorno, Theodor W. (1991), *The Culture Industry: Selected Essays on Mass Culture*, Routledge, London.

Althusser, Louis (1971), *Lenin and Philosophy and Other Essays*, London: New Left Books.

Altman, Dennis (2002), *Global Sex* (new edition), Chicago: University of Chicago Press.

Anderson, Kristin J. and Cavallaro, Donna (2002), 'Parents or Pop Culture? Children's Heroes and Role Models', *Childhood Education*, vol. 78, no. 3, pp. 161–168.

Arbuthnot, L. and Seneca, G. (1982), 'Pretext and Text in Gentlemen Prefer Blondes', reprinted in Erens, Patricia, ed. (1991), *Issues in Feminist Film Criticism*, Bloomington: Indiana University Press.

Arlidge, John (2001), 'Straights and Gays Take to Same Lifestyle', *Guardian*, 27 May, www.guardian.co.uk

Assibey-Mensah, George O. (1997), 'Role Models and Youth Development: Evidence and Lessons From the Perceptions of African-American Male Youth', *The Western Journal of Black Studies*, vol. 21, no. 4, pp. 242–251.

Awan, Fatimah (2007), 'Young People, Identities, and the Media', unpublished PhD thesis, Bournemouth: Bournemouth University.

Babygirl_Gigi (2007), 'Ugly Betty!', posted 15 April, http://babygirlgigi.vox.com

Baehr, Helen and Dyer, Gillian, eds (1987), *Boxed In: Women and Television*, London: Pandora.

Baehr, Ted (2006), 'Time Warner Promotes Terrorism and Anti-Christian Bigotry in New Leftist Movie, "V for Vendetta"', *World Net Daily*, 17 March, www.wnd.com/news/article.asp?article_id=49317

Barker, Gary T. (2005), *Dying to Be Men: Youth, Masculinity and Social Exclusion*, London: Routledge.

Bartlett, Nancy H., Vasey, Paul L. and Bukowski, William M. (2000), 'Is Gender Identity Disorder in Children a Mental Disorder?', *Sex Roles*, vol. 43: no. 11–12, pp. 753–785.

Barton, Laura (2007), 'Girl Wonders', *Guardian*, 4 July, www.guardian.co.uk

Bartsch, Robert A., Burnett, Teresa, Diller, Tommye R. and Rankin-Williams, Elizabeth (2000), 'Gender Representation in Television Commercials: Updating an Update', *Sex Roles*, vol. 43, nos 9/10, pp. 735–743.

Baudrillard, Jean (1988), *America*, London: Verso.

Baudrillard, Jean (1994), *Simulacra and Simulation*, Ann Arbor: University of Michigan Press.

BBC (2006a), 'Super Surfers Oust Couch Potatoes', 8 March, http://news.bbc.co.uk/1/hi/business/4784518.stm

BBC (2006b), 'Online Video "Eroding TV Viewing"', 27 November, http://news.bbc.co.uk/1/hi/entertainment/6168950.stm

BBC (2007), 'Body Image Survey: Results', 20 February, www.bbc.co.uk/radio1/news/newsbeat/070220_body_image.shtml

BBC Online (2000a), 'Blair to Take "Paternity Holiday"', 8 April, www.bbc.co.uk/news

BBC Online (2000b), 'Models Link to Teenage Anorexia', 30 May, www.bbc.co.uk/news

BBC Online (2001a), 'Cambridge's "Macho" Culture', 30 January, www.bbc.co.uk/news

BBC Online (2001b), 'Poor Body Image Plagues Women', 9 May, www.bbc.co.uk/news

Beck, Ulrich (2002), 'A Life of One's Own in a Runaway World: Individualization, Globalization and Politics', in Beck, Ulrich and Beck-Gernsheim, Elisabeth eds, *Individualization*, London: Sage.

Beck, Ulrich and Beck-Gernsheim, Elisabeth (2002), *Individualization*, London: Sage.

Beezer, A., Grimshaw, J. and Barker, M. (1986), 'Methods for Cultural Studies Students', in Punter, D., ed., *Introduction to Contemporary Cultural Studies*, London: Longman.

Bell, Vikki, ed. (1999), *Performativity and Belonging*, London: Sage.

Benson, Susan (1997), 'The Body, Health, and Eating Disorders', in Woodward, Kathryn, ed., *Identity and Difference*, London: Sage.

Berger, John (1972), *Ways of Seeing*, London: Penguin.

Billboard (2007), 'Billboard 2006 Year In Music: Top 25 Tours', www.billboard.com/bbcom/yearend/2006/touring/top_tours.jsp

Blunkett, David (2006), *The Blunkett Tapes: My Life in the Bear Pit*, London: Bloomsbury.

BMA Board of Science and Education (2000), *Eating Disorders, Body Image and the Media*, London: British Medical Association.

Borden, Richard J. (1975), 'Witnessed Aggression: Influence of an Observer's Sex and Values on Aggressive Responding', in *Journal of Personality and Social Psychology*, vol. 31, no. 3, pp. 567–573.

Bourland, Julia (2000), *The Go-Girl Guide: Surviving Your 20s with Savvy, Soul and Style*, Lincolnwood, Chicago: Contemporary Books.

Brannon, Linda (2007), *Gender: Psychological Perspectives – Fifth Edition*, Boston: Allyn and Bacon.

Bristow, Joseph (1997), 'Discursive Desires', *Sexuality*, London: Routledge.

Brooke, Jill (1997), 'Gay Characters Don't Always Cost TV Ad Dollars', *CNN.com*, 9 April, www.cnn.com/showbiz/9704/09/ellen/index.html

Brooks, Ann (1997), *Postfeminisms: Feminism, Cultural Theory and Cultural Forms*, London: Routledge.

Bryant, Christopher G. A. and Jary, David, eds (2001), *The Contemporary Giddens: Social Theory in a Globalizing Age*, Basingstoke: Palgrave.

Buckingham, David (1993), 'Boys' Talk: Television and the Policing of Masculinity', in Buckingham, David, ed., *Reading Audiences: Young People and the Media*, Manchester: Manchester University Press.

Buckingham, David (1996), *Moving Images: Understanding Children's Emotional Responses to Television*, Manchester: Manchester University Press.

Buckingham, David and Bragg, Sara (2004), *Young People, Sex and the Media: The Facts of Life?*, Basingstoke: Palgrave Macmillan.

Bunting, Madeleine (2001), 'Loadsasex and Shopping: A Woman's Lot', 9 February, *Guardian*, www.guardian.co.uk

Butler, Judith (1990), *Gender Trouble: Feminism and the Subversion of Identity*, London: Routledge.

Butler, Judith (1997), *The Psychic Life of Power: Theories in Subjection*, Stanford: Stanford University Press.

Butler, Judith (1999), 'Revisiting Bodies and Pleasures', in Bell, Vikki, ed., *Performativity and Belonging*, London: Sage.

Butler, Judith (2004), *Undoing Gender*, London: Routledge.

Butler-Bowdon, Tom (2003), *50 Self-Help Classics*, London: Nicholas Brealey.

Campbell, Denis, and Asthana, Anushka (2007), 'Catwalk Ban for Under-16 Models', 8 July, *Observer*, www.guardian.co.uk

Carver, Charles S. and Scheier, Michael F. (2006), *Perspectives on Personality – 5th Edition*, Boston: Allyn and Bacon.

Carver, Terrell, and Chambers, Samuel, eds (2007), *Judith Butler's Precarious Politics: Critical Encounters*, London: Routledge.

Cashmore, Ellis (2006), *Celebrity/Culture*, London: Routledge.

Catalyst (2007), 'Catalyst Releases 2006 Census of Women in Fortune 500 Corporate Officer and Board Positions', 21 February, www.catalyst.org/pressroom/press_releases/2006_Census_Release.pdf

Chauncey, George (1994), *Gay New York: Gender, Urban Culture, and the Making of the Gay Male World 1890–1940*, New York: Basic Books.

Clare, Anthony (2001), *On Men: Masculinity in Crisis*, London: Arrow.

Cohan, Steven, and Hark, Ina Rae, eds (1993), *Screening the Male: Exploring Masculinities in Hollywood Cinema*, London: Routledge.

Cohen, Nicole (2007), 'On Ugly Betty', posted 27 January, www.shamelessmag.com/blog

Coleman, Robin R. Means, ed. (2002), *Say It Loud!: African-American Audiences, Media, and Identity*, London: Routledge.

Coltrane, Scott and Messineo, Melinda (2000), 'The Perpetuation of Subtle Prejudice: Race and Gender Imagery in 1990s Television Advertising', *Sex Roles*, vol. 42, nos 5/6, pp. 363–389.

Cottle, Simon, ed. (2001), *Ethnic Minorities and the Media: Changing Cultural Boundaries*, Maidenhead: Open University Press.

Cronin, Anne M. (2000), 'Consumerism and "Compulsory Individuality"': Women, Will and Potential', in Ahmed, Sara, Kilby, Jane, Lury, Celia, McNeil, Maureen and Skeggs, Beverley, eds, *Transformations: Thinking Through Feminism*, London: Routledge.

Currie, Dawn H. (1999), *Girl Talk: Adolescent Magazines and Their Readers*, Toronto: University of Toronto Press.

Davies, Bob (2007), 'Seven Things I Wish Pro-Gay People Would Admit', National Association for Research and Therapy of Homosexuality website, www.narth.com/docs/7things.html.

Davis, D. M. (1990), 'Portrayals of Women in Prime-time Network Television: Some Demographic Characteristics', *Sex Roles*, vol. 23, nos 5/6, pp. 325–332.

Davis, Kathy (1995), *Reshaping the Female Body: The Dilemma of Cosmetic Surgery*, London: Routledge.

De Certeau, Michel (1984), *The Practice of Everyday Life*, Berkeley: University of California Press.

Deveaux, Monique (1994), 'Feminism and Empowerment: A Critical Reading of Foucault', *Feminist Studies*, vol. 20, no. 2, pp. 223–247.

DeWolf, Rose (1997), 'ABC, Others Don't See Advertisers Fleeing from a Lesbian-themed Ellen', 6 March, *Philadelphia Daily News*, www3.newstimes.com/archive97/mar0697/tvc.htm

Dittmar, Helga, Lloyd, Barbara, Dugan, Shaun, Halliwell, Emma, Jacobs, Neil and Cramer, Helen (2000), 'The "Body Beautiful": English Adolescents' Images of Ideal Bodies', *Sex Roles*, vol. 42, nos 9/10, pp. 887–915.

Douglas, Susan J. (1995), *Where the Girls Are: Growing Up Female with the Mass Media*, London: Penguin.

Downing, John and Husband, Charles (2005), *Representing 'Race': Racisms, Ethnicity and the Media*, London: Sage.

Doyle, Laura (2000), *The Surrendered Wife: A Practical Guide to Finding Intimacy, Passion, and Peace with a Man*, New York: Simon & Schuster.

Dyer, Gillian (1987), 'Introduction', in Baehr, Helen and Dyer, Gillian, eds, *Boxed In: Women and Television*, London: Pandora.

Easton Ellis, Bret (1991), *American Psycho*, London: Picador.

Edwards, Tim (1997), *Men in the Mirror: Men's Fashion, Masculinity and Consumer Society*, London: Cassell.

Edwards, Tim (1998), 'Queer Fears: Against the Cultural Turn', *Sexualities*, vol. 1, no. 4, pp. 471–484

Elasmar, Michael; Hasegawa, Kazumi and Brain, Mary (1999), 'The Portrayal of Women in US Prime Time Television', *Journal of Broadcasting and Electronic Media*, vol. 44, no. 1, pp. 20–34.

Elliot, Gregory, ed. (1994), *Althusser: A Critical Reader*, Oxford: Blackwell.

Ellis, Thomas (2005), *The Rantings of a Single Male: Losing Patience with Feminism, Political Correctness ... and Basically Everything*, Austin: Rannenberg.

Equal Opportunities Commission (2005), 'Jobs for the Boys?', 2 September, www.eoc.org.uk/Default.aspx?page=17429

Equal Opportunities Commission (2006), 'Free to Choose – Tackling Gender Barriers to Better Jobs', 31 March, www.eoc.org.uk/Default.aspx?page=17332

Equal Opportunities Commission (2007), 'Black and Asian Women Are "Missing" from Almost a Third of Workplaces', 15 March, www.eoc.org.uk/Default.aspx?page=20064

ESRC (2006), 'Change Needed to Ensure Women Secure Business Loans', 16 August, www.esrc.ac.uk/ESRCInfoCentre/PO/releases/2006/august/women.aspx

Faith, Karlene (1997), *Madonna: Bawdy and Soul*, Toronto: University of Toronto Press.

Faludi, Susan (1991), *Backlash: The Undeclared War Against Women*, London: Vintage.

Faludi, Susan (1999), *Stiffed: The Betrayal of the Modern Man*, London: Chatto & Windus.

Family Research Council (2001), 'Position Statement', www.frc.org

Family Research Council (2007), 'Homosexuality In Your Child's School', www.frc.org/get.cfm?i=BC06D02

Farrell, Warren (2001), *The Myth of Male Power*, New York: Penguin.

Ferree, Myra Marx, Lorber, Judith and Hess, Beth B., eds (1999), *Revisioning Gender*, London: Sage.

Ferretter, Luke (2005), *Louis Althusser*, London: Routledge.

Fiske, John (1989a), *Understanding Popular Culture*, London: Unwin Hyman.

Fiske, John (1989b), *Reading the Popular*, London: Unwin Hyman.

Fiske, John (1989c) 'Moments of Television: Neither the Text Nor the Audience', in Seiter, Ellen, *et al.*, *Remote Control: Television, Audiences and Cultural Power*, London: Routledge.

Foucault, Michel (1980), *Power/Knowledge: Selected Interviews and Other Writings 1972–1977*, edited by Colin Gordon, New York: Pantheon.

Foucault, Michel (1990), *The Care of the Self: The History of Sexuality Volume Three*, translated by Robert Hurley, London: Penguin.

Foucault, Michel (1992), *The Use of Pleasure: The History of Sexuality Volume Two*, translated by Robert Hurley, London: Penguin.

Foucault, Michel (1998), *The History of Sexuality, Volume I: The Will To Knowledge*, London: Penguin.

Foucault, Michel (2000), *Essential Works of Foucault 1954–1984: Ethics*, edited by Paul Rabinow, London: Penguin.

Fraker, Pamela (2001), 'The Hypocrisy of So-Called Women's Magazines', *Voices: The Women's College Magazine at Santa Monica College*, vol. 2, no. 1, Spring, www.smc.edu/voices/volume2_1/politics/Women's%20Magazines.htm

Frank, Lisa and Smith, Paul, eds (1993), *Madonnarama: Essays on Sex and Popular Culture*, Pittsburgh: Cleis Press.

Frazer, Elizabeth (1987), 'Teenage Girls Reading *Jackie*', *Media, Culture and Society*, vol. 9, pp. 407–425.

Friedan, Betty (1963), *The Feminine Mystique*, Penguin: London.

Frisby, David (2002), *Georg Simmel: Revised Edition*, London: Routledge.

Frosh, Stephen, Phoenix, Ann and Pattman, Rob (2001), *Young Masculinities: Understanding Boys in Contemporary Society*, Basingstoke: Palgrave Macmillan.

Future Beauty & Body Visions (2006), Conference brochure, 20–21 September, www.beauty-visions.com

Ganahl, Dennis J., Prinsen, Thomas J. and Netzley, Sara Baker (2003), 'A Content Analysis of Prime Time Commercials: A Contextual Framework of Gender Representation', *Sex Roles*, vol. 49, nos 9/10, pp. 545–551.

Garfinkel, Harold (1984), *Studies in Ethnomethodology*, Cambridge: Polity.

Gateward, Frances K. and Pomerance, Murray, eds (2002), *Sugar, Spice, and Everything Nice: Cinemas of Girlhood*, Detroit: Wayne State University Press.

Gauntlett, David (1995), *Moving Experiences: Understanding Television's Influences and Effects* [first edition], London: John Libbey.

Gauntlett, David (1997), *Video Critical: Children, the Environment and Media Power*, London: John Libbey. (Online version available at www.artlab.org.uk/videocritical).

Gauntlett, David (1998), 'Ten Things Wrong with the "Effects Model"', in Dickinson, Roger, Harindranath, Ramaswani and Linné, Olga, eds, *Approaches to Audiences – A Reader*, London: Arnold.

Gauntlett, David (2000), *Web.Studies: Rewiring Media Studies for the Digital Age*, London: Arnold.

Gauntlett, David (2001), 'The Worrying Influence of "Media Effects" Studies', in Barker, Martin and Petley, Julian, eds, *Ill Effects: The Media/Violence Debate – Second Edition*, Routledge: London.

Gauntlett, David (2002), *Media, Gender and Identity: An Introduction* [first edition], Routledge, London.

Gauntlett, David (2005), *Moving Experiences, Second Edition: Media Effects and Beyond*, London: John Libbey.

Gauntlett, David (2007), *Creative Explorations: New Approaches to Identities and Audiences*, London: Routledge.

Gauntlett, David (2008), 'Self-help books and the pursuit of a happy identity', extended version of the material given here, available at www.theory head.com

Gauntlett, David and Hill, Annette (1999), *TV Living: Television, Culture and Everyday Life*, London: Routledge.

Gauntlett, David and Holzwarth, Peter (2006), 'Creative and Visual Methods for Exploring Identities', *Visual Studies*, vol. 21, no. 1, April, pp. 82–91.

Gauntlett, David and Horsley, Ross, eds (2004), *Web.Studies, 2nd Edition*, London: Arnold.

Giddens, Anthony (1991), *Modernity and Self-Identity: Self and Society in the Late Modern Age*, Cambridge: Polity.

Giddens, Anthony (1992), *The Transformation of Intimacy*, Cambridge: Polity.

Giddens, Anthony (1998), *The Third Way: The Renewal of Social Democracy*, Cambridge: Polity.

Giddens, Anthony (1999), *Runaway World: How Globalisation is Reshaping Our Lives*, London: Profile Books.

Giddens, Anthony (2000), *The Third Way and Its Critics*, Cambridge: Polity.

Giddens, Anthony (2006), *Europe in the Global Age*, Cambridge: Polity.

Giddens, Anthony (2007), *Over To You, Mr Brown: How Labour Can Win Again*, Cambridge: Polity.

Giddens, Anthony and Pierson, Christopher (1998), *Conversations with Anthony Giddens: Making Sense of Modernity*, Cambridge: Polity.

Gill, Rosalind (2007), *Gender and the Media*, Cambridge: Polity.

Goffman, Erving (1959), *The Presentation of Self in Everyday Life*, London: Penguin.

Gogoi, Pallavi (2006), 'Mattel's Barbie Trouble', *Business Week*, 18 July, www.businessweek.com

Gratch, Alon (2001), *If Men Could Talk, This Is What They Would Say*, London: Arrow.

Gratch, Alon (2006), *If Love Could Think: Using Your Mind to Guide Your Heart*, New York: Three Rivers Press.

Gray, Ann (1992), *Video Playtime: The Gendering of a Leisure Technology*, London: Routledge.

Gray, Herman (2004), *Watching Race: Television and the Struggle for 'Blackness'* (new edition), Minnesota: University of Minnesota Press.

Gray, John (1993), *Men Are From Mars: Women Are From Venus*, London: Thorsons.

Greer, Germaine (1999), *The Whole Woman*, London: Doubleday.

Grogan, Sarah (1999), *Body Image: Understanding Body Dissatisfaction in Men, Women and Children*, London: Routledge.

Gunter, Barrie (1995), *Television and Gender Representation*, London: John Libbey.

Gutting, Gary (2005a), 'Michel Foucault: A User's Manual', in Gutting, Gary, ed.,

A Cambridge Companion to Foucault: Second Edition, Cambridge: Cambridge University Press.

Gutting, Gary (2005b), *Foucault: A Very Short Introduction*, Oxford: Oxford University Press.

Hacking, Ian (1986), 'Self-Improvement', in Couzens Hoy, David, ed. *Foucault: A Critical Reader*, Oxford: Blackwell.

Hagell, Ann and Newburn, Tim (1994), *Young Offenders and the Media: Viewing Habits and Preferences*, London: Policy Studies Institute.

Hall, Stuart (1973), 'Encoding/Decoding', reprinted in Hall, Stuart, Hobson, Dorothy, Lowe, Andrew and Willis, Paul, eds (1980), *Culture, Media, Language*, London: Hutchinson.

Hall, Stuart (1983), 'The Great Moving Right Show', in Hall, Stuart and Jacques, Martin, eds, *The Politics of Thatcherism*, London: Lawrence & Wishart.

Hall, Stuart (1988), *The Hard Road to Renewal*, London: Verso.

Hall, Stuart (1997), 'Cultural Identity and Diaspora', in Woodward, Kathryn, ed., *Identity and Difference*, London: Sage.

Halperin, David M. (1994), *Saint Foucault: Towards a Gay Hagiography*, New York: Oxford University Press.

Halpern, Sue (1999), 'Susan Faludi: The Mother Jones Interview', *Mother Jones*, September/October, www.motherjones.com/mother_jones/SO99/faludi.html

Hardiman, Michael (2000), *Ordinary Heroes: A Future for Men*, Dublin: Newleaf.

Harding, Jennifer (1998), *Sex Acts: Practices of Femininity and Masculinity*, London: Sage.

Hargreaves, Duane A. and Tiggemann, Marika (2003), 'Female "Thin Ideal" Media Images and Boys' Attitudes Toward Girls', *Sex Roles*, vol. 49, nos 9/10, pp. 539–544.

Harris, Anita (2004), *Future Girl: Young Women in the Twenty-First Century*, New York: Routledge.

Hart, Kylo-Patrick R. (2000), 'Representing Gay Men on American Television', *The Journal of Men's Studies*, vol. 9, no. 1, pp. 59–79.

Helmanis, Lisa (2006), *How to Be an Irresistible Woman: How to Charm and Attract Everyone You Meet*, London: Carlton.

Hermes, Joke (1995), *Reading Women's Magazines: An Analysis of Everyday Media Use*, Cambridge: Polity.

Hill, Annette (1997), *Shocking Entertainment: Viewer Response to Violent Movies*, Luton: John Libbey Media.

Hill, Annette (2004), *Reality TV: Audiences and Popular Factual Television*, London: Routledge.

Hill, Annette (2007), *Restyling Factual TV: Audiences and News, Documentary and Reality Genres*, London: Routledge.

Hise, Richard T. (2004), *The War Against Men*, Oakland: Elderberry Press.

Holliday, Ruth (1999), 'The Comfort of Identity', *Sexualities*, vol. 2, no. 4, pp. 475–491.

Holliday, Ruth (2004), 'Reflecting the Self', in Knowles, Caroline and Sweetman, Paul, eds, *Picturing the Social Landscape: Visual Methods and the Sociological Imagination*, London: Routledge.

Hollows, Joanne, Hutchings, Peter, and Jancovich, Mark, eds (2000), *The Film Studies Reader*, London: Arnold.

Holmes, Su and Redmond, Sean, eds (2006), *Framing Celebrity: New Directions in Celebrity Culture*, London: Routledge.

hooks, bell (1982), *Ain't I a Woman: Black Women and Feminism*, London: Pluto.

hooks, bell (1992), *Black Looks: Race and Representation*, Boston: South End Press.

hooks, bell (1996), *Reel to Real: Race, Sex, and Class at the Movies*, London: Routledge.

hooks, bell (2000), *Feminist Theory: From Margin to Center – Second Edition*, London: Pluto.

hooks, bell (2005), *Sisters of the Yam: Black Women and Self-Recovery*, South End Press Classics edition, Boston: South End Press.

Horkheimer, Max and Adorno, Theodor W. (1979), *Dialectic of Enlightenment*, London: Verso.

Huffman, Karen (2006), *Psychology in Action – 8th Edition*, New York: Wiley.

Humm, Maggie (1997), *Feminism and Film*, Edinburgh: Edinburgh University Press.

Icon (2004), *Gender Identity Disorder*, San Diego: Icon Health Publications.

Inter-Parliamentary Union (2007), 'Women in National Parliaments: Situation as of 31 May 2007', www.ipu.org/wmn-e/classif.htm

Jackson, Peter, Brooks, Kate and Stevenson, Nick (1999), 'Making Sense of Men's Lifestyle Magazines', *Environment and Planning D: Society and Space*, vol. 17, pp. 353–368.

Jackson, Peter, Stevenson, Nick and Brooks, Kate (2001), *Making Sense of Men's Lifestyle Magazines*, Cambridge: Polity.

Jackson, Stevi (1996), 'Ignorance is Bliss, When You're Just Seventeen', *Trouble and Strife*, no. 33, summer.

Jameson, Fredric (1991), *Postmodernism, or the Cultural Logic of Late Capitalism*, London: Verso.

Jansz, Jeroen and Martis, Raynel G. (2007), 'The Lara Phenomenon: Powerful Female Characters in Video Games', *Sex Roles*, vol. 56, nos 3–4, pp. 141–148.

Jeffers, Susan (2007), *Feel the Fear and Do It Anyway: 20th Anniversary Edition*, London: Vermilion.

Jeffords, Susan (1993), 'Can Masculinity Be Terminated?', in Cohan, Steven and Hark, Ina Rae, eds, *Screening the Male: Exploring Masculinities in Hollywood Cinema*, London: Routledge.

Jones, Liz (2001a), 'Why It's All Over for Nova', *Observer*, 6 May, www.guardian.co.uk

Jones, Liz (2001b), 'I Expose the Guilty Fashion Editors Who Drive Young Women to Starve Themselves', *The Mail on Sunday*, 15 April, pp. 32–33.

July, William II (2001), *Understanding the Tin Man: Why So Many Men Avoid Intimacy*, New York: Broadway Books.

Jung, John (1986) 'How Useful is the Concept of Role Model?', *Journal of Social Behavior and Personality*, vol. 1, no. 4, pp. 525–536.

Kane, Pat (2000), 'Dispatches from the Genderquake Zone', *Independent*, 14 August, www.independent.co.uk

Kaplan, E. Ann (1983), *Women and Film: Both Sides of the Camera*, London: Methuen.

Kaplan, E. Ann (1992), Review of *Gender Trouble*, *Signs*, vol. 17, no. 4, pp. 843–848.

Kaplan, E. Ann (1993), 'Madonna Politics: Perversion, Repression, or Subversion? Or Masks and/as Master-y', in Schwichtenberg, Cathy, ed., *The Madonna Connection: Representational Politics, Subcultural Identities, and Cultural Theory*, Boulder: Westview Press.

Kaspersen, Lars Bo (2000), *Anthony Giddens: An Introduction to a Social Theorist*, Oxford: Blackwell.

Kendall, Gavin and Wickham, Gary (1999), *Using Foucault's Methods*, London: Sage.

Kirby, Vicki (2006), *Judith Butler: Live Theory*, London: Continuum.

Kirkham, Pat and Thumim, Janet, eds (1993), *You Tarzan: Masculinity, Movies and Men*, London: Lawrence & Wishart.

Kirkham, Pat and Thumim, Janet, eds (1995), *Me Jane: Masculinity, Movies and Women*, London: Lawrence & Wishart.

Knowles, Caroline and Sweetman, Paul, eds (2004), *Picturing the Social Landscape: Visual Methods and the Sociological Imagination*, London: Routledge.

Koch, Richard (1997), *The 80/20 Principle*, London: Nicholas Brealey.

Koch, Richard (2004), *Living the 80/20 Way*, London: Nicholas Brealey.

Kohlberg, L. (1966), 'A Cognitive-developmental Analysis of Children's Sex-role Concepts and Attitudes', in Maccoby, E. E., ed., *The Development of Sex Differences*, Stanford: Stanford University Press.

Latham, Mark (2006), 'Real Men Aren't Weasel-word-wielding Toss-bags', *The Age*, 25 September, www.theage.com.au

Lauzen, Martha M. and Dozier, David M. (1999), 'Making a Difference in Prime Time: Women on Screen and Behind the Scenes in the 1995–96 Television Season', *Journal of Broadcasting and Electronic Media*, vol. 43, no. 1, pp. 1–19.

Lauzen, Martha M., Dozier, David M. and Cleveland, Elizabeth (2006), 'Genre Matters: An Examination of Women Working Behind the Scenes and On-screen Portrayals in Reality and Scripted Prime-Time Programming', *Sex Roles*, vol. 55, no. 7–8, pp. 445–455.

Layard, Richard (2006), *Happiness: Lessons from a New Science*, London: Penguin.

Lee Simmons, Kimora (2006), *Fabulosity: What It Is and How to Get It*, New York: HarperCollins.

Lehman, Peter, ed. (2001), *Masculinity: Bodies, Movies, Culture*, London: Routledge.

Lentricchia, Frank (1982), 'Reading Foucault (Punishment, Labor, Resistance)', *Raritan* 2.1, pp. 41–70.

Lind, Rebecca Ann (2003), *Race/Gender/Media: Considering Diversity Across Audience, Content, and Producers*, Boston: Allyn & Bacon.

Lindenfield, Gael (2000), *The Positive Woman: Simple Steps to Optimism and Creativity*, London: HarperCollins.

Lloyd, Fran, ed. (1993), *Deconstructing Madonna*, London: Batsford.

Lloyd, Moya (2007), *Judith Butler: Key Contemporary Thinkers*, Polity: Cambridge.

Macdonald, Myra (1995) *Representing Women: Myths of Femininity in the Popular Media*, London: Arnold.

McGee, Micki (2005a), 'Belabored: The Cult of Life as a Work of Art', *The Chronicle of Higher Education*, 16 September, Section: The Chronicle Review, vol. 52, no. 4, p. B17.

McGee, Micki (2005b), *Self-Help Inc.: Makeover Culture in American Life*, New York: Oxford University Press.

McGraw, Phillip C. (2001), *Life Strategies: Doing What Works, Doing What Matters*, London: Vermilion.

Machin, David and Van Leeuwen, Theo (2006), *Global Media Discourse: A Critical Introduction*, London: Routledge.

McKee, Robert (1999), *Story*, London: Methuen.

McNair, Brian (2002), *Striptease Culture: Sex, Media, and the Democratisation of Desire*, London: Routledge.

McNeil, J. (1975), 'Feminism, Femininity and the Television Shows: A Content Analysis', in *Journal of Broadcasting*, vol. 19, pp. 259–269.

McRobbie, Angela (1999), *In the Culture Society: Art, Fashion and Popular Music*, London: Routledge.

McRobbie, Angela (2004), 'The rise and rise of porn chic', *The Times Higher Educational Supplement*, 2 January, subscribers-only archive at www.thes.co.uk

McRobbie, Angela (2005), 'Cutting Girls Down to Victoria Beckham's Size', *The Times Higher Educational Supplement*, 14 October, subscribers-only archive at www.thes.co.uk

McRobbie, Angela (2006), 'Post-feminism and Popular Culture: Bridget Jones and the New Gender Regime', in Curran, James and Morley, David, eds, *Media and Cultural Theory*, London: Routledge.

Maio, Kathi (1991), *Popcorn and Sexual Politics*, Santa Cruz: Crossing Press.

Malchiodi, Cathy (1998), *Understanding Children's Drawings*, London: Jessica Kingsley.

Malik, Sarita (2002), *Representing Black Britain: Black and Asian Images on Television*, London: Sage.

Malim, Tony and Birch, Ann (1998), *Introductory Psychology*, London: Macmillan.

Marketdata (2006), *The US Market for Self-Improvement Products and Services*, Tampa: Marketdata Enterprises.

Martin, C. L. (1991), 'The Role of Cognition in Understanding Gender Effects', *Advances in Child Development and Behaviour*, vol. 23, pp. 113–149.

Martin, Rux (1988), 'Truth, Power, Self: An Interview with Michel Foucault, October 25, 1982', in Martin, Luther H., Gutman, Huck and Hutton, Patrick H. eds, *Technologies of the Self: A Seminar with Michel Foucault*, Amherst: University of Massachusetts Press.

Meštrović, Stjepan G. (1998), *Anthony Giddens: The Last Modernist*, London: Routledge.

Mesure, Susie (2007), 'Stress and the City: Dead Girl's Father on Suicide Watch', *Independent*, 10 June, www.independent.co.uk

Miles, B. (1975), *Channelling Children: Sex Stereotyping as Primetime TV*, Princeton: Women on Words and Images.

Miller, Stephen H. (2000), 'Just Folks', *Independent Gay Forum*, 15 December, www.indegayforum.org/articles/miller32.html

Mills, Sara (2003), *Michel Foucault: Routledge Critical Thinkers*, London: Routledge.

MiM (1999), 'MiM Campaign to Shield Children from Prurient Magazine Covers at Supermarket Checkout Counters', *Morality in Media* (New York), www.moralityinmedia.org/badcosmo2.html

MiM (2000), 'Supermarkets Can Refuse to Allow Their Checkouts to be Used for the Open Display of "Pornographic or Indecent Talk"; "Common Decency Requires Nothing Less"', *Morality in Media* (New York), Press Release, 9 October, www.moralityinmedia.org/storelet10.html

MiM (2006), 'Morality in Media and American Decency Association Call for Magazine Coverup at Supermarket Checkout Lanes', *Morality in Media*, Press Release, 29 June , www.moralityinmedia.org/mediaIssues/supmktmags.htm

MORI (2001), 'Poll Shows Prejudice Rife as Stonewall Launches New Project to Combat Discrimination', MORI Polls and Surveys Archive, 19 June, www.mori.com/polls

Morley, David and Chen, Kuan-Hsing, eds (1996), *Stuart Hall: Critical Dialogues in Cultural Studies*, London: Routledge.

Mulvey, Laura (1975), 'Visual Pleasure and Narrative Cinema', *Screen*, vol. 16, no. 3, pp. 6–18.

Muncer, Steven, Campbell, Anne, Jervis, Victoria and Lewis, Rachel (2001), '"Ladettes," Social Representations, and Aggression', *Sex Roles*, vol. 44, nos 1/2, pp. 33–44.

Nathanson, Paul and Young, Katherine K. (2001), *Spreading Misandry: The Teaching of Contempt for Men in Popular Culture*, Montreal, Quebec: McGill-Queen's University Press.

Nathanson, Paul and Young, Katherine K. (2006), *Legalizing Misandry: From*

Public Shame to Systemic Discrimination Against Men, Montreal, Quebec: McGill-Queen's University Press.

National Centre for Social Research (2000), 'British Social Attitudes: Focusing on Diversity – The 17th Report: 2000–01 Edition', NCSR Press Release, 28 November, www.natcen.ac.uk

National Statistics (2001), *Population Trends: Spring 2001*, London: The Stationery Office.

National Statistics (2006a), 'Lifestyles: Men Spend More Time Watching TV than Women', 16 October, www.statistics.gov.uk

National Statistics (2006b), 'Civil Partnerships: Over 15,500 Formed by September 2006', 4 December, www.statistics.gov.uk

Nauta, Margaret M. and Kokaly, Michelle L. (2001), 'Assessing Role Model Influences on Students' Academic and Vocational Decisions', *Journal of Career Assessment*, vol. 9, no. 1, pp. 81–99.

New Scientist (2005), 'Fatherhood and Apple Pie', 27 August, p. 41.

Newport, Frank (2001), 'American Attitudes Toward Homosexuality Continue to Become More Tolerant', Gallup website, 4 June, www.gallup.com/poll/releases/pr010604.asp

Nixon, Sean (1996), *Hard Looks: Masculinities, Spectatorship and Contemporary Consumption*, London: UCL.

Nussbaum, Martha (1999), 'The Professor of Parody', *The New Republic*, 22 February. Accessed at *The New Republic Online*: www.tnr.com/archive/0299/022299/nussbaum022299.html

O'Brien, Martin, Penna, Sue and Hay, Colin, eds (1999), *Theorising Modernity: Reflexivity, Environment and Identity in Giddens' Social Theory*, Harlow: Addison Wesley Longman.

O'Keefe, Tracie and Fox, Katrina, eds (2003), *Finding the Real Me: True Tales of Sex and Gender Diversity*, San Francisco: Jossey-Bass.

Ogletree, Shirley Matile and Drake, Ryan (2007), 'College Students' Video Game Participation and Perceptions: Gender Differences and Implications', *Sex Roles*, vol. 56, no. 7–8, pp. 537–542.

Orbach, Susie (1993), *Hunger Strike: The Anorectic's Struggle as a Metaphor for Our Age*, London: Penguin.

Osborne, Peter and Segal, Lynne (1994), 'Gender as Performance: An Interview with Judith Butler', *Radical Philosophy*, 67 (summer).

Palmer, Patricia (1986), *The Lively Audience: A Study of Children Around the TV Set*, Sydney: Allen & Unwin.

Pennington, Donald C., Gillen, Kate and Hill, Pam (1999), *Social Psychology*, London: Arnold.

Penny, Laurie (2007), 'Where the Size-zero Debate Goes Awry', *The F Word* website, www.thefword.org.uk/features/2007/07/size_zero

Pew Research Center (2004a), 'Americans and Canadians: The North American

Not-so-odd Couple', 14 January, Pew Global Attitudes Project, http://pewglobal.org

Pew Research Center (2004b), 'A Global Generation Gap: Adapting to a New World', 24 February, Pew Global Attitudes Project, http://pewglobal.org

Pew Research Center (2006), 'Pragmatic Americans Liberal and Conservative on Social Issues', 3 August, The Pew Research Center for the People and the Press, http://people-press.org

Pew Research Center (2007), 'As Marriage and Parenthood Drift Apart, Public Is Concerned about Social Impact: Generation Gap in Values, Behaviors', 1 July, The Pew Research Center, http://pewresearch.org

Phares, E. Jerry and Chaplin, William F. (1998), *Introduction to Personality: Fourth Edition*, New York: Longman.

Phillips, E. Barbara (1978), 'Magazines' Heroines: Is *Ms.* Just Another Member of the Family Circle?', in Tuchman, Gaye, Kaplan Daniels, Arlene and Benét, James, eds, *Hearth and Home: Images of Women in the Mass Media*, New York: Oxford University Press.

Polling Report (2007), 'Law and Civil Rights', www.pollingreport.com/civil.htm

Posener, Jill (1982), *Spray It Loud*, London: Routledge & Kegan Paul (see also www.jillposener.com).

Procter, James (2004), *Stuart Hall*, London: Routledge.

Prosser, Jon, ed. (1998), *Image-Based Research: A Sourcebook for Qualitative Researchers*, London: RoutledgeFalmer.

Pruzinsky, Thomas and Cash, Thomas F., eds (2004), *Body Image: A Handbook of Theory, Research, and Clinical Practice*, New York: Guilford.

Rapping, Elayne (1996), *The Culture of Recovery: Making Sense of the Self-Help Movement in Women's Lives*, Boston: Beacon Press.

Red Pepper (2005), 'Guerilla Guides: Help yourself', March, www.redpepper.org.uk/gg/x-Mar2005-guerillaguides.htm

Richardson, Diane (2000), *Rethinking Sexuality*, London: Sage.

Ricoeur, Paul (1992), *Oneself as Another*, translated by Kathleen Blamey, Chicago: University of Chicago Press.

Rojek, Chris (2001), *Celebrity*, London: Reaktion Books.

Rosen, Marjorie (1973), *Popcorn Venus*, New York: Avon Books.

Rumsey, Nicola and Harcourt, Diana (2007), *The Psychology of Appearance*, Maidenhead: Open University Press.

Said, Edward W. (1983), *The World, the Text, and the Critic*, Cambridge, Massachusetts: Harvard University Press.

Salih, Sara (2002), *Judith Butler: Routledge Critical Thinkers*, London: Routledge.

Sarup, Madan (1996), 'Foucault: Sex and the Technologies of the Self', *Identity, Culture and the Postmodern World*, Edinburgh: Edinburgh University Press.

Scaff, Lawrence A. (2000), 'Georg Simmel', in Ritzer, George, ed., *The Blackwell Companion to Major Social Theorists*, Oxford: Blackwell.

Scheibe, C. (1979), 'Sex Roles in TV Commercials', *Journal of Advertising Research*, vol. 19, pp. 23–28.

Schirato, Tony and Yell, Susan (1999), 'The "New" Men's Magazines and the Performance of Masculinity', *Media International Australia*, no. 92, August, pp. 81–90.

Schlesinger, Philip, Dobash, R. Emerson, Dobash, Russell P. and Weaver, C. Kay (1992), *Women Viewing Violence*, London: British Film Institute Publishing.

Schlessinger, Laura (1995), *Ten Stupid Things Women Do To Mess Up Their Lives*, New York: Harper Perennial.

Schlessinger, Laura (1998), *Ten Stupid Things Men Do To Mess Up Their Lives*, New York: Harper Perennial.

Schwichtenberg, Cathy, ed. (1993), *The Madonna Connection: Representational Politics, Subcultural Identities, and Cultural Theory*, Boulder: Westview Press.

Segal, Lynne (1997), 'Sexualities', in Woodward, Kathryn, ed., *Identity and Difference*, London: Sage.

Simmel, Georg (1971), *On Individuality and Social Forms*, Chicago: University of Chicago Press.

Simmel, Georg (2004), *The Philosophy of Money: Third Enlarged Edition*, edited by David Frisby, translated by Tom Bottomore and David Frisby, London: Routledge.

Simonds, Wendy (1996), 'All Consuming Selves: Self-Help Literature and Women's Identities', in Grodin, Debra and Lindlof, Thomas R., eds, *Constructing the Self in a Mediated World*, London: Sage.

Skeggs, Beverley (1997), *Formations of Class and Gender: Becoming Respectable*, London: Sage.

Smith, Sharon (1972), 'The Image of Women in Film: Some Suggestions for Future Research', *Women and Film*, no. 1, pp. 13–21.

Smith, Tom W. (1999), 'Marriage Wanes as American Families Enter New Century', National Opinion Research Center at the University of Chicago, 24 November, www-news.uchicago.edu/releases/99/991124.family.shtml

Smith, Tom W. (2000), *Changes in the Generation Gap, 1972–1998*, GSS Social Change Report No. 43, Chicago: National Opinion Research Center, University of Chicago.

Soghomonian, Talia (2005), 'The Pussycat Dolls – Purrfect Girl Power Pop', www.musicomh.com/interviews/pussycat-dolls_1105.htm

Sönser Breen, Margaret and Blumenfeld, Warren J., eds (2005), *Butler Matters: Judith Butler's Impact on Feminist and Queer Studies*, London: Ashgate.

Spicer, Andrew (2001), *Typical Men: The Representation of Masculinity in Popular British Culture*, London: I. B. Tauris.

Stacey, Jackie (1987), 'Desperately Seeking Difference', reprinted in Kaplan, E. Ann, ed. (2000), *Feminism and Film*, Oxford: Oxford University Press.

Stald, Gitte and Tufte, Thomas, eds (2001), *Global Encounters: Media and Cultural Transformation*, Luton: University of Luton Press.

Starr, Alexandra (1999), 'You've Got a Long Way to Go, Baby: Women's Magazines

Continue to Create – and Exploit – Women's Anxiety', *Washington Monthly*, vol. 31, no. 10, www.washingtonmonthly.com

Stevenson, Nick; Jackson, Peter and Brooks, Kate (2000), 'The Politics of "New" Men's Lifestyle Magazines', *European Journal of Cultural Studies*, vol. 3, no. 3, pp. 369–388.

Strachan, Alex (2007), 'Life is Beautiful for Ugly Betty Star America Ferrera', *Dose*, 22 January, www.dose.ca

Strinati, Dominic (1995), *An Introduction to Theories of Popular Culture*, London: Routledge.

Sullivan, Andrew (2000), 'Dumb and Dumber', *The New Republic*, 15 June, www.thenewrepublic.com/062600/trb062600.html

Sussman, Dalia (2007), 'Poll: Hillary Clinton as Role Model', 19 July, *The Caucus: Political Blogging from the New York Times*, http://thecaucus.blogs.nytimes.com/2007/07/19/

Tasker, Yvonne (1998), *Working Girls: Gender and Sexuality in Popular Cinema*, London: Routledge.

Templar, Richard (2002), *The Rules of Work*, London: Pearson Education.

Templar, Richard (2006), *The Rules of Life*, London: Pearson Education.

Thussu, Daya K., ed. (2006), *Media on the Move: Global Flow and Contra-flow*, London: Routledge.

Tuchman, Gaye (1978), 'Introduction: The Symbolic Annihilation of Women by the Mass Media', in Tuchman, Gaye, Kaplan Daniels, Arlene and Benét, James, eds, *Hearth and Home: Images of Women in the Mass Media*, New York: Oxford University Press.

Tucker, Kenneth H. Jr (1998), *Anthony Giddens and Modern Social Theory*, London: Sage.

United Nations (2006), 'Women Still Struggle to Break Through Glass Ceiling in Government, Business, Academia', 8 March, www.un.org/womenwatch/daw/csw/csw50/PressReleaseIWD8March.pdf.

US Department of Labor (2002), 'Women's Bureau Publication Offers Statistics on Women-Owned Businesses', 9 December, www.dol.gov/wb/media/pressusdl05.htm

Valenti, Jessica (2007), *Full Frontal Feminism: A Young Woman's Guide to Why Feminism Matters*, Emeryville: Seal Press.

Valls-Fernández, Federico and Martínez-Vicente, José Manuel (2007), 'Gender Stereotypes in Spanish Television Commercials', *Sex Roles*, vol. 56, nos 9/10, pp. 691–699

Van Zoonen, Liesbet (1994), *Feminist Media Studies*, London: Sage.

Vernon, Polly (1999), 'Girls at Our Best', 27 October, *The Guardian*, www.guardian.co.uk

Vogler, Christopher (1999), *The Writer's Journey: Second Revised Edition*, London: Pan.

Walter, Natasha (1998), *The New Feminism*, London: Little, Brown.

Whelehan, Imelda (2000), *OverLoaded: Popular Culture and the Future of Feminism*, London: Women's Press.

Wilke, Michael (2000), 'Advertisers Battle Dr Laura', *The Commercial Closet*, 29 May, www.commercialcloset.org

Wilke, Michael (2001), 'CBS Show Heightens Gay TV Presence', *The Commercial Closet*, 4 March, www.commercialcloset.org

Williams, J. E. and Best, D. L. (1977), 'Sex Stereotypes and Trait Favorability on the Adjective Check List', *Educational and Psychological Measurement*, 37, 101–110.

Williams, J. E. and Best, D. L. (1990), *Measuring Sex Stereotypes: A Multination Study (Revised Edition)*, Newbury Park: Sage.

Williams, Zoe (2002), 'Just Fancy…' (interview with Kim Cattrall), *Guardian Weekend*, 5 January, pp. 14–19.

Williams, Zoe (2007), 'Wake up. Feminism is More than Just Capitalism with Tits', *Guardian*, 4 July, www.guardian.co.uk

WIMN's Voices (2007), 'An Open Letter to Ugly Betty's America Ferrera', posted 19 January, www.wimnonline.org/WIMNsVoicesBlog

Winship, Janice (1987), *Inside Women's Magazines*, London: Pandora.

Wykes, Maggie and Gunter, Barrie (2005), *The Media and Body Image*, London: Sage.

Ziglar, Zig (1998), *Success for Dummies*, Foster City: IDG Books.

INDEX

Related titles from Routledge

The Media Student's Book
Fourth Edition
Gill Branston and Roy Stafford

The Media Student's Book is a comprehensive introduction for students of media studies. It covers all the key topics and provides a detailed, lively and accessible guide to concepts and debates. This fourth edition, newly in colour, has been thoroughly revised, re-ordered and updated, with many very recent examples and expanded coverage of the most important issues currently facing media studies. It is structured in four main parts, addressing key concepts, media practices, media debates and the resources available for individual research.

Individual chapters include: Interpreting media * Narratives * Genres and other classifications * Institutions * Questions of representation * Ideologies and power * Industries * Audiences * Advertising and branding * Research * Production organisation * Production techniques * Distribution * Documentary and 'reality TV' * Whose globalisation? * 'Free choices' in a 'free market'?

Chapters are supported by case studies which include: Ways of interpreting * *CSI: Miami* and crime fiction * J-horror and the *Ring* cycle * Television as institution * Images of migration * News * The media majors * The music industry, technology and synergy * Selling audiences * Celebrity, stardom and marketing * Researching mobile phone technologies * Contemporary British cinema.

The authors are experienced in writing, researching and teaching across different levels of pre-undergraduate and undergraduate study, with an awareness of the needs of those students. The book is specially designed to be easy and stimulating to use with:
* marginal terms, definitions, references (and even jokes), allied to a comprehensive glossary
* follow-up activities, suggestions for further reading, useful websites and resources plus a companion website to support the book at www.routledge.com/textbooks/0415371430/
* references and examples from a rich range of media forms, including advertising, television, films, radio, newspapers, magazines, photography and the Internet.

ISBN13: 978-0-415-37142-1 (hbk)
ISBN13: 978-0-415-37143-8 (pbk)

Available at all good bookshops
For ordering and further information please visit: www.routledge.com